The Future of
ISIS

The Future of
ISIS

Regional and International Implications

EDITED BY

Feisal al-Istrabadi *and* Sumit Ganguly

BROOKINGS INSTITUTION PRESS
Washington, D.C.

The Brookings Institution is a private nonprofit organization devoted to research, education, and publication on important issues of domestic and foreign
policy. Its principal purpose is to bring the highest quality independent research
and analysis to bear on current and emerging policy problems. Interpretations
or conclusions in Brookings publications should be understood to be solely
those of the authors.

Library of Congress Cataloging-in-Publication Data
Names: Ganguly, Sumit, editor. | Al-Istrabadi, Feisal, editor.
Title: The future of ISIS : regional and international implications / [edited by]
    Sumit Ganguly and Feisal Al-Istrabadi.
Description: Washington, D.C. : Brookings Institution, 2018. | Includes
    bibliographical references and index.
Identifiers: LCCN 2018012373 (print) | LCCN 2018018368 (ebook) | ISBN
    9780815732174 (ebook) | ISBN 9780815732167(pbk. :alk. paper)
Subjects: LCSH: IS (Organization) | Middle East—History—21st century. |
    Intelligence service—United States. | United States—Foreign relations—
    Middle East. | Middle East—Foreign relations—United States.
Classification: LCC HV6433.I722 (ebook) | LCC HV6433.I722 F88 2018
    (print) | DDC 363.325—dc23
LC record available at https://lccn.loc.gov/2018012373

9 8 7 6 5 4 3 2 1

Typeset in Bembo

Composition by Westchester Publishing Services

Contents

Acknowledgments

It is with pleasure that we acknowledge the many individuals and organizations without whom this book would not have been possible.

This book is the result of a conference convened jointly by the Center for the Study of the Middle East (CSME) and the Center for American and Global Security (CAGS) at the School of Global and International Studies (SGIS) in Bloomington, Indiana, October 7–8, 2016. The conference could not have taken place without a contribution from F. Wallace Hays. His sustained and generous support of CSME over the years is greatly appreciated and has allowed CSME to embark on many valuable activities in which it could not have otherwise engaged. Thanks are also due to Indiana University Vice President for International Affairs David Zaret, who also provided support, thereby ensuring the continuance of the university's well-deserved reputation for Hoosier Hospitality.

The editors gratefully express their thanks to William Finan, director of the Brookings Institution Press. His initial interest in this proposal, his help in formulating the questions submitted to each author, his attendance at the conference in Bloomington, and his steady encouragement over the months have been invaluable. We are also grateful to Janet Walker and Elliott Beard, both at Brookings, and Brian Ostrander, project editor with Westchester Publishing Services, for the thousand things they did to make the book come together.

PART I

Ideology and Externalities

1

Introduction

An End to ISIS?

Feisal al-Istrabadi *and* Sumit Ganguly

The Islamic State in Iraq and Syria (ISIS throughout this volume) seemed to rise dramatically in 2014, taking over Iraq's second-largest city, Mosul, in four hours. A frenzy of activity and hand-wringing ensued, both amongst the ranks of policymakers in various capitals and in the media. Indeed, no major observer of the region, in or out of government, had seen this rise coming, and U.S. officials, starting with the president, had been openly dismissive of ISIS while touting what they deemed to be their far more important success against al Qaeda. Yet here was ISIS achieving what al Qaeda had never even aspired to do in the course of its existence: taking over territory through military means from two governments that had previously controlled it. Overnight, ISIS erased the internationally recognized border between Iraq and Syria and proclaimed the existence of its so-called caliphate and named its amir al-muminin—commander of the faithful—an Iraqi, Ibrahim Awad al-Badri, known by his nom de guerre, Abu Bakr al-Baghdadi.

The backdrop to these events, however, was far less dramatic. ISIS had been building for years. Particularly in Iraq, as the Sunni insurgency was

3

largely defeated—or at least reduced in size—in the wake of the surge of U.S. troops in 2007 and subsequently, what was then known as the Islamic State in Iraq rose to displace al Qaeda. The organization that was to become ISIS began to grow and metastasize. ISIS's leadership initially sought refuge in Syria as the regime of Bashar al-Assad began to lose its iron-fisted control over much of the country, especially in parts of the predominantly Sunni areas. In the meantime, the Baghdad government, under the leadership of Prime Minister Nuri al-Maliki, began to renege on promises made to Iraq's Sunni population that had been negotiated by General David Petraeus and Ambassador Ryan Crocker during the surge, promises to which Baghdad had agreed.

As the United States withdrew its forces from Iraq at the end of 2011, many in the Sunni community were seething with anger at Maliki, and a genuine sense of Sunni disenfranchisement began to take root. This sense of disenfranchisement became the vehicle of the initially slow infiltration of ISIS from across the Syrian frontier back into Iraq, especially in Anbar Governorate, as Maliki sent troops violently to disperse what had largely been peaceable demonstrations. It was this infiltration that set the groundwork for the dramatic rise of ISIS from Mosul southward in June 2014. By then, however, ISIS had controlled significant territory in Syria and had controlled Raqqah, its nominal capital, for two years. To borrow a phrase from a different context, the surprise to the policymaking class in the United States and the region occasioned by the "sudden" rise of ISIS in 2014 seems to have been occasioned by yet another failure of imagination. Tensions in Iraq were sufficiently high by the beginning of 2013 that one of the authors of this introduction predicted the reignition of a civil war.[1] Even if the particulars of ISIS's rise might not have been precisely predictable, that there would be a palpable and significant response to provocation of the Sunnis was eminently predictable.

This volume fills a niche not hitherto occupied by other publications on ISIS: the lessons learned and pitfalls to be avoided in the future. The express intention of the book is to deal with ISIS as a strategic issue going forward, from the perspectives of the regional powers as well as the United States and its engagement in the region. The book is primarily intended for policymakers and policy analysts. Equally, however, in that it brings together internationally renowned experts from the academy, most of whom have significant real-world experience, its analysis is also targeted to other academics and their students.

The book is divided into five parts, each consisting of two chapters. Part I, which includes this introduction, looks at ideologies and externalities. Part II examines intelligence failures and ponders whether the rise of ISIS in so spectacular a fashion, especially in Iraq in 2014, betokens an inability on the part of U.S. intelligence services to assess the real threat ISIS posed at a discrete moment in history. Part III examines issues relating to local actors, focusing especially on Syria and Afghanistan. Part IV assesses the often divergent agendas of the powers combating ISIS in Syria and Iraq. Part V concludes with an examination of U.S. interests in the fight against ISIS.

A final note on nomenclature: The extent of the territory ISIS claimed was dramatic. The English translation of the second "S" in ISIS as "Syria" fails adequately to convey the original Arabic. In the context of this terrorist organization, the use of the word "Sham" in Arabic does not merely denote modern-day Syria. Instead, as any native speaker of Arabic understands, al-Dawlah al-Islamiyyah fil al-Iraq wa al-Sham refers to Bilad al-Sham—that is, Greater Syria. Thus ISIS's claim is for dominion over a large swath of territory that encompasses all of modern-day Iraq, Syria, Lebanon, Jordan, Israel, and Palestine. It was thus a matter of negotiation between the editors of this volume and the publisher as to whether the second "S" should be more accurately translated as Levant or Syria. In the end, it was agreed that Syria is the more commonly used translation.

Chapter Summaries

After this introduction, Nukhet Sandal considers the vexed and elusive issue of ISIS's ideology and governance using the public theology framework. Too many commentators on ISIS glibly assert that it attempts to return Islam to its past, failing to note how thoroughly modern a phenomenon it actually is, especially in its utter totalitarianism, but also in its engagement with modern media. Sandal divides her inquiry into four analytical dimensions: substantive, spiritual, spatial, and temporal. She begins by rejecting the trope that ISIS is merely a terrorist organization, noting that, at the very least, it can and should be considered a revolutionary and revanchist pseudo- or emerging state (irrespective of its ultimate fate of having lost the territory it once controlled). Indeed, she notes that it sees itself as the "ultimate political unit for the Muslims" and behaves like a state to the extent that it provides services such as health care and other public services.

Sandal dismisses the argument over whether ISIS is Islamic or un-Islamic. She notes that, analytically, it suffices to note that it acts in the name of religion—as other groups from other religions also do—and that it is able to rally followers and adherents. She convincingly traces the development of ISIS from its roots in Salafi jihadism through al Qaeda. Still, she argues that the issue of whether to place ISIS within or outside Islam should not be taken up by policymakers and politicians. Rather, she argues that it should be left to theologians and scholars of Islam. She notes, however, the rise of ISIS as a phenomenon occurring in light of interventions in Islamic countries and the need, therefore, for policymakers to consider such second-order consequences when setting policy. She concludes by noting that a principal factor contributing to the rise of such organizations as ISIS and its fellow travelers is the lack of good governance in states where such groups do occur. To Sandal, it is axiomatic that promotion of good governance and building capacity should constitute an important part of the fight against such groups arising in the future.

Erik J. Dahl begins the consideration of intelligence failures in Part II. He notes, to begin with, that some have argued that there were no intelligence failures in the lead-up to June 2014. These voices assert that warnings were given, but that senior administration officials simply failed to heed them. Although there may be some truth to this line of argument, Dahl observes that senior intelligence officials have conceded that they did indeed underestimate ISIS's strength and its ability to challenge the post-2003 dispensation in Iraq. Dahl himself argues that the intelligence community (IC) did fail properly to assess the threat that ISIS constituted. Dahl's chapter adds insight to the scholarly literature about these failures, which, as he notes, has too often ignored them. He does so in part by analyzing the statements of public officials about what went amiss and examines a controversy about the management of intelligence by the U.S. Central Command (CENTCOM). Disturbingly, he concludes that the failures attendant to the failure to appreciate the danger actually posed by ISIS in 2014 are not isolated but are indicative of a larger set of challenges as the IC assesses the dangers posed by nonstate actors.

Dahl traces the failures that culminated in the losses of territory in June 2014 back to February 2011, ten months before the United States withdrew its forces from Iraq. At that time the director of national intelligence publicly testified that, while al Qaeda in Iraq would continue to be a security problem, he believed it would be unable to control "territory from which to launch attacks." Others, most notably Defense Intelligence Agency Director Michael Flynn, did eventually warn of rising risks, but the warnings from other administration officials were general and contained such pap as Deputy Assistant Secretary of State Brett McGurk's statement in November 2013 that "the next year may be pivotal." Dahl argues that there were two principal failures. They are (1) that the United States lacked a physical presence in Iraq to assess adequately the virtue of the U.S. withdrawal, and (2) that what assets were present on the ground were focused on military operations and were simply unavailable to contribute to an understanding of the greater threat that was gathering. He concludes his chapter by noting that the ultimate failure to predict the rise of ISIS may well be structural, to the extent that it is extremely difficult to understand and forecast "intangible events" such as the rise of social movements or regional instability.

Part II concludes with James J. Wirtz's consideration of the issue. He asks what it means to say that the failure to predict the rapid rise of ISIS was an intelligence failure; like Dahl, he notes that the IC did warn generally of a deteriorating situation. Wirtz notes the inherent tension between, on the one hand, the need for intelligence analysts to be at a remove from policymakers and thus to ensure the objectivity of their analyses. On the other is the imperative for the IC to be able to provide "actionable intelligence" to those same policymakers. In the context of the rise of ISIS in 2014 he argues that it would have required the ability of an analyst to connect de-Baathification by the U.S. administrator in Iraq in 2003 with the rise of ISIS a decade later—in effect having to predict the rise of ISIS by recognizing "the impetus it received from U.S. policy." Indeed, given the manner in which briefings are conducted, he observes that an analyst would only make this connection if he were "directly asked this question by public officials," something he says "defies credulity."

Significantly, Wirtz argues that, although officials were warning of al Qaeda–like threats, ISIS in fact represents a qualitatively different type of threat. This new threat involves taking and holding territory and declaring emirates that could provide safe haven for its operatives, all while wearing down the United States and weakening its resolve to fight. Among the new tactics developed by ISIS was to take children from captive territories and train them in ISIS's ideology and combat methods as a way of increasing its numbers. These tactics made ISIS not a "normal" clandestine actor, in Wirtz's view, and made detection difficult. Its use of social media and the Internet for recruiting also made its actions extremely difficult to track. Like Dahl, Wirtz concludes that this confluence of events may well recur in the future with respect to other, similar actors, making the "intelligence failure" with respect to ISIS a possible "harbinger of things to come."

Part III is an examination of local actors. Kevin Martin assesses Syria and Iraq, placing the events that occurred there in their historical and regional contexts, particularly the various regional conflicts. He argues that, because organizations such as ISIS did not arise ex nihilo, preventing the rise of similar organizations will also have to consider the historical and regional contexts. In Syria he identifies a number of ongoing problems that will have an impact on future attempts to restore peace. Perhaps most disturbing is the regime's current practice of "demographic reengineering"—that is, limiting the return of certain refugee populations to particular areas. Exacerbating the problems in Syria are the number of armed militias, both internal militias and those from Lebanon, Iraq, and Iran, that are taking part in the fighting. The fact that so many different groups are fighting the Syrian regime—many supported by regional states—has benefited the government, as none seems capable of genuinely challenging it in areas where it is in control. That is also true of the cacophonous political opposition.

Martin sees ISIS as "very much the product of Iraq-specific historical experiences," including decades of personalized tyranny, militarism, sectarianism, and foreign intervention. Iraq, like Syria, has internal and regional militias supporting the government, including the popular mobilization units (PMUs), many of which are supported by Iran. Iran aside, Martin notes that Iraq and Syria have moved much closer since 2011, including by sharing intelligence information. Iraq, too, faces myriad Sunni insurgent groups of varying significance and with various degrees of support from the region. Both Iraq and Syria must balance power among the diverse groups in the country and fend off regional interference.

Amin Tarzi's chapter discusses a group often overlooked in the literature on ISIS and is this volume's only specific consideration of Afghanistan and Pakistan. Tarzi notes that several disgruntled groups there began pledging allegiance to ISIS in 2013 and 2014, leading to a formal announcement of Islamic State–Khurasan Province (ISKP) in 2015. The causes of their disgruntlement ranged from personal grievances to theological disputes, though others were simply "awed" by the evident success ISIS achieved in both Syria and Iraq. Like ISIS, ISKP seeks the erasure of international boundaries. Khurasan, in its conception, encompasses Afghanistan, Pakistan, the Central Asian republics, parts or all of Iran, and even parts or all of India. According to Tarzi, ISKP has successfully recruited sympathizers from the Federally Administered Tribal Areas (FATA) in Pakistan, as well as from among Afghans, and by 2015 U.S. commanders had noted that the group was "operationally emergent" in Afghanistan. Tarzi warns that, as Taliban members become disenchanted with that organization, ISKP may well come to fill the vacuum; in the event, it already had 3,000 members by 2016, though estimates at this writing (in 2017) are that they number some 2,000.

Just as Martin does for Syria and Iraq, Tarzi underscores the importance of understanding the indigenous factors that gave rise to ISKP by exploring the mythologies surrounding Khurasan and the troubled history of Afghanistan over the past four decades. As in the Middle East proper, various groups contest the ground in Afghanistan, such as the Taliban, al Qaeda, and ISKP. Interestingly, he notes that instances of sectarian violence in Afghanistan have been relatively few. Indeed, the Taliban has rejected ISKP's targeting of Shia, but the familiar alignment of regional players will take its toll in Afghanistan, too. Tarzi suggests intriguingly that, if the Kabul government loses its grip on whatever territory it now controls, Iran might well calculate that the Taliban are its least threatening alternative. He cautions that, as ISIS loses territory in Iraq, its followers might seek refuge amongst ISKP fighters in Afghanistan. Much of the solution lies in the hands of Pakistan, which has failed to secure the vacuum in the FATA, where ISKP germinated. Improving relations between Kabul and Islamabad would also assist in keeping ISKP marginalized, though better relations have been elusive in the post-2001 era.

Part IV examines the U.S. and regional powers. Hussein Banai begins his chapter with a discussion of the U.S.-led effort against ISIS in Syria and Iraq. He notes that the United States created a sixty-eight-member coalition to combat the group, though some prominent countries are excluded from this neocoalition of the (ostensibly) willing. Those excluded include Russia, China, Iran, and the Syrian government itself. Of course, both Russia and Iran have intervened, the latter through elite units of Iran's Revolutionary Guards, which have provided ground troops alongside their Iraqi counterparts. (It might be added that, operationally, the United States may have been effectively providing air cover for Iranian troops in Iraq, a truly bizarre set of affairs, if true.) Banai identifies the five pillars of the coalition's strategy as: military; stopping recruitment and flow of foreign fighters; cutting off funding sources to ISIS; humanitarian assistance and stabilizing liberated areas; and countering ISIS's propaganda. He evaluates the coalition's success in the areas as generally positive, though he says that attempts to stabilize newly liberated cities and towns have had mixed results. This latter conclusion is, of course, worrying, as stabilization will be a sine qua non for winning the peace, as it were.

Banai notes that a major weakness of the coalition is that many Sunni states regard ISIS as at base a check, however much of an unpleasant one, on Iran and its regional hegemonic aspirations. Similarly, Turkey has its own objectives in the fight against ISIS, particularly respecting Kurdish aspirations in the region. He quotes prior scholarship to the effect that these divergent regional responses to ISIS should be evaluated according to the "jolts" that the Middle East has received, including the 2003 war and the reform movements that began in 2011. In the event, he places the blame for the rise of ISIS on regional state failure and "institutional ineptitude."

Reminiscent of Sandal's prescription for avoiding a recurrence of ISIS, Banai advocates renewed emphasis on state-building in the region, even while noting the unpopularity of such efforts. He acknowledges that such endeavors cost billions of dollars, but counters that the failure to engage in them has resulted in great human costs also, including death and destruction throughout the region. He concludes by recommending that an international commission be established to explore the reasons behind the rise of ISIS and to make policy recommendations designed to prevent its ability to thrive. He also recommends the establishment of a "regional trusteeship" among some of the leading regional players to promote cooperation between them.

In his chapter, Feisal al-Istrabadi writes that several factors have limited the ability of the United States to defeat ISIS, especially in Iraq. He argues that one of those is the failure of the United States to articulate or intermediate a vision amongst Iraqis for what would constitute the post-ISIS dispensation. While it is self-evident that the all-Iraqi forces have been fighting against ISIS, there is no vision of what it is they have been fighting for. He also argues that the current administration has inherited a complex and, at times, incoherent alliance structure that hampers the ability of the United States to articulate a convincing narrative of its goals in fighting ISIS. Each of its major regional allies has its own interests, and many of them regard the fight against ISIS as secondary to other national interests. Thus the United States is allied with Iraq in the fight against ISIS there, but Iraq is allied with Iran both in Iraq (meaning the United States is de facto allied with Iran) and Syria, where the United States has been nominally supporting groups fighting Iran's ally, Bashar al-Assad. In Syria, where the United States has never had a positive policy, Russia has stepped in, first cautiously to ensure that Assad did not fall, then more vigorously with the evident intention of supporting his effort to recapture as much territory as reasonably possible. Istrabadi concludes that this morass of competing interests has made a coherent U.S. policy in either Iraq or Syria exceptionally difficult.

Istrabadi argues that the continued presence of ISIS threatens U.S. interests and that its defeat once and for all is essential to the preservation of those interests. He cautions against the possibility of future incarnations of ISIS-like organizations rising if the political outcome in Iraq and Syria post-ISIS does not result in genuine power-sharing and a sense of enfranchisement on the part of a broad mass of the respective populations. He argues the United States ought to resist the temptation to disengage once the battle is won; it must instead continue to use its influence in favor of a decent and mutually acceptable settlement. Combating corruption and reconciliation must top the agenda, along with political reform. Istrabadi agrees with Banai that state institutions must be reconstituted, but he notes specifically the need to reform the armed and security services so that professional cadres, rather than political hacks, are promoted and integrated as the best protection against ethno-confessional strife. Although he acknowledges that the United States cannot dictate these terms in either country, Istrabadi believes that the United States ought to use its considerable influence—particularly in Iraq—in this direction.

Part V, on U.S. interests, concludes this book. Risa Brooks begins her chapter by noting that an overarching imperative of U.S. policy since the September 11 attacks has been to deny terrorist organizations sanctuary from which they can plot attacks on the United States. Although she accepts this effort as legitimate, she also cautions against overestimating the threat that ISIS constitutes in carrying out "complex attacks" within the United States. She distinguishes between "lone-wolf" attacks and "complex attacks" by noting that the latter involve networks of operatives, aim at targets that are hardened by security defenses, involve phased or simultaneous attacks or a campaign of clustered attacks, and employ lethal and technically sophisticated weapons. Holding territory, as ISIS did in Iraq and Syria, promotes a group's ability to carry out complex attacks, since camps facilitate building training facilities and the cultivation of "specialized expertise," such as engineering skills. Still, the remoteness of the territory ISIS controls means that its ability to launch complex attacks is attenuated. Brooks notes that the spatial separation can be overcome, as was done on September 11, but planning for those attacks took years, and it is far less likely that ISIS-like groups could infiltrate the United States in the post-2001 security environment. Moreover, she notes the lack of "community sanctuaries" in the United States, where such plotters could hide.

Brooks concludes her analysis by pointing out that the threat of ISIS is "more qualified" than it is "sometimes characterized." Importantly, she says that her analysis has two policy implications. First, law enforcement agencies should be careful not to employ counterproductive strategies in dealing with local Muslim populations that have demonstrated their willingness to expose suspected extremists. Second, regarding U.S. policy in the Middle East, she suggests that the U.S. provision of air support to local militaries shows "promise," as distinct from maintaining a large U.S. footprint in the region.

Peter Krause ends this book. He begins his analysis with a good news/bad news paradigm. The good news in this view is that ISIS does not threaten the most crucial U.S. regional interests, namely the rise of a regional hegemon or the proliferation of nuclear weapons. The bad news is that it does constitute a threat to other U.S. interests, such as the stability of regional allies and the prevention of terrorist attacks. Krause identifies the central difficulty in fighting ISIS as the fact that it is in effect a three-headed monster. It is at once a state that, at its peak, controlled territory the size of Indiana; a transnational insurgency that seeks to spread chaos and overrun established regimes; and a revolutionary movement that works to "reshape societies and spread an extreme ideology." To fail to fight it on any one of these fronts, in Krause's view, means a long and frustrating "future of tactical victories and strategic defeats." Still, he maintains that there is a paradox in the threat-to-interest calculation that ISIS poses to the United States. The most significant U.S. interests are the ones that ISIS is least capable of harming (regional hegemony, nuclear proliferation), while what he identifies as secondary interests are the ones ISIS is most capable of harming (democracy promotion and regional peace and stability).

Krause posits a strategy for defeating ISIS that begins with defeating the forces of sectarianism and polarization. (It could be noted parenthetically that, in fact, far from defeating sectrarianism, the United States has embraced one side of the sectarian divide, rather than finding ways of bridging it.) Krause supports a policy of rolling back ISIS's territorial acquisitions in the region. As other contributors to this book have alluded, especially Martin, Banai, and Istrabadi, Krause agrees that good governance would constitute an important front in the fight against ISIS, especially, one presumes, as an effective ideology. Finally, Krause argues that, to defeat ISIS, it will be necessary to match "needs with ends," calling therefore for an end to announcing lofty policy goals without devising the means to achieve them.

Two interrelated themes emerge from virtually every chapter in this book, and they are quite timely viewed from the perspective of the first year and a half of the Trump administration. The first is that U.S. policy has focused on military confrontations in its fight against radical Islamic militant movements in the Middle East, particularly in Iraq. Thus, for instance, the United States surged its forces in Iraq in 2006 and 2007 to confront al Qaeda, but once the spike in violence subsided, U.S. forces went home. The Bush administration negotiated an agreement to withdraw all U.S. forces from the country by the end of 2011, and the Obama administration was in no mood to extend the presence of its forces there. (In fairness, neither did Prime Minister Maliki, who sensed he could wrest domination of the country without the interference of U.S. forces.)

The military withdrawal itself had several ramifications. Intelligence sharing between the sides declined perilously. Equally significant, the engagement of U.S. diplomats in Iraq substantially decreased, particularly during the Obama administration. Critical irritants between the competing political camps were dismissed as internal politics and of no consequence to U.S. policy in the region, even as Maliki began issuing arrest warrants for his political rivals and surrounding their houses with tanks. In the end, al Qaeda gave way to the rise of ISIS and the need for yet another buildup of U.S. forces in the region.

These considerations, then, lead to the second overarching theme that emerges from this book: the need for sustained U.S. diplomatic engagement in confronting the underlying causes that give rise to organizations such as ISIS. Organizations such as ISIS have arisen in various countries throughout the Middle East and elsewhere in part owing to a breakdown of ordinary politics in those countries. In Syria, for instance, the despotic regime of Bashar al-Assad failed to engage with critics or adequately respond to reasonable demands of demonstrators for reform. It chose, instead, to fire on unarmed civilians. Although the United States lacked the requisite influence in Damascus to mediate between Assad and his critics, the United States had such an ability in Iraq but simply chose not to use its good offices. Where the United States failed to engage in diplomacy, it was forced to rely on a military response instead.

These lessons should not be lost on a new administration still finding its sea legs. The announced policy of increasing reliance on the U.S. military capability at the expense of diplomacy augurs ill for vital U.S. interests. As the president has surrounded himself by retired and active-duty generals, experienced U.S. diplomats are leaving the State Department in droves, as the agency's budget suffers dramatic cuts hitherto unseen. One of the lessons of Iraq, for instance, should have been that the military surge would have been inefficacious by itself had U.S. officials not engaged in diplomacy with the belligerents and brokered a political solution to the grievances of the parties. It is because those solutions broke down that ISIS emerged.

At this writing, ISIS has suffered devastating military defeats, losing control of virtually all the territory it once controlled in Iraq and Syria. Yet even in these two countries, military operations continue to root out cells of the organization. It is almost certain that such cells will continue to exist into the indefinite future, and that is to say nothing of franchisees of ISIS in Africa and parts of Asia, including Afghanistan and South Asia. For the United States to continue to rely primarily (or even exclusively) on its military options means that new life will be continually breathed into these groups. To deprive such groups of the oxygen they need to exist, America's diplomats will need to be engaged, again, to help mediate the politics away from extremism toward creating a modus vivendi between elites. Otherwise, the peoples of the region—and American service men and women—will be condemned to repeat the cycle of the past decade and a half.

Note

1 "Iraq seems now to be perched on yet another Fearonian precipice. The Sunna, perhaps convinced their power in Baghdad has waned permanently, are poised to unleash yet another round of violence. . . . They are no doubt calculating, as Maliki rounds up the representatives they voted for, that in another five years, he will have been able to consolidate power even more effectively, making now the relatively optimal time to re-ignite their insurgency." Feisal Amin Rasoul al-Istrabadi, "Sectarian Visions of the Iraqi State: Irreconcilable Differences?," in *Social Difference and Constitutionalism in Pan-Asia*, edited by Susan H. Williams (Cambridge University Press, 2014), pp. 225–26. This analysis was written in 2013 and published in February 2014.

2

"Apocalypse Soon"

Revolutionary Revanchism of ISIS

Nukhet Sandal

As I was writing this chapter in late 2017, the Iraqi forces had just re-taken the last ISIS-held town. ISIS might be facing its end, but it is too early to claim that we will not witness its branches or its new manifestations in the near future. It is certain that new jihadi organizations will continue to emerge, and existing ones will change shape in response to the changing global political landscape. This is therefore a critical moment to look back at ISIS and discuss various elements of the organization's ideology to prepare for what might be next.

There are many debates surrounding the ideology of ISIS. Through reports, articles, and books, scholars and practitioners have tried to capture exactly what the group stood for. It is not possible to make predictions about future jihadi organizations or to fight against this particular type of radicalism and savagery without understanding the ideology ISIS espoused. However, it is also important to recognize that the group's multiple characteristics cannot be reduced to just one word. ISIS was not like al Qaeda or any other jihadi organization we have seen before. So how can we have a meaningful conversation about the ideology of ISIS if it was not something we had seen before, and if there were many factors that led to its birth and evolution?

Analyzing ISIS's governance and ideology using the public theology framework, this chapter investigates the religious, political, and territorial factors involved in the organization's operations. This framework is useful, especially for analysts who are not scholars of Islamic studies, to navigate through the complex map of doctrines and aspirations of ISIS. Public theology is a perspective on an issue, such as governance, that is produced or publicly advocated by a religious institution or authority, that is expressed by a group of people who distinguish their practice and perspective from other traditions, and that informs the public discussions of these issues in multiple ways, including political opposition, violent or nonviolent protest, and publications.[1] The public theology of a particular issue includes human interpretation of what is relevant and to what extent particular religious premises are evident in the public arena. In the context of ISIS, it is not a judgment of what is "really" Islamic or jihadi, but how the group has redefined these notions in its every day practice. International relations scholar Fawaz Gerges, for example, calls Salafi jihadism "a traveling ideology," and as such it is "nourished on the ideas that can be tailored to fit the predilections and whims of every wave, providing nourishment, sustenance and motivations to new adherents."[2] Public theology is an organizing framework for understanding the "ISIS version" of this "traveling ideology" and its implications for governance.

The chapter also assumes an epistemic lens and emphasizes how ISIS reformulated the existing understandings of Islamic governance and jihadism. This is not an entirely new position; in their edited book, Christina Hellmich and Andreas Behnke frame the discussion of al Qaeda's origins and strategy under "the epistemology of terrorism."[3] An epistemic lens encourages the analyst to question what remains constant, what has changed, and what networks made a difference in the understanding of this new form of jihadism. With their reframing of the conventional Salafi jihadi ideology, ISIS leaders and preachers devised new interpretation of jihadism and Islamic governance.[4] They shaped the conventional ideologies of jihadi governance within the political parameters delineated by the territory they control and the time frame they operate in. Their attempts to reformulate jihadi doctrines of governance and warfare can be seen in the numerous speeches, publications, treatises, and even syllabi written specifically for the jihadis.[5]

Elsewhere, I have formulated the dimensions of the public theology framework as substantive, spiritual, and spatial. In line with these components of public theology, the chapter is divided into three sections. The first section covers essential questions regarding the identity of ISIS. Was it a state, as it called itself? Was it just another terrorist group? The second section focuses on the theological aspects of the organization's ideology. What did the organization mean when it declared it was Islamic? How do contemporary scholars view its religious identity? The third section focuses on the territorial aspects of the group's governance and warfare. What difference does it make that the organization was primarily located in the Levant, and not in South Asia or sub-Saharan Africa? What kind of territorial factors and legacies shaped the group's public theology of governance? While reviewing these dimensions, the chapter maintains a forward-looking stance and examines what each factor means for jihadi movements in general.

Substantive Dimension: ISIS, Statehood, and the Caliphate

Was ISIS really a state, as it claimed to be? Or was it a group of thugs and wannabes, as President Obama once casually implied?[6] The question does not have a simple answer, but many analysts agree that ISIS was more than a terrorist organization. Audrey Kurth Cronin, professor of international security, argues that ISIS was not a terrorist organization but a "pseudo-state led by a conventional army."[7] In a provocative article, political scientist Stephen Walt agrees with Cronin's diagnosis and reminds readers that state-building has been a brutal enterprise for centuries (he gives multiple examples that include the Bolsheviks, the Maoists, and the creation of the United States among others), and "movements that were once beyond the pale sometimes end up accepted and legitimized, if they manage to hang onto power long enough."[8] From these perspectives, ISIS was not an anomaly; it operated like just another emerging state, regardless of its ideology.

What ISIS was engaged in at the height of its power, however, was not traditional state-building. The group followed what it called "prophetic methodology," which was based on an attempt to closely follow prophet Muhammad's and early Muslims' example in governance and warfare. In this spirit, ISIS revived the institution of the caliphate (khilafah) when, in a June 2014 audio recording, it declared its leader, Abu Bakr al-Baghdadi, to be caliph. A caliph is the supreme religious and civil ruler in the Islamic tradition. The last caliph was the heir to the Ottoman throne, Abdülmecid II. In March 1924, Mustafa Kemal Atatürk, the founder of the Republic of Turkey, and the new political elite abolished the caliphate post in Turkey in an attempt to make the country secular. The Muslim world has not had a caliph since then. Even when the post was in existence a caliph did not fully function as the leader of the Muslim world; the post lost its influence and became merely symbolic within a couple of centuries of Islam's birth. ISIS took pride in giving life to a long-defunct political and religious institution, and its leaders emphasized that a caliphate does not have any ethnic, racial, or regional allegiance and occasionally exploits the nationalist, ethnic, and racial tensions in the West.[9]

The declaration of a caliphate was not a straightforward process even within jihadi circles. ISIS had its roots in al Qaeda in Iraq, and the group's evolution as an independent organization had already disturbed al Qaeda's leadership. Declaring the caliphate further strained existing relations. Al Qaeda's and the Taliban's spiritual leader was Mullah Mohammad Omar until 2015. The designation of Baghdadi as caliph in 2014 challenged both the spiritual leadership of Mullah Omar and undermined al Qaeda's political authority. The fact that Mullah Omar was away from the public eye for a long time contributed to the challenges associated with the leadership competition. Mullah Omar was so removed from the day-to-day politics of al Qaeda that in 2015, when the Afghan government announced that Mullah Omar had died in 2013, the news was not received with much surprise. ISIS founders and leaders always regarded al Qaeda as lackadaisical, and they wanted to create the ultimate Islamic political unit with a leader who would have authority over the Muslim world. The desire for this utmost power led them to claim the caliphate, the only political entity that would give them the legitimacy they desired.

Seeing itself as the ultimate political unit for Muslims, ISIS behaved like a state and boasted about providing health care and public services in the territories it commanded. Its glossy publications featured photos of street-cleaning services, cancer treatment for children, and care homes for the elderly. The group issued its own currency system "in an effort to disentangle the Ummah from the corrupt interest-based global financial system."[10] It called on Muslims to move to the caliphate and told them that it was a sin to live in any other setting (Dar al-Kufr) now that there was a purely Islamic entity (Dar al-Islam).

Since ISIS encouraged hijrah (religious migration to the land of Islam), it came as no surprise that it attracted many foreign fighters. Fighters from more than eighty countries joined the organization. Members had different incentives and reasons for joining ISIS. The religious knowledge of these fighters, for the most part, was rudimentary. According to the organization's jihadi employment documents submitted by 4,030 foreign recruits, which were acquired by the Syrian opposition site Zaman al-Wasl and shared with the Associated Press, 70 percent of recruits defined themselves as having just "basic" knowledge of sharia (the lowest level the recruits could pick), around 24 percent were categorized as having an "intermediate" knowledge, and just 5 percent considered themselves advanced students of Islam.[11] In other words, most of the recruits joined ISIS for political reasons or for adventure, not because they had a solid grasp of and wanted to follow a coherent religious ideology. Governing these people within a pseudo-state structure proved to be challenging. ISIS leadership had concerns about how foreign fighters from different backgrounds and their families would adjust to the new lifestyle and their expectations. Being a terrorist organization operating from behind the scenes and trying to govern territories are two different projects. Although ISIS had significant resources, it still needed to meet the expectations of the newcomers, some of whom were coming from established states with decent services and infrastructure. Reflecting these tensions, the group made a point to warn that "the Khilafah is a state whose inhabitants and soldiers are human beings. They are not infallible angels. You may see things that need improvement and that are being improved."[12]

ISIS operated as an expansionist political unit. Most states and organizations agree to operate within the political system, and they usually care about outside legitimacy.[13] ISIS did not have such international legitimacy concerns or allies in the conventional sense because it rejected the concept of the modern state, international treaties, and borders. It demanded *bay'a* (allegiance) from other political and Islamic groups in the region and worldwide. The allegiances it secured were prominently featured in its media outlets, including its magazine, *Dabiq*. Not all of these allegiances were religion based. Michael Weiss and Hassan Hassan note that many tribes joined the organization not because they endorsed its ideology; the tribal allegiances were driven predominantly by power politics.[14] Therefore it is crucial not to overestimate the power of ideology, especially in settings where there is a political vacuum that threatens the existence of groups and organizations.

As part of its territorial expansion strategy, ISIS portrayed its aims as unequivocally religious. To illustrate, it tried to justify its battles against Kurdish paramilitary groups of the region like Yekîneyên Parastina Gel and Partiya Karkerên Kurdistanê. "Our war with Kurds is a religious war. It is not a nationalistic war—we seek the refuge of Allah," proclaimed ISIS; "we do not fight Kurds because they are Kurds. Rather we fight the disbelievers amongst them, the allies of the Crusaders and Jews in their war against the Muslims."[15] ISIS regularly called the Kurdish groups it was fighting against "commies," "terrorists," and "Assad regime supporters" with "numerous flimsy female 'fighters.'"[16]

Despite its aspirations to statehood and a territorial base, ISIS tried to increase its reach through attacks in multiple settings globally. These attacks did not need to be coordinated with the organization; mere inspiration and the attacker's testimony were good enough for ISIS. In the 2016 nightclub shooting in Orlando, Florida, the perpetrator, Omar Mateen, stated that he was a "soldier" of the organization, and he expressed his admiration for Tamerlan Tsarnaev and the Boston Marathon bombings, noting that it was now his "turn."[17] The definition and character of lone-wolf attacks have changed considerably in the past decade. Especially after the Boston Marathon bombing perpetrated by the Tsarnaev brothers, who were inspired by al Qaeda, "terrorism by inspiration" and lone-wolf attacks have been prominently featured and endorsed in jihadi publications. ISIS spokesperson Abu Muhammad al-Adnani was quoted as saying, "If you can kill a disbelieving American or European . . . kill him in any manner or way however it may be. Do not ask for anyone's advice and do not seek anyone's verdict."[18] This pragmatic flexibility enabled ISIS to take advantage of any violent act committed by self-proclaimed sympathizers and supporters. In short, because it was convenient, terrorism by inspiration became part of the unconventional apocalyptic state's "foreign policy tool kit," and one can expect this mode of terrorism to be part of future terrorist organizations, regardless of their ideology.

Spiritual Dimension: "The Religious" in the "Islamic"

The debate over what is "real" Islam is beyond the scope of this chapter. Any reasonable analyst will grant that ISIS is not representative of Muslims or Islam. However, it would be naive to dismiss an organization that called itself Islamic and used frequent references to Islamic texts and traditions simply as "un-Islamic." Graeme Wood, the journalist who wrote the controversial "What ISIS Really Wants," stated that ISIS was indeed Islamic, and that "the religion preached by its most ardent followers derives from coherent and even learned interpretations of Islam."[19] Some disagree with Wood's argument; some scholars, for example, have argued that ISIS's interpretation was not coherent and not consistent with the rich Islamic legal tradition.[20] This ongoing conversation is intellectually stimulating, but it does not change the fact that there will be many violent organizations and groups in the future that claim religious identities in order to rally followers. Even if scholars showed that ISIS violated many Islamic precepts, it is doubtful that this argument would have a significant impact on the group's recruitment.

ISIS described itself as jihadi Salafi. Salafism is a branch of Sunni Islam that is based on emulating the actions of the Salafs ("righteous predecessors") and living as one would have in the early days of Islam. Combined with jihadism, the ideology's focus becomes the military conquests, symbols, and strategies of the early Islamic era. The organization's interpretation and enactment of this ideology, however, was much stricter and more focused than that of any other organization that described itself as jihadi. Political analyst Shiraz Maher, in his detailed survey of jihadi Salafism, states that ISIS constituted the "most dramatic physical manifestation of Salafi-Jihadi doctrine in the modern era, serving a dualistic purpose between temporal and cosmic ends."[21] ISIS indeed espoused a distinct apocalyptic ideology. The apocalyptic revanchism of the organization that promised divine justice had an influence on disillusioned Muslim youth both in the Middle East and in other regions.

In Islamic eschatology, the scenario of apocalypse usually includes the symbolism of the imam and savior Mahdi, who is expected to establish his rule in the world and who, with the second coming of Jesus, will fight against the antichrist. A scholar of militant Islamism, William McCants, drew attention to the fact that, unlike in prior Islamic apocalyptic movements, the Mahdi did not feature prominently in the contemporary ISIS doctrine; the caliphate is the "locus of the group's apocalyptic imagination."[22] In other words, despite the strong emphasis on the "end of the world" discourse, the apocalyptic narrative of the group focused more on the near future than on the present. Political historian Jean-Pierre Filiu situated the resurgence of this type of Sunni apocalyptic thinking within a contemporary framework that is delineated by occurrences like the 1979 Islamic Revolution, the U.S. invasions of Afghanistan and Iraq, and increasing Shiite fanaticism about the apocalypse in Iran and Iraq.[23] ISIS's ideology, in this sense, was not just apocalyptic but also quintessentially revanchist. It showcased blood and suffering, and continuously promised violent revenge and domination of the West, going beyond the apocalyptic battle scenes. It fed on the frustrations of the local communities with foreign interventions and unfulfilled promises, and it exploited the disenfranchisement of youth worldwide.

ISIS espoused a takfiri ideology. A takfiri is a Muslim who declares another Muslim to be a nonbeliever (kafir). ISIS prioritized purifying the Islamic world and territories under its control more than organizing attacks abroad. According to the group's takfiri perspective, the Shia Muslims were regarded as apostates because their practice and ideology were considered to be later additions to the original Quranic precepts. ISIS designated many other types of Muslims as *murtaddin* (one who turns away from religion). For example, any Muslim who participated in man-made political systems, through voting or public service, was considered an apostate.

No organization's ideology can be imagined independent of its leader. In this vein, ISIS's public theology of governance could partly be attributed to its de facto founder, Abu Musab al-Zarqawi. Zarqawi was the head of al Qaeda in Iraq until he was killed in 2006. A prominent Salafi cleric who influenced al Qaeda's intellectual framework, Abu Muhammad al-Maqdisi, was Zarqawi's mentor, although Zarqawi's zeal went beyond even Maqdisi's. Despite his training under Maqdisi, Zarqawi represented an epistemic break from the rest of the al Qaeda leadership. His background was different from that of Osama bin Laden and Ayman al-Zawahiri, both of whom were from wealthy families and had strong educational backgrounds (Zawahiri studied medicine, and bin Laden had a degree in public administration, whereas Zarqawi was a high school dropout who later studied under Maqdisi's tutelage). After spending some time in Afghanistan, Zarqawi established Jama'at al-Tawhid wal-Jihad (the Group of God's Unity and Jihad) in 2002 and pledged lukewarm allegiance to Osama bin Laden in 2004, which resulted in the organization becoming al Qaeda in Iraq. Zarqawi's strong condemnation of Shiism and his uncompromising takfiri attitude made both Zawahiri and Maqdisi uncomfortable.

When he moved to Iraq, Zarqawi found the jihadis in the region too complacent. In his 2004 letter to the al Qaeda leadership, Zarqawi complained that the jihadis in Iraq were behaving too cautiously and were proud not to have lost lives in their struggle. "That should change," Zarqawi wrote, as "we have told them in our many sessions with them that safety and victory are incompatible."[24] Al Qaeda did not like Zarqawi's fanaticism and the strict implementation of the takfiri ideology. In line with Zarqawi's vision, the number of Muslims killed by ISIS was higher than the number of other victims, which shows that ISIS prioritized "purifying" the "Land of Islam" over organizing attacks abroad. This priority conflicted with al Qaeda's desire to target non-Muslims (with a focus on the United States and its allies) and its concerns about maintaining unity in the Muslim world. Although al Qaeda was more reserved in its public statements regarding ISIS, the latter was vocal about its distaste especially for Zawahiri and the Taliban and their "soft" approach toward the Shia. In an article the group stated that Zawahiri's policies toward the Shia "were clearly based upon his deviant belief that they are 'Muslims.'"[25] In the same article, to Zawahiri's statement that no Islamic state had systematically killed the Shia, ISIS responded that since the Shia had had political aspirations since the Safavid Empire it was now acceptable to kill them.

Following up on the differences of perspective between ISIS and al Qaeda, Jessica Stern and J. M. Berger posited that "where al-Qaida framed its pitch to potential recruits in relatable terms as 'doing the right thing', ISIS seeks to stimulate more than to convince."[26] Al Qaeda, for example, did not use slaves because of its concerns about public opinion and legitimacy. It emphasized "hearts and minds" in the Muslim world, and one can even argue that it wanted to become mainstream. Adam Gadahn, former spokesman and media adviser for al Qaeda, once wrote in a letter that jihadi forums are not ideal for al Qaeda interviews because they are "biased towards (Salafists) and not any Salafist, but the Jihadi Salafist, which is just one trend of the Muslims trends. The Jihad Salafist is a small trend within a small trend."[27] Al Qaeda, for the most part, has had clear political goals even if they are far-fetched. ISIS, on the other hand, was millenarian. In its worldview there was no possibility of a compromise or negotiation with other political actors, and the group did not care about public opinion in the Muslim world.

The religious claims of ISIS did not go unopposed. Muslims worldwide condemned the group's actions, and many Muslim organizations declared ISIS "un-Islamic." For example, 126 scholars of Islam penned a famous letter to Baghdadi, explaining in detail why specific actions such as torture, disfiguring the dead, forcible conversions, and slavery are forbidden in Islam.[28] ISIS published articles against such statements and initiatives. In a *Dabiq* article entitled "Islam Is the Religion of Sword, not Pacifism," the group states:

There is a slogan repeated continuously by apologetic "du'at" when flirting with the West and that is their statement: "Islam is the religion of peace," and they mean pacifism by the word peace. They have repeated this slogan so much to the extent that some of them alleged that Islam calls to permanent peace with kufr and the kafirin. How far is their claim from the truth, for Allah has revealed Islam to be the religion of the sword, and the evidence for this is so profuse that only a zindiq (heretic) would argue otherwise.[29]

In another issue of *Dabiq*, in an article called "Wala' and Bara' vs. American Racism," they stated:

"Islamic" preachers and writers often do so with humanistic undertones that seek to portray Islam as a religion of peace that teaches Muslims to coexist with all. Deluded by the open-ended concept of "tolerance," they cite numerous ayat and ahadith that—rightfully so—serve to demonstrate that racial hatred has no place in Islam, but they do so for the purpose of advancing an agenda that attempts to "Islamize" more "liberal" concepts that the kuffar apply across the board for achieving evil, such as political pluralism, freedom of religion, and acceptance of sodomites.[30]

The group also strongly condemned interreligious dialogue initiatives:

Francis is taking the route traveled by his counterparts from the apostate "scholars" at al-Azhar and in Medina, namely the path of overlooking the clear call to warring against shirk and its people throughout the Quran and Sunnah—and instead altering the religion to fit some devilish "inter-faith" fantasy, far removed from the truth, which one is naturally inclined to seek. This is all part of a plan to demilitarize Islam or, to put it more correctly, to remove the clearly Quran- and Sunnah-based duty of waging jihad against pagans until all the world is ruled by the Shari'ah.[31]

In short, ISIS followed major religious initiatives and arguments against its policies and governance, and took the time and energy to boldly respond. It argued that Islam was a religion of the sword and there could not be any compromise. Although the group claimed a religious identity and performed gruesome executions, there was nothing uniquely religious about the nature of its violence. Stathis Kalyvas, a political science professor, noted that "there is nothing particularly Islamic or jihadi about the organization's violence" and the practices used by ISIS "have been used by a variety of insurgent incumbent actors in civil wars across time and space."[32] He recommended analyzing ISIS as a "revolutionary" actor that happened to be Islamist, rather than as either simply an Islamist actor or a sectarian one.[33] This interpretation is consistent with Cronin's and Walt's analyses; the group might have been Islamist, but it exhibited the character of a revolutionary pseudo-state and analyses should take this political qualification into account.

Spatial Dimension: Territorial Underpinnings in Perspective

An organization's ideology is intimately tied to the time and space it operates in. ISIS was, for the most part, the result of the political vacuum created by the American invasion of Iraq and hasty withdrawal from the region after promising the Sunni groups full participation in the new Iraqi political system. Unfulfilled promises and the early withdrawal consolidated the existing frustrations with Arab authoritarian regimes and frequent foreign interventions. Not surprisingly, the group's ideology was shaped by the political factors that gave birth to it. Fawaz Gerges confirms that, in his conversations with Iraqi tribal leaders, many acknowledged that their sons joined ISIS not because of its Islamist ideology but as a means of resistance to the sectarian central authority in Iraq and its regional patron Iran.[34] The unique conditions created by the invasion, such as the disbanding of the Iraqi Army and the establishment of special detention facilities, helped bring together disillusioned actors with a jihadi orientation and experience. Abu Ahmed, a senior official in ISIS, once stated that Camp Bucca (the detention center where he met Baghdadi for the first time) was an extraordinary opportunity for jihadis in that it brought them all together in a physically safe environment; "Here [in Camp Bucca], we were not only safe, but we were only a few hundred metres away from the entire al-Qaida leadership."[35]

From mid-2013 to mid-2014, ISIS extended its territories to Syria. The group's expansion to Syria was possible because of failed governance and civil war. Weiss and Hassan remind readers that ISIS benefited from the absence of a "Syrian" jihadi discourse in war-ravaged Syria and that the group had a monopoly on the global Salafi jihadist narrative. In April 2013 Baghdadi unilaterally declared the group's jurisdiction over Syria and named the organization "the Islamic State of Iraq and al-Sham." The expansion created further complications with al Qaeda. Baghdadi did not heed the stark warnings and insisted on the group's independence. Cole Bunzel noted that this division divided the jihadi ideologues; one group dominated by younger jihadis supported Baghdadi, whereas another group of senior jihadis denounced ISIS's defiance.[36]

ISIS also signaled how seriously it took the territory and region it operated in. It put great symbolic emphasis on the Syrian city of Dabiq, near Aleppo, after which the group named its magazine. In Islamic eschatology, Dabiq is one of the sites where the caliphate will meet the armies of "Rome" (there are different interpretations of what "Rome" stands for; the most common one is any army of "the West"). ISIS actually wanted to draw the United States and its ally armies to the region; it was part of its revolutionary revanchist theology. One of the group's famous statements noted, "If one examined the battleground of Sham, he would see that the military factions before ISIS's official expansion fell mostly into four categories: (1) Islamic factions with an international agenda; (2) 'Islamic' factions with a nationalist agenda (leaders have a Salafi background and soldiers engage in more religious practices than those in the third category); (3) nationalist factions with an 'Islamic' agenda; and (4) secularist factions with a democratic agenda (Free Syrian Army)."[37] In that political landscape ISIS prided itself on being the only authentic Islamic unit, fighting against all the others that are Islamic in name only.

ISIS's public theology of governance and its ideology are unique to the time period it operated in, while the group was a product of the historical perspectives and understandings of jihadism. Today's communication technologies, for example, change the color of ideologies and redefine in-group discussion parameters by increasing the reach of any organization's message. McCants reminds us that the biggest split in the global jihadist community happened with the advent of new forms of social media such as Twitter, where, unlike on private discussion boards, discussants with unpalatable views cannot be silenced.[38] Radical groups can market their ideologies online and provide sympathizers with concrete instructions on how to carry out attacks.

ISIS had observable ideological underpinnings that cannot be captured comprehensively in a chapter-length treatment. Wahhabism, the ultra-conservative Islamic doctrine founded by Muhammad Ibn Abd al-Wahhab in the eighteenth century, was one such influence. The doctrine aimed to purge the religion of practices that did not exist in the Qu'ran or in the initial years of the birth of Islam, such as tomb visitation. Abd al-Wahhab made a pact with Muhammed bin Saud, a prominent tribal leader who was in control of a critical portion of the Arabian Peninsula. The pact has continued into the political structure of contemporary Saudi Arabia. Hassan traced many of the extremist religious concepts that constitute ISIS's ideology to Saudi Arabia's Sahwa (Islamic awakening) movement in the 1970s and a similar movement in Egypt, where Salafism and political Islam merged.[39]

There are also individuals whose legacies cannot be underestimated in the formation of ISIS's ideology and governance. Among them are Ibn Taymiyya, Sayyid Qutb, Abdullah al-Muhajir, Abu Bakr Naji, Sayyid Imam Sharif, and Abu Musab Al-Suri. Ibn Taymiyya, a medieval Sunni Muslim theologian, was the main intellectual influence behind Wahhabism; he espoused a literal interpretation of the Qu'ran, and his writings endorsed takfiri approaches; he believed that if a Muslim does not practice the "right" interpretation of Islam then he should be severely punished. Egyptian author and leading Muslim Brotherhood member Sayyid Qutb's revolutionary Islamism also played a role, albeit much less direct than Taymiyya and Wahhabism. In his famous *Ma'alim fi-l-Tariq* (Milestones), Qutb defended the use of physical force and jihad to bring down existing organizations and authorities. "Given Qutb's advocacy of systemic change," John Calvert maintained, "his influence has been strongest among Islamist militants who adopt the methods of 'direct action' to bring about a theocratic state."[40] Abdullah al-Muhajir's treatises (such as the *Introduction to the Jurisprudence of Jihad*) are known to have influenced Zarqawi's worldview. Muhajir argued that Muslims are obligated to leave lands of infidelity that submit to positive law, that "siding with apostates against Muslims is the greatest infidelity of all, and that Islam does not differentiate between military and civilians."[41]

Al Qaeda strategist Abu Bakr Naji's 2004 online manifesto, *The Management of Savagery*, also undergirded the ISIS strategy. Deriving insights from Ibn Taymiyya, Naji divided the path to statehood into three stages: exercising the power of vexation and exhaustion; the administration of savagery; and taking power and establishing the state.[42] Naji was skeptical of the former treatises on jihad; he cautioned in *The Management of Savagery* that "the political, security, and military books which the heretical movements published—such as the Brothers—are more dangerous than books of others because they mix their writings with proofs from the Book [the Qur'an] and the Sunna and events from the sira after they have distorted them."[43] In addition to Abdullah al-Muhajir's book and Abu Bakr Naji's *The Management of Savagery*, Gerges counted *The Essentials of Making Ready* (for Jihad) by Sayyid Imam Sharif (also known as Abdel-Qader Ibn Abdel-Aziz or Dr. Fadl) among the three manifestos that "represent the most extreme thinking within the Salafi jihadist movement and the degeneration of this ideology into Fiqh Damaa (the jurisprudence of blood)."[44] Abu Musab Al Suri's contributions to jihadi strategy (epitomized by his book-length manifesto *The Call to Global Islamic Resistance* and individual shorter writings, including his occasional articles called "Jihadi Experiences" in al Qaeda's magazine, *Inspire*) most likely played a role in shaping the ideology and strategy a jihadi organization should follow. In his work, Suri emphasized the importance of joining both open fronts and individual operations, and he advised transforming the resistance into a strategic phenomenon, "after the pattern of the Palestinian intifada against the occupation forces, the settlers and their collaborators . . . but on a broader scale, originally comprising the entire Islamic world."[45]

ISIS is unique to its time and should not be conflated with other Islamic groups and movements. Ahmed al-Hamdan, a well-known jihadi Salafist and a former student of Maqdisi, wrote in his famous "Methodological

Difference between ISIS and Al Qaida" that it would be a mistake to say that ISIS was a part of the Salafi jihadi movement for they have destroyed the Salafi Jihadi methodology and attacked its iconic leaders.[46] This iconoclasm might well be interpreted as a natural next step in the jihadi trajectory that exhausted its conventional methods and experienced a political transformation. In that sense it is critical to follow influential jihadi theologians worldwide to observe what kind of intellectual currents are in development.

Looking Ahead: The Legacy of ISIS and Future Jihadi Movements

There are too many dimensions of ISIS's existence and thinking to be reduced to ideology. ISIS challenged the traditional conception of a terrorist organization. It transformed parts of a once authoritarian country into a religious-cult-like political unit and started showcasing its brutality through multiple media channels. ISIS might be territorially defeated, yet its members are now escaping to different continents to take part in other organizations. It is obvious that there will be groups in the future who will carry the caliphate banner and take lessons from the ISIS experience. The same goes for attacks "by inspiration." Lone-wolf attacks existed before ISIS. However, ISIS made the most efficient use of the jihad sympathizers, and it continuously and publicly encouraged these attacks. The number of attempts might have been relatively low, but when an attack happened, it usually resulted in a high number of casualties.

ISIS was considered jihadi Salafi, but not like the groups that came before it. It was a revolutionary revanchist organization that made frequent use of apocalyptic imagery and narratives. Its understanding of governance was shaped by its leaders and by the territories it operated in, and it borrowed perspectives from different sources in history. It was the outcome of a series of failed jihadi projects, evolving theoretical perspectives on governance, changing technologies, the Western legacy in the region, personal feuds, and most important, a political vacuum. Even when a group is physically defeated, its members and sympathizers live on, and its ideology is not destroyed. Political vacuums and foreign interventions prepare the ground for radicals who have coherent enough ideologies to rally the frustrated masses that are facing existential threats.

The ideological battle against jihadi groups is also a sensitive one. Politicians should avoid weighing in on the religious debate and using theological terms. It is critical to keep in mind that overt political support for one group might discredit it in the eyes of potential followers. Atheel al-Nujaifi, who was the governor of Ninevah Governorate between 2009 and 2015, once said that "this issue [ISIS] has to be resolved not by Maliki, but as a Sunni project. We have to struggle against ISIS with our Sunni way. It is not a fight for Shiites or Maliki's supporters. Maliki cannot fight ISIS."[47] Outside intervention in the politics of ideology makes matters even worse and gives ammunition to radicals. Theological debate about how Islamic a group is or is not should be left to theologians and scholars of Islam.

As this chapter notes, many groups and tribes pledged allegiance to ISIS as a means of self-preservation. Looking ahead, this is one fact that policymakers should remember. Even when there is a significant religious identity present, political units, including tribes, operate to protect their existence and, if possible, extend their influence. The Realpolitik dimension sometimes got lost in the widely distributed dramatic imagery produced by ISIS and the sensational reporting of the organization's executions and advances. Especially given the ISIS recruits' low level of religious knowledge, it is clear that something beyond religion was at play in the organization's operational success. The major policy lesson here is to pay more attention to state-building and cooperating with leaders around the world to prevent power imbalances and vacuums.

In order to prevent ISIS from reappearing in the future, the focus should primarily be on good governance and capacity-building in conflict-ridden societies. If communities feel disenfranchised and their basic needs are not met, they are more likely to join jihadi movements. That is why it is critical to partner with or provide support to local policymakers to build infrastructures and create systems where concerns can be aired through political platforms. In Iraq, for example, a solid power-sharing system between Sunni and Shia communities that will alleviate their existential concerns is essential. Similarly, in Syria, the end of the civil war and a focus on reconstruction and reconciliation, albeit challenging, could prove to be the most effective solution against jihadi organization recruitment and radicalization. Relying only on military capabilities and operations, in the absence of reliable partnerships, will likely alienate local communities and make matters worse.

Another policy that would help the battle against radicalization would be to minimize ambitious foreign policy engagements and interventions abroad. ISIS and many other jihadi organizations used the Western military presence in the Middle East and South Asia to justify their actions. In the absence of broad international consensus, foreign interventions rarely produce desired results and are likely to weaken political structures that are not able to cope with radicalization.

On the domestic politics front, it is critical to have democratic systems with a strong civil society presence and multiple channels through which citizens and residents can convey their concerns. When fighting terrorist organizations, reducing the problem to identity politics and singling out religious or national groups might have short-term political benefits, but in the long term those actions will only help radical organizations recruit adherents. Even if it claims a religious identity, ISIS and other jihadi organizations constitute a direct threat to more Muslims than non-Muslims. Portraying the tension as one between the West and Islam is not only analytically fallacious and factually incorrect, but also practically dangerous. Therefore, while keeping necessary intelligence facilities in place, it is crucial to treat all citizens and residents equitably and take measures to decrease alienation and disenfranchisement in democratic societies.

Notes

1 Nukhet Sandal, "The Clash of Public Theologies? Rethinking the Concept of Religion in Global Politics," *Alternatives: Global, Local, Political* 37 (2012): 70.

2 Fawaz Gerges, *ISIS: A History* (Princeton University Press, 2016), p. 35.

3 Christina Hellmich and Andreas Behnke, *Knowing al Qaeda: The Epistemology of Terrorism* (New York: Routledge, 2012). The individual chapters in the book do not go into the components or mechanisms of an epistemic theory of terrorism (or of al Qaeda), but the framing is still worth noting.

4 I have explored the epistemic dimension of religious leadership in times of conflict in *Religious Actors in Conflict Transformation* (Cambridge University Press, 2017).

5 On Osama bin Laden's syllabus for new recruits, see "The Course of Islamic Studies for Soldiers and Members" (https://assets.documentcloud.org /documents/2729966/Jihad-101.pdf).

6 "The analogy we use around here sometimes, and I think is accurate, is if a jayvee team puts on Lakers uniforms, that doesn't make them Kobe Bryant," Barack Obama told the *New Yorker*. See David Remnick, "Going the Distance: On and Off the Road with Barack Obama," *New Yorker*, January 27, 2014.

7 Audrey Kurth Cronin, "ISIS Is Not a Terrorist Group," *Foreign Affairs* (March/April 2015): 88.

8 Stephen Walt, "What Should We Do if the Islamic State Wins?," *Foreign Policy*, June 10, 2015.

9 "Khilafah Declared," *Dabiq*, no. 1, July 2014, p. 6.

10 "The Currency of the Khilafah," *Dabiq*, no. 5, November 2014, p. 18.

11 Aya Batrawy, Paisley Dodds, and Lori Hinnant, "'Islam for Dummies': IS Recruits Have Poor Grasp of Faith," Associated Press, August 15, 2016 (http://bigstory.ap.org/article/9f94ff7f1e294118956b049a51548b33/islamic -state-gets-know-nothing-recruits-and-rejoices).

12 "Advice for Those Embarking upon Hijrah," *Dabiq*, no. 3, September 2014, p. 33.

13 For an analysis of the Taliban's diplomacy, for example, see Paul Sharp, "Mullah Zaeef and Taliban Diplomacy," *Review of International Studies* 29, no. 4 (2003): 481–98.

14 Michael Weiss and Hassan Hassan, *ISIS: Inside the Army of Terror* (New York: Regan Arts, 2015), p. 209.

15 Abu Muhammad al-Adnani, "Indeed Your Lord Is Ever Watchful," *Dabiq*, no. 4, October 2014, p. 9.

16 See, for example, "The Crusade Serving Iran and Russia," *Dabiq*, no. 4, October 2014, p. 38.

17 Quoted in Steve Visser and John Couwels, "Orlando Killer Repeatedly References ISIS, Transcript Shows," CNN, September 24, 2016 (www.cnn .com/2016/09/23/us/orlando-shooter-hostage-negotiator-call/).

18 Abu Muhammad al-Adnani, "Foreword," *Dabiq*, no. 6, December 2014, p. 4.

19 Graeme Wood, "What ISIS Really Wants," *The Atlantic*, March 2015.
20 See, for example, Robert Wright, "The Clash of Civilizations that Isn't," *New Yorker*, February 25, 2015.
21 Shiraz Maher, *Salafi Jihadism: The History of an Idea* (Oxford University Press, 2016).
22 William McCants, *The ISIS Apocalypse* (New York: St. Martin's, 2015), p. 143.
23 Jean-Pierre Filiu, *Apocalypse in Islam*, translated by M. B. DeBevoise (University of California Press, 2011).
24 Abu Mus'ab al-Zarqawi, "Zarqawi Letter" (English translation), State Department Archive, February 2004 (https://2001-2009.state.gov/p/nea/rls/31694.htm).
25 "The Rafidah: From Ibn Saba to the Dajjal," *Dabiq*, no. 14, April 2016, p. 39.
26 Jessica Stern and J. M. Berger, "Thugs Wanted—Bring Your Own Boots: How ISIS Attracts Foreign Fighters to Its Twisted Utopia," *The Guardian*, March 9, 2015.
27 Adam Gadahn, "Letter from Adam Gadahn" (English translation), January 2011 (https://www.ctc.usma.edu/posts/letter-from-adam-gadahn-english-translation-2).
28 Open Letter to Al-Baghdadi (http://www.lettertobaghdadi.com/).
29 "Islam Is the Religion of Sword, Not Pacifism," *Dabiq*, no. 7, February 2015, p. 20.
30 "Wala' and Bara' vs. American Racism," *Dabiq*, no. 11, September 2015, p. 19.
31 "In the Words of the Enemy," *Dabiq*, no. 15, July 2016, p. 76.
32 Stathis Kalyvas, "The Logic of Violence in the Islamic State's War," *Washington Post*, July 7, 2014.
33 Ibid.
34 Gerges, *ISIS*, p. 14.
35 Quoted in Martin Chulov, "ISIS: The Inside Story," *The Guardian*, December 11, 2014.
36 Cole Bunzel, "From Paper State to Caliphate: The Ideology of the Islamic State," Analysis Paper 19, Brookings Project on U.S. Relations with the Islamic World (Brookings, March 2015).
37 "Irja': The Most Dangerous Bid'ah," *Dabiq*, no. 8, March 2015, p. 52.
38 McCants, *The ISIS Apocalypse*, p. 95.
39 Hassan Hassan, "The Sectarianism of the Islamic State: Ideological Roots and Political Context," Carnegie Endowment for International Peace Paper (Washington, June 13, 2016) (http://carnegieendowment.org/2016/06/13/sectarianism-of-islamic-state-ideological-roots-and-political-context-pub-63746).

40 John Calvert, *Sayyid Qutb and the Origins of Radical Islamism* (Oxford University Press, 2013), p. 4.

41 Motaz al-Khateeb, "Daesh's Intellectual Origins: From Jurisprudence to Reality," Al Jazeera, January 18, 2015 (http://studies.aljazeera.net/en/dossiers /decipheringdaeshoriginsimpactandfuture/2014/12/2014123981882756 .html).

42 Abu Bakr Naji, *Management of Savagery: The Most Critical Stage through Which the Umma Will Pass*, translated by William McCants, 2004 (https://azelin .files.wordpress.com/2010/08/abu-bakr-naji-the-management-of-savagery -the-most-critical-stage-through-which-the-umma-will-pass.pdf).

43 Ibid., p. 99.

44 Fawaz A. Gerges, "The Three Manifestos that Paved the Way for Islamic State," *Los Angeles Times*, April 15, 2016.

45 Abu Musab Al Suri, "Jihadi Experiences," *Inspire,* no. 10 (2013): p. 24.

46 Ahmad Al-Hamdan, "Methodological Difference between ISIS and Al-Qaeda," Al-Muwahideen Media, December 30, 2015, p. 45 (https:// almuwahideenmedia.files.wordpress.com/2016/02/methodological.pdf).

47 Atheel al-Nujaifi interview with Fehim Tastekin, "'Sunni Project' Needed to Fight ISIS, Says Mosul Governor," *Al Monitor,* June 16, 2014 (www.al -monitor.com/pulse/originals/2014/06/tastekin-isis-sunnis-mosul-iraq -turkey-syria-erbil-kirkuk.html).

PART II

Intelligence Failures

3

Not Your Father's Intelligence Failure

Why the Intelligence Community Failed to Anticipate the Rise of ISIS

Erik J. Dahl

The rapid rise of the Islamic State in Iraq and Syria (ISIS) in 2013 and early 2014 caught many observers by surprise and led to charges that American intelligence had failed to anticipate and understand the growing threat. Not all experts have agreed that there was any intelligence failure; some have claimed that the American intelligence community (IC) actually did a good job of warning about ISIS but that the Obama administration failed to listen. Senior intelligence officials, however, have acknowledged that they underestimated ISIS and overestimated the capability of the Iraqi security forces combating it, and this chapter argues that the American intelligence community did indeed fail to properly assess the growing threat from ISIS.

Although there has been considerable discussion in the media about a possible intelligence failure concerning the rise of ISIS, there has been relatively little careful examination of the issue in the policy or scholarly literature.[1] Most scholars who have studied the question have concluded there was an intelligence failure. David Siman-Tov and Yotam Hacohen, for example, write, "The meteoric rise of the Islamic State in June 2014 stunned the intelligence organizations in the United States."[2] Ephraim Kam argues that U.S. intelligence was not alone in failing to understand the danger as the group rose to prominence in 2014:

> Less than a year before, no government or intelligence community in the nations most affected by ISIS predicted the force, scope, or speed of its emergence. . . . Not even one actor seems to have envisaged that by the middle of 2014, the organization would control one third of Syria and one quarter of Iraq, infiltrate into other countries, and threaten the future of states, the stability and survivability of regimes, and the way of life of large population groups.[3]

This chapter adds to the literature by first examining what U.S. intelligence and national security leaders said about the threat from ISIS and its predecessor organization al Qaeda in Iraq (AQI) in the years before it exploded to prominence in 2014. These statements and reports from government agencies and officials tended to lag behind the development of the threat and often provided little more than reviews of past events and broad-based warnings of potential dangers to come. These official assessments are then compared with the view from outside experts during the same time period, who similarly tended to provide warnings about the continuing threat from al Qaeda–affiliated groups but little appreciation that the greatest threat would come from AQI and then ISIS.

The chapter next reviews the statements by senior government leaders, including President Barack Obama, about the intelligence failure and the debate in the media and among experts over who is to blame for it. The subsequent section examines a separate controversy about intelligence and ISIS over the management of intelligence at the headquarters of U.S. Central Command (CENTCOM), the major U.S. military command responsible for fighting ISIS. The chapter concludes by considering the reasons for the intelligence failure to understand ISIS and argues that the failure to anticipate ISIS is more than simply another in a long list of American intelligence failures. This most recent failure is an example of the many new challenges facing the American intelligence community today as it continues to grapple with nonstate actors and other unconventional threats.

Assessments of the Threat

The strength of ISIS came to world attention when its forces moved into Fallujah, Iraq, on New Year's Day 2014. Then in June 2014 the city of Mosul fell to ISIS, and the Iraqi Army failed to stop it as soldiers dropped their uniforms and fled. Did American intelligence warn policymakers that this might happen? Did they see it coming, or were they caught flat-footed, as critics have charged? This section reviews the public record about what American intelligence agencies and senior officials were saying about ISIS (and its predecessor AQI), focusing on the period before 2014.

It should be acknowledged that the only assessments available are those that have been made public. We do not know what information IC agencies and officials were providing during this time in classified channels, and some observers have claimed that the classified record shows a history of significantly more detailed and perceptive warnings than are reflected here. But until those classified warnings are made available, such as through the work of a blue-ribbon commission empowered to investigate the ISIS intelligence failure, the public record is all we have to go on.

U.S. Government Assessments

Before the summer of 2013, most intelligence leaders and other senior government officials assessed al Qaeda in Iraq as a serious threat, but it was usually not high on their list of concerns. For example, in his annual congressional testimony in February 2011, Director of National Intelligence (DNI) James Clapper said that AQI "will be a persistent security problem," but he added, "we believe it is unlikely AQI will be able to achieve its larger strategic goals of controlling territory from which to launch attacks."[4] In January 2012 Clapper warned that al Qaeda's regional affiliates, including al Qaeda in Iraq, would surpass the remnants of "core" al Qaeda in terms of threats to U.S. interests; and of AQI, he said, "we are watchful for indications that AQI aspires to conduct attacks in the West."[5]

In a media conference call in April 2012, an unnamed senior U.S. counterterrorism official said, "AQI in Iraq is still a very dangerous, potent, lethal organization." The official said the intelligence community had expected some increase in AQI operations following the U.S. withdrawal from Iraq, but added, "I do think that a piece of good news is that the Iraqi security forces are actually doing a decent job of keeping up with AQI. But it is certainly a battle and AQI is a well-armed adversary."[6]

In March 2013 the commander of U.S. Central Command, Marine General James Mattis, gave his annual congressional testimony on the posture of Central Command. His prepared statement had only one reference to al Qaeda in Iraq as "a sustained violent AQI threat."[7] Clapper's prepared testimony that same month was stronger: he noted that the 2012 attack on U.S. facilities in Benghazi, Libya, and the 2013 attack on an Algerian oil facility demonstrated the threat represented by al Qaeda affiliates and splinter groups such as al Qaeda in Iraq: "Since the 2011 withdrawal of US forces, AQI has conducted nearly monthly, simultaneous, coordinated country-wide attacks against government, security, and Shia civilian targets."[8] But he also added in his remarks before the Senate Intelligence Committee, "AQI almost certainly lacks the strength to overwhelm Iraqi security forces."[9]

The State Department issues an annual assessment on terrorism, and its 2012 assessment, published in May 2013, noted that "Al-Qa'ida in Iraq (AQI)—even with diminished leadership and capabilities—continued to conduct attacks across Iraq."[10] By the middle of 2013 threat assessments were becoming more dire, and in July 2013 David Shedd, acting deputy director of the Defense Intelligence Agency (DIA), said at a conference that al Qaeda–affiliated groups were gaining strength in Syria: "Over the last two years they've grown in size, they've grown in capability, and ruthlessly have grown in effectiveness."[11] Then, in September 2013, a senior administration official told reporters on a conference call that the danger from ISIS was growing: "This is really a major and increasing threat to Iraq's stability . . . and it's an increasing threat to us."[12]

One of the strongest warnings came in November 2013, when Deputy Assistant Secretary of State Brett McGurk warned in congressional testimony, "Internally and regionally, pressures continue to build, exacerbated by a resurgent terrorist network led by al Qaeda's Iraq-based affiliate, now known publicly as the Islamic State of Iraq and the Levant (AQ/ISIL). The next year in Iraq may be pivotal."[13]

In early 2014 these warnings became more urgent. Clapper's January 2014 testimony focused on other issues, but noted that Iraq was facing a rising challenge from AQI, and the civil war in Syria was contributing to increased attacks by AQI.[14] Lt. Gen. Michael Flynn, then the DIA director, was more outspoken and testified on February 11, 2014, that "ISIL probably will attempt to take territory in Iraq and Syria in 2014."[15]

In March 2014, General Lloyd Austin, who was then commander of U.S. Central Command, testified that the security situation in Iraq had deteriorated significantly, "exacerbated by the active presence of Al Qaeda (through the Islamic State of Iraq and the Levant) and the steady influx of jihadists coming into Iraq from Syria."[16] The 2013 State Department assessment, issued in April 2014, noted that al Qaeda in Iraq now called itself ISIL, had increased the violence of its attacks, and had expanded from Syria into Iraq.[17]

Since 2014 ISIS has been a major concern. The 2014 State Department report, issued in June 2015, began by stating, "Major trends in global terrorism in 2014 included the Islamic State in Iraq and the Levant's (ISIL's) unprecedented seizure of territory in Iraq and Syria."[18] DNI Clapper's February 2015 testimony included considerable discussion of ISIS/ISIL, and in February 2016 Clapper described it as "the preeminent global terrorist threat."[19]

This history of official assessments of AQI and ISIS shows that IC leaders did provide a number of high-level strategic warnings about the threat. But these warnings were often tempered, couched as "on the one hand, on the other hand" assessments that are commonly found in the intelligence community, such as the assessments into early 2013 that AQI was diminished but still represented a threat. And even when the assessments became more dire in late 2013 and early 2014, they were still very general, with little indication in the public record of specific, actionable warnings that might have been useful for decisionmakers.

The View from Outside Experts

The public record suggests American intelligence agencies were slow to recognize the rising threat from ISIS. But how does that record compare with the assessments of nongovernmental experts and scholars? Did outside experts have a clearer view of the rising threat from ISIS than intelligence officials did?[20] In early and mid-2013, terrorism experts were warning of the growing threat from al Qaeda–affiliated groups, but al Qaeda in the Arabian Peninsula (AQAP) was widely considered to be the affiliate that presented the greatest threat, and there was little appreciation that al Qaeda in Iraq would soon rise to such deadly prominence.

In July 2013 the House Foreign Affairs Committee held a subcommittee hearing on the threat from al Qaeda affiliates.[21] Some of that testimony appears prescient today; Frederick W. Kagan, for example, said of AQI: "The group is expanding its capabilities at an accelerating rate, and the Iraqi Security Forces appear to be unable to contain it, despite numerous offensive and defensive operations."[22] But Kagan also reflected the conventional wisdom by noting, "Almost all analysts agree that AQAP poses a direct and immediate threat to the U.S. homeland for the excellent reason that it has already attempted attacks against us on three separate occasions."[23] The focus on AQAP was also seen in September 2013, when the House Homeland Security Committee Subcommittee on Counterterrorism and Intelligence held a hearing on the threat from that group, with several speakers warning it was the al Qaeda affiliate that presented the greatest threat to the U.S. homeland.[24]

In September 2013 the Bipartisan Policy Center warned of the threat from al Qaeda and its affiliated groups, including al Qaeda in Iraq, al Qaeda in the Arabian Peninsula, and al Qaeda in the Islamic Maghreb. The center's report stated, "It is too soon to predict the long-term threat posed by al Qaeda and allied groups as the movement is undergoing a transition that may end up proving to be its last gasp; but the right set of circumstances in the unstable Middle East could also revive the network." The report stated that AQI had increased its attacks in Iraq since American troops pulled out of the country at the end of 2011, and that AQI was involved in the Syrian civil war. It warned that "the group is perhaps more threatening and consequential today than it has been at any time since the height of its power in 2006." But the report also noted that senior American officials assessed AQAP as posing "the greatest immediate threat from a jihadist group to the United States."[25]

In December 2013 two subcommittees of the House Foreign Affairs Committee held a joint hearing on the resurgence of al Qaeda in Iraq, and the testimony they heard was much more alarming. Daniel Byman testified that the group "has seemingly returned from the dead," while Kenneth M. Pollack said that "AQI has been one of the principal culprits in the worsening violence across Iraq."[26] The testimony of these respected terrorism experts mirrored the warnings of government officials at the same time, but by then—less than a month before ISIS occupied Fallujah—the warnings may have been too late.

Acknowledging the Failure

Senior U.S. intelligence officials have acknowledged that the IC underestimated the ISIS threat. Admiral Michael Rogers, director of the National Security Agency (NSA), said, "I'll only speak for me and for NSA—I wish we'd been a little stronger about" the threat.[27] Director of National Intelligence Clapper said that the IC made the same mistake with ISIS that it did in Vietnam: it underestimated the enemy's will to fight. He told an interviewer: "What we didn't do was predict the will to fight. That's always a problem. We didn't do it in Vietnam. We underestimated the Viet Cong and the North Vietnamese and overestimated the will of the South Vietnamese. In this case, we underestimated ISIL and overestimated the fighting capability of the Iraqi army."[28] In September 2014, in an interview with CBS's *60 Minutes*, when President Obama was asked about Clapper's comments he acknowledged that the United States had underestimated the rise of ISIS and overestimated the ability of the Iraqi military.[29]

There has been controversy over what Obama believed about the threat from ISIS and what advice and assessments he received. If there is a single quote that seems to sum up the failure to understand the rise of ISIS, it came from Obama in an interview with the *New Yorker* published on January 27, 2014. He described ISIS as a junior varsity basketball team: "The analogy we use around here sometimes, and I think is accurate, is if a jayvee team puts on Lakers uniforms that doesn't make them Kobe Bryant."[30] The White House later argued that Obama had not been talking about ISIS, but in the context of the full article it did seem clear that the president was referring to—and discounting the threat from—ISIS.[31]

It is possible that Obama's "jayvee team" comment was a reflection of the advice he was getting at the time. Jeffrey Goldberg of *The Atlantic* published a favorable article about the president in April 2016, in which he wrote: "Early in 2014, Obama's intelligence advisers told him that ISIL was of marginal importance. According to administration officials, General Lloyd Austin, then the commander of Central Command, which oversees U.S. military operations in the Middle East, told the White House that the Islamic State was 'a flash in the pan.'"[32] Goldberg noted that Austin's spokesman denied he had made such a statement.[33] But by late spring 2014, Goldberg wrote, Obama's view of ISIS had shifted to consider it a much more serious threat. Obama explained to advisers, according to Goldberg, that he saw ISIS as representing a truly new and dangerous threat, in the way that the Joker was presented in the Batman movie *The Dark Knight*:

> "There's a scene in the beginning in which the gang leaders of Gotham are meeting," the president would say. "These are men who had the city divided up. They were thugs, but there was a kind of order. Everyone had his turf. And then the Joker comes in and lights the whole city on fire. ISIL is the Joker. It has the capacity to set the whole region on fire. That's why we have to fight it."[34]

Whose Failure Was It?

Not all observers believe American intelligence failed to properly assess and warn about the threat from ISIS. Former CIA official Paul Pillar defends the IC against charges of failure, suggesting that there may have been more warnings about ISIS than are publicly known: "It is remarkable how, when anything disturbing goes bump in the night overseas, the label 'intelligence failure' gets quickly and automatically applied by those who have no basis whatever for knowing what the intelligence community did or did not say—in classified, intra-governmental channels—to policymakers." He added that although there is a tendency to believe that surprises should not happen, "This belief disregards how much that is relevant to foreign policy and national security is unknowable, no matter how brilliant either an intelligence service or a policymaker may be."[35]

Some analysts—especially those critical of the Obama administration—have argued that the failure lies not with the intelligence community, which had warned about ISIS, but with senior officials who disregarded the warnings. Former U.S. representative and chair of the House Intelligence Committee Mike Rogers said, "This was not an intelligence community failure, but a failure by policy makers to confront the threat."[36] Fox News reported in September 2014 that, according to an unnamed Pentagon official, "detailed and specific intelligence about the rise of ISIS" was included in the President's Daily Brief for at least a year before June 2014.[37] Critics cited that report to claim that Obama had ignored warnings from the intelligence community.[38]

There have been a number of unconfirmed reports that intelligence agencies did in fact provide specific warning. The *Daily Beast*, for example, reported that the failure of the Iraqi military to stand up to ISIS was no surprise: "Both the CIA and the Defense Intelligence Agency have issued reported analysis for nearly a year warning that Iraq's military would not be able to stand up against a sustained campaign from ISIS."[39] And in July 2014, amid growing discussion in the press about intelligence failure, a CIA spokesman was quoted in the *Washington Times* saying, "Anyone who has had access to and actually read the full extent of CIA intelligence products on ISIL and Iraq should not have been surprised by the current situation."[40] We do not have these intelligence reports, and without them we cannot have a full accounting of the intelligence picture available; but the public record to date does not appear to support the argument that the IC was providing such prescient warning.

The CENTCOM Intelligence Controversy

Alongside the complaints about a failure by the intelligence community to foresee the rise of ISIS, there has been a separate controversy over the management of intelligence at U.S. Central Command headquarters. Civilian analysts complained they were pressured by senior officers to put a positive spin on their assessments of the efforts against the Islamic State, and those charges led to investigations by the Department of Defense (DoD) inspector general (IG) and by a joint task force in the U.S. House of Representatives. In addition, Democratic members of the House Permanent Select Committee on Intelligence (HPSCI) conducted their own inquiry.

The controversy arose in May 2015 when a DIA analyst assigned to CENTCOM headquarters filed a complaint with the DIA inspector general charging that senior CENTCOM intelligence officials had modified intelligence assessments "to present an unduly positive outlook on CENTCOM efforts to train the ISF and combat ISIL."[41] The senior Iraq analyst at CENTCOM, Gregory Hooker, reportedly was the leader of a group of analysts who complained that their intelligence assessments were changed to be more optimistic by Major General Steven Grove, the CENTCOM senior intelligence officer, and his civilian deputy, Gregory Ryckman.[42] More than fifty analysts filed complaints with the Pentagon IG in July 2015.[43] A survey of Central Command staff members conducted between August and October 2015 found that more than 40 percent of analysts were concerned that there were flaws in the integrity of the intelligence analysis and in how their work was handled.[44]

David Shedd, a former acting director of the DIA, wrote that the charges by the analysts suggested a very serious problem might exist: "If the allegations are determined to be well founded it would mean that top brass at a combatant command violated the sacrosanct professional code of intelligence to provide objective analysis, free of political bias and personal agendas. The fact that as many as 50 analysts reportedly signed the complaint filed with the inspector general suggests the problem is not a stand-alone case but systematic."[45]

The House Joint Task Force found that changes that had been made at the CENTCOM intelligence directorate led to attempts to distort or suppress negative assessments, and to the production of intelligence assessments that were more positive than was warranted by the judgments of other members of the IC or by actual events.[46] The HPSCI Democratic inquiry also criticized the CENTCOM policies, finding: "CENTCOM created an overly insular process for producing intelligence assessments on ISIL and Iraq Security Forces (ISF)—one that at times deviated from analytical best practices; stalled the release of intelligence products; limited the ability of CENTCOM analysts to coordinate with IC experts; insufficiently accommodated dissenting views; and negatively influenced the morale of CENTCOM analysts."[47]

There is some evidence that politicization at CENTCOM directly affected strategic assessments that reached national leaders: CBS News reported that the CENTCOM senior intelligence officer, Grove, on one occasion in 2015 "blocked a negative assessment of Iraq's military from the President's Daily Brief, a top secret intelligence summary viewed only by the president and his closest advisors."[48] But the problems at CENTCOM appear to have occurred largely during and after a leadership turnover within the intelligence directorate in the summer of 2014.[49] By that time ISIS's strength was clear, making it unlikely that the suppression of negative assessments contributed to an underestimation of ISIS's capabilities during 2013 and earlier, while ISIS was becoming a major force and such assessments would presumably have been most useful.

The DoD IG released its report in January 2017, which stated, "In sum . . . we did not substantiate the most serious allegation, which was that intelligence was falsified."[50] The IG also found there was insufficient evidence to substantiate the claims of some analysts that intelligence had been distorted or suppressed in order to provide a more optimistic view of conflict against ISIS. But the IG did find what it called "a strong perception among many intelligence analysts" that intelligence leaders were attempting to distort reporting on ISIS, and it identified several weaknesses in the CENTCOM intelligence process that appear to have led to such a perception.[51] It also found that some officials in other intelligence agencies believed that although CENTCOM's intelligence assessments were not systematically distorted, they were more optimistic than those of the other agencies.[52]

The CENTCOM controversy reflects what may be a larger problem for intelligence, which is the apparent tendency of senior officials—especially military leaders—to minimize threats and put the capabilities of U.S. forces and allies in a positive light. One journalist has described "the longstanding cultural differences between intelligence analysts, whose job is to warn of potential bad news, and military commanders, who are trained to promote 'can do' optimism."[53] Such optimism can make it difficult for civilian decisionmakers to arrive at objective threat assessments. Barack Obama, for example, indicated that he took the views of military commanders into account; in May 2015, after Jeffrey Goldberg of *The Atlantic* noted that Ramadi had just fallen to ISIS and asked the president whether he believed we were losing the war, Obama replied, "No, I don't think we're losing, and I just talked to our CENTCOM commanders and the folks on the ground."[54]

Reasons for Failure

The American intelligence community underestimated the potential threat from ISIS and overestimated the ability of the Iraqi security forces to counter that threat. We can understand the reasons behind that intelligence failure at two levels: specific causes of this particular failure, and reasons that can be seen in many cases of intelligence failures.

What Were the Specific Causes of This Failure?

Commentators have pointed to several reasons why American intelligence failed to foresee the rising strength of ISIS. Nelly Lahoud and Liam Collins, for example, believe the counterterrorism community failed to properly analyze the trajectory of ISIS dating back to at least 2006, and that part of the problem was with an "al Qaeda fixation," as there was "a post-9/11 bias toward understanding the threat emanating from jihadi groups around the world through the lens of AQ."[55] But there appear to have been two primary causes of the failure: first, that the United States lacked the physical presence in Iraq and Syria that would have been needed to establish intelligence networks; and second, that those intelligence assets that were available against ISIS were focused mainly on providing direct support to military operations and not on gaining a broader understanding of the threat.

U.S. intelligence capabilities against AQI and later ISIS were limited in Iraq after the withdrawal of U.S. forces at the end of 2011. Kam writes that "the CIA station in Baghdad was, at that time, the biggest CIA station in the world, with hundreds of operators and researchers. Following the departure from Iraq in late 2011, intelligence coverage shrank as the need was reduced and the CIA presence was scaled back."[56] The United States resumed occasional surveillance flights over Iraq in 2013 and attempted to create a joint intelligence center to share information with the Iraqis, but these efforts reportedly garnered only modest results.[57] Similar limitations hobbled American intelligence in Syria, especially after the U.S. embassy in Damascus was closed in 2012 for security reasons.[58]

Without an on-the-ground physical presence, intelligence agencies were limited to using technical collections systems such as signals intelligence and aerial reconnaissance. These capabilities can provide useful targeting and other technical data, but they cannot provide a full a picture of the threat unless they are complemented by human intelligence—which can only be developed by having personnel in place. And to compound the problem, these technical capabilities have mostly been used to support military operations, especially those aimed at finding and killing terrorist targets under the rubric of "Find, Fix, and Finish." Sarah Chayes, a journalist who served as a special adviser to Joint Chiefs of Staff Chairman Admiral Michael Mullen, argues that this has been a problem ever since the 9/11 attacks, as intelligence priorities have moved away from strategic-level analysis and toward more direct military support. "What you had is a drift of the intelligence community toward essentially being a paramilitary organization, the intelligence gathering and analysis being in support of that sort of paramilitary activity: basically finding and fixing targets."[59]

Broader Patterns of Intelligence Failure

The failure to foresee the rise of ISIS demonstrates several of the same problems that can be found in the long litany of American intelligence failures dating back to Pearl Harbor, but more recently including failures to anticipate the Iranian Revolution in 1979, the end of the Cold War, and the Arab Spring.[60] One lesson from these past failures is that even when strategic intelligence is good, specific tactical warning of a rising threat—such as a future attack—is rarely available.[61] This appears to have been the case here. For several years before 2014, officials understood that ISIS represented a long-term, serious threat; but they did not know—they probably could not know—that soon ISIS would become the most prominent face of that threat.

This level of understanding—good at the strategic level but weak at the operational and tactical levels—is evident in a story told by former acting CIA director Michael Morell. In February 2013, Tom Donilon, the national security adviser, asked Morell and the National Counterterrorism Center (NCTC) director, Matt Olsen, to meet with the president to describe what the threat from international terrorism would look like in the years ahead. Morell writes, "The overarching theme of my presentation—almost two years ago to the day of the writing of this book and well before the rise of ISIS—was that the war against Islamic extremism was far from over and that this war would be one that would be fought by multiple generations."[62] Looking back today, Morell's warning appears to have been a very good strategic assessment—but one wonders, what could a policymaker have done with such a broad-based warning?

Although several intelligence and military leaders did warn about the threat from ISIS in the years before 2014, the history of intelligence failure shows that it is not enough to simply mention a potential threat to a decisionmaker. A possibly apocryphal story about Henry Kissinger exemplifies this problem. Once when he was secretary of state, Kissinger was briefed about a coup attempt that had taken place somewhere in the world. He complained that he should have known about it ahead of time, only to be told by his intelligence briefer, "But we warned, you, sir." Kissinger reportedly replied, "Yes, but you didn't persuade me."[63]

Another lesson from the ISIS case that resembles earlier failures is that no intelligence agency can predict the future. As Kam writes, "Part of the assessment and forecasting difficulty is that no source, no matter how good, can report what will happen."[64] This lesson may sound banal or trite, but there is a debate in the intelligence literature about whether it is reasonable to expect intelligence professionals and agencies to make accurate predictions about the future.[65]

Some experts have not been optimistic about the ability of intelligence agencies to anticipate conflict; former CIA director and secretary of defense Robert Gates, for example, said in a speech at West Point in February 2011: "I must tell you, when it comes to predicting the nature and location of our next military engagements, since Vietnam, our record has been perfect. We have never once gotten it right."[66] But the intelligence community does acknowledge that warning of future threats is part of its job: the National Intelligence Strategy for 2014 identifies "anticipatory intelligence" as one of its foundational mission objectives, stating that "the IC will improve its ability to foresee, forecast, and alert the analytic community of potential issues of concern and convey early warning to national security customers."[67] And during his confirmation process as CIA director, John Brennan responded to a written question from the Senate Intelligence Committee by stating, "With billions of dollars invested in C.I.A. over the past decade, policy maker expectations of C.I.A.'s ability to anticipate major geopolitical events should be high."[68]

Not Your Father's Intelligence Failure

Although some aspects of the ISIS intelligence failure resemble problems seen previously, as a whole it appears to be more than simply another instance of the same old intelligence failure. The failure against ISIS represents something new and even more troubling for the American intelligence community because it illustrates the challenges intelligence faces today from new types of threats, and in particular from nonstate actors.

Senior intelligence officials have been warning for several years that today's world is in many ways more dangerous, and more difficult for the intelligence community to analyze, than it has been in the past. Director of National Intelligence Clapper, for example, testified in 2014, "Looking back over my now more than half a century in intelligence, I've not experienced a time when we've been beset by more crises and threats around the globe."[69] More recently, when Clapper announced that he would be retiring at the end of President Obama's second term, he told the House Intelligence Committee, "Our nation is facing the most diverse array of threats that I've seen."[70] CIA Director John Brennan said, "I've never seen a time when we have been confronted with such an array of very challenging, complex and serious threats to our national security, and issues we have to grapple with."[71]

Kam writes that the rise of ISIS was an example of these new and more difficult challenges for intelligence. As difficult as it is to anticipate and predict traditional strategic surprises such as the outbreak of war or major terrorist attacks, it is much more difficult to understand and forecast intangible events and processes such as the rise of social movements or regional instability.[72]

These challenges are even greater because intelligence is more than ever today a part of public discourse, meaning that its failures—or even perceived failures—are magnified. A number of experts have argued that the American intelligence community is facing a crisis as it attempts to grapple with this wider array of challenges and with a more complex information environment. Josh Kerbel of the DIA calls this a "Kodak moment" for the intelligence community,[73] while former U.S. representative Jane Harman, president of the Woodrow Wilson Center, argues that "rearranging the deck chairs will not be enough to prepare the intelligence community for the challenges that lie ahead."[74]

Where to Go from Here?

The problems that led to the inability to anticipate the rise of ISIS continue to affect American intelligence today. For example, despite some indications of increasing focus on human intelligence, critics of the Pentagon and the intelligence community charge that American military and intelligence agencies still rely too much on technical collection, such as signals intelligence and drone surveillance, at the expense of on-the-ground human intelligence, or traditional spying.[75] James Clapper has acknowledged the intelligence community's limited ability to understand the capabilities and intentions of ISIS, especially in areas such as Syria that are usually denied to American personnel: "I'm not going to fib to you, the intelligence challenges in Syria are quite profound because we're not there on the ground and that makes it a very challenging intelligence problem," he said at a conference in October 2014.[76]

In addition, statements by top military leaders indicate that their intelligence priority continues to be supporting the targeting and killing of ISIS leaders. This is clearly a key function for intelligence, but the sensors and capabilities that are likely to provide good targeting intelligence are not likely to help assess the future threat more than a few days or weeks down the road.[77]

American intelligence is very good at the tactical level of finding and finishing specific targets such as terrorist leaders. And as we have seen above, it also tends to be good at the other end of the spectrum, providing very broad and general strategic intelligence and warning on potential future threats such as ISIS. But what is lacking is intelligence about and an understanding of the environment where these threats develop—the kind of operational-level intelligence that would be required in order to understand the capabilities and intentions of ISIS or other groups, and to help leaders decide what needs to be done about such threats. Michael Flynn, who was then the director of intelligence for U.S. and allied forces in Afghanistan, recognized this problem in 2010 when he criticized "the tendency to overemphasize detailed information about the enemy at the expense of the political, economic, and cultural environment that supports it."[78]

How can the American intelligence community develop this kind of operational-level intelligence on ISIS and other threats? First, it should abandon the "stovepipe" model that has shaped the IC through most of its modern existence, in which security concerns and the need for specialization have pushed intelligence personnel to work in small, tightly compartmented cells, apart from one another. Intelligence experts have long recognized the difficulties with that model, and much of the intelligence reform effort following 9/11 was to create intelligence centers, such as the National Counterterrorism Center, that would bring analysts and collectors from a wide variety of disciplines together under one roof to coordinate their efforts on a problem. More recently, however, there has been growing recognition within the IC that more needs to be done to encourage greater use of intelligence fusion centers and all-source analysis that brings together human, signals, and other sources of intelligence. One positive impact of the ISIS intelligence failure may be that it will spur progress in this area. At the CIA, for example, John Brennan directed a restructuring that he believed will be more effective in understanding and countering ISIS and other global threats by bringing together analysts, collectors, computer hackers, and others in "mission centers."[79]

Second, the intelligence community—and in particular the military intelligence community—needs to make greater use of open-source intelligence and increase its focus on political, economic, and cultural factors. American intelligence excels at the technical collection of data, but it often fails to understand human behavior. As a study by the National Research Council noted, "Open sources can be particularly useful when analyzing human behavior, such as economic, political, religious, and cultural developments."[80]

Third, intelligence agencies should increase their use of the tool of net assessment, which involves not only understanding the enemy but also understanding the capabilities of one's own forces and those of one's allies. Part of the problem with ISIS was that the intelligence community was not equipped to assess the strength of the Iraqi Army; as Kam argues, "assessing one's own capabilities is not part of the mandate of the intelligence community."[81] Within the American intelligence and national security establishment the only place where such work is done is in the Pentagon's Office of Net Assessment.[82] As the importance of nonstate actors continues to increase, and the lines between friend and foe, and ally and enemy, become more and more blurred, it is crucial that intelligence agencies move beyond the old thinking that their only concern is with understanding the enemy.

Finally, intelligence leaders need to address the unfortunate fact that intelligence assessments—especially public, official assessments—almost always lag behind the development of the threat. If intelligence reports are to be useful for decisionmakers, they should precede the threat, not follow it. But as we saw in the case of ISIS, American intelligence assessments are more often than not playing catch-up.

We can see this lag clearly in the State Department's annual terrorism assessments, which are not issued until well into the year after they attempt to cover. But the same is true of other official U.S. government documents and statements. The National Intelligence Strategy, for example, is issued only occasionally, and the strategy for 2014 did not even mention ISIS, although it did refer to al Qaeda.[83] Even less frequently made public are National Intelligence Estimates (NIEs); the last publicly known NIE on the terrorist threat to the United States was published in 2007.[84] As a result, the DNI's annual testimony is probably the most authoritative and regularly updated public threat assessment made available by American intelligence, but it does not get the attention it deserves. To address the problem of intelligence lag, and to help decisionmakers deal with future threats before they have fully developed, the American intelligence community needs to redouble its efforts to provide anticipatory intelligence, both in classified and in public channels.

Notes

1 Exceptions include Nelly Lahoud and Liam Collins, "How the CT Community Failed to Anticipate the Islamic State," *Democracy and Security* 12, no. 3 (2016) (www.tandfonline.com/doi/full/10.1080/17419166.2016 .1207448); and Ephraim Kam, "The Islamic State Surprise: The Intelligence Perspective," *Strategic Assessment* 18 (October 2015): 21–31.

2 David Siman-Tov and Yotam Hacohen, "The Islamic State as an Intelligence Challenge," in *The Islamic State: How Viable Is It?*, edited by Yoram Schweitzer and Omer Einav (Tel Aviv: Institute for National Security Studies, 2016), p. 58.

3 Kam, "The Islamic State Surprise," p. 21.

4 James R. Clapper, Worldwide Threat Assessment of the U.S. Intelligence Community for the House Permanent Select Committee on Intelligence, February 10, 2011, p. 14.

5 James R. Clapper, Worldwide Threat Assessment of the U.S. Intelligence Community for the Senate Select Committee on Intelligence, January 31, 2012, p. 3.

6 Office of the Director of National Intelligence, "Media Conference Call: Background Briefing on the State of Al Qaida," April 27, 2012, transcript (www.dni.gov/files/documents/Newsroom/Speeches%20and%20Inter views/Media%20Conference%20Call%20-%20Background%20brief ing%20on%20the%20state%20of%20Al%20Qaida.pdf).

7 James N. Mattis, "The Posture of U.S. Central Command," testimony before the Senate Armed Services Committee, March 5, 2013, p. 15.

8 James R. Clapper, Worldwide Threat Assessment of the U.S. Intelligence Community, Senate Select Committee on Intelligence, March 12, 2013, p. 4.

9 "Remarks as delivered by James R. Clapper," Senate Select Committee on Intelligence, March 12, 2013, p. 9 (www.dni.gov/files/documents /Intelligence%20Reports/WWTA%20Remarks%20as%20delivered%20 12%20Mar%202013.pdf).

10 U.S. Department of State, *Country Reports on Terrorism 2012*, May 2013, p. 105 (www.state.gov/j/ct/rls/crt/2012/209982.htm).

11 Eric Schmitt and Mark Mazzetti, "U.S. Intelligence Official Says Syrian War Could Last for Years," *New York Times*, July 20, 2013.

12 Kevin Liptak, "How Could Obama Have 'Underestimated' ISIS?," CNN .com, September 30, 2014 (www.cnn.com/2014/09/29/politics/obama -underestimates-isis/).

13 Testimony of Deputy Assistant Secretary Brett McGurk, House Foreign Affairs Subcommittee on the Middle East and North Africa, November 13, 2013.

14 James R. Clapper, Worldwide Threat Assessment of the U.S. Intelligence Community, Senate Select Committee on Intelligence, January 29, 2014, p. 15.

15 Peter Baker and Eric Schmitt, "Many Missteps in Assessment of ISIS Threat," *New York Times*, September 29, 2015.

16 Lloyd J. Austin III, "The Posture of U.S. Central Command," testimony before the Senate Armed Services Committee, March 6, 2014, p. 22.

17 U.S. Department of State, *Country Reports on Terrorism 2013*, chap. 1, "Strategic Assessment" (www.state.gov/j/ct/rls/crt/2013/index.htm).

18 Country Reports on Terrorism 2014, June 2015 (www.state.gov/j/ct/rls/crt /2014/), p. 7.

19 James R. Clapper, Worldwide Threat Assessment of the U.S. Intelligence Community, Senate Armed Services Committee, February 26, 2015; James R. Clapper, remarks as delivered to the Senate Armed Services Committee hearing on the IC's Worldwide Threat Assessment, February 9, 2016

(www.dni.gov/files/documents/2016-02-09SASC_open_threat_hearing _transcript.pdf), p. 2.

20 Although this section focuses on assessments by scholars and other experts, it should be noted that there were warnings in the media in 2013 about the rising strength of ISIS. See, for example, Liz Sly, "Foreign Extremists Dominate Syria Fight," *Washington Post*, October 1, 2013. For other examples of warnings about ISIS from other sources, see Jennifer Rubin, "Obama's False 'Intelligence Failure' Claim," *Washington Post*, September 29, 2014.

21 U.S. House Foreign Affairs Committee, Subcommittee Hearing: Global al-Qaeda: Affiliates, Objectives, and Future Challenges, July 18, 2013, testimony (https://foreignaffairs.house.gov/hearing/subcommittee-hearing -global-al-qaeda-affiliates-objectives-and-future-challenges/).

22 Frederick W. Kagan, "The Continued Expansion of Al Qaeda Affiliates and Their Capabilities," statement before the House Committee on Foreign Affairs, July 18, 2013, p. 4.

23 Ibid, p. 3.

24 U.S. House Homeland Security Committee, Subcommittee Hearing: Understanding the Threat to the Homeland from AQAP, September 18, 2013, testimony (https://homeland.house.gov/hearing/subcommittee-hearing -understanding-threat-homeland-aqap/).

25 Ibid.; Bipartisan Policy Center, *Jihadist Terrorism: A Threat Assessment*, Report (Washington, September 2013), pp. 11, 31, 28.

26 Daniel Byman, "The Resurgence of al-Qaeda in Iraq," prepared testimony before the joint hearing of the Terrorism, Nonproliferation, and Trade Subcommittee and the Middle East and North Africa Subcommittee of the House Committee on Foreign Affairs, December 12, 2013, p. 1; Kenneth M. Pollack, "The Resurgence of al-Qaeda in Iraq," testimony before the same hearing, p. 1.

27 Quoted in Baker and Schmitt, "Many Missteps."

28 David Ignatius, "James Clapper: We Underestimated the Islamic State's 'Will to Fight,'" *Washington Post*, September 18, 2014.

29 Obama: U.S. Underestimated Rise of ISIS in Iraq and Syria," CBSnews.com, September 28, 2014 (www.cbsnews.com/news/obama-u-s-underestimated -rise-of-isis-in-iraq-and-syria/).

30 David Remnick, "Going the Distance," *New Yorker*, January 27, 2014.

31 Glenn Kessler, "Spinning Obama's Reference to Islamic State as a 'JV' Team," *Washington Post*, September 3, 2014.

32 Jeffrey Goldberg, "The Obama Doctrine," *The Atlantic*, April 2016.

33 On the debate over Austin's statement, see also Rowan Scarborough, "Shifting Blame, White House Faults War General's 2014 ISIS Assessment as He Departs," *Washington Times*, March 30, 2016.

34 Goldberg, "The Obama Doctrine."

35 Paul R. Pillar, "ISIS and the Politics of Surprise," *National Interest*, October 3, 2014.

36 Baker and Schmitt, "Many Missteps."

37 "Strong Intelligence on ISIS: President's Daily Brief," foxnews.com, September 2, 2014 (http://nation.foxnews.com/2014/09/02/briefed-daily-isis -year-and-still-pres-obama-called-them-jv-and-still-he-has-no-strategy).

38 Fred Fleitz, "ISIS Is the President's Intelligence Failure," Center for Security Policy, September 2, 2014 (www.centerforsecuritypolicy.org/2014/09 /02/isis-is-the-presidents-intelligence-failure/).

39 Eli Lake, "Why the White House Ignored All Those Warnings about ISIS," *Daily Beast*, July 6, 2014 (www.thedailybeast.com/articles/2014/07/06/why -the-white-house-ignored-all-those-warnings-about-isis.html).

40 Bill Gertz, "CIA Blew It in Iraq, Blamed for Failing to Warn about Rise of Islamic State," *Washington Times*, July 1, 2014.

41 *Initial Findings of the U.S. House of Representatives Joint Task Force on U.S. Central Command Intelligence Analysis*, August 10, 2016, p. 3 (www.documentcloud .org/documents/3010857-Initial-Findings-of-the-U-S-House-of.html).

42 Mark Mazzetti and Matt Apuzzo, "Military Analyst Again Raises Red Flags on Progress in Iraq," *New York Times*, September 23, 2015.

43 Shane Harris and Nancy A. Youssef, "50 Spies Say ISIS Intelligence Was Cooked," *Daily Beast*, September 9, 2015 (www.thedailybeast.com/articles /2015/09/09/exclusive-50-spies-say-isis-intelligence-was-cooked.html).

44 Deb Riechmann, "House Chairman: Military Files, Emails Deleted amid Probe," Associated Press, February 25, 2016; Paul McLeary and Dan De Luce, "Top House Lawmaker Accuses Pentagon of Obstructing Intel Probe," Foreignpolicy.com, February 26, 2016 (http://foreignpolicy.com/2016/02/26 /exclusive-top-house-lawmaker-accuses-pentagon-of-obstructing-intel -probe/). The survey was reportedly a routine survey conducted by the DNI at all seventeen agencies of the IC.

45 David Shedd, "In Defense of the ISIS Intelligence Whistleblowers," *Defense One*, September 21, 2015 (www.defenseone.com/ideas/2015/09/defense -isis-intelligence-whistleblowers/121604/).

46 *Initial Findings of the U.S. House of Representatives Joint Task Force*, p. 11.

47 House Permanent Select Committee on Intelligence, Press Release, August 11, 2016, "HPSCI Democrats Release Findings of Investigation into CENTCOM Intelligence Analysts" (http://democrats.intelligence.house .gov/press-release/hpsci-democrats-release-findings-investigation-centcom -intelligence-analysis).

48 Jim Axelrod and Emily Rand, "Investigation Reveals CENTCOM General Delayed Intel on ISIS Fight Meant for the President," CBSnews.com, September 22, 2016 (www.cbsnews.com/news/did-a-centcom-general -delay-intelligence-meant-for-the-president/).

49 *Initial Findings of the U.S. House of Representatives Joint Task Force*, p. 6.

50 U.S. Department of Defense Inspector General, *Unclassified Report of Investigation on Allegations Relating to USCENTCOM Intelligence Products*, January 31, 2017, p. 188.

51 Ibid., pp. 189–90.

52 Ibid., p. 97.

53 Elisabeth Bumiller, "Intelligence Reports Offer Dim View of Afghan War," *New York Times*, December 14, 2010.

54 Jeffrey Goldberg, "'Look, It's My Name on This': Obama Defends the Iran Nuclear Deal," theatlantic.com, May 21, 2015 (www.theatlantic.com /international/archive/2015/05/obama-interview-iran-isis-israel/393782 /#ISIS).

55 Lahoud and Collins, "How the CT Community Failed," p. 2. Note that Lahoud and Collins write that there was ample open source reporting that could have provided a better understanding of ISIS, but they don't cite specific evidence.

56 Kam, "The Islamic State Surprise," pp. 26–27.

57 Baker and Schmitt, "Many Missteps."

58 Greg Miller and Joby Warrick, "U.S. Spy Efforts Lag in Syria," *Washington Post*, July 24, 2012; Ken Dilanian, "U.S. Has a Big Blind Spot in Syria," *Los Angeles Times*, July 25, 2012.

59 Jeff Seldin, "Analysis: Concerns Rise about U.S. Intel Capabilities on IS," Voice of America, October 23, 2014 (www.voanews.com/a/analysis-concerns -rise-on-us-intelligence-cababilities-on-islamic-state/2493534.html).

60 For a useful review of the literature on intelligence failures, see Daniel Byman, "Intelligence and Its Critics," *Studies in Conflict and Terrorism* 39, no. 3 (2016): 260–80.

61 Daniel Byman notes this phenomenon in "The Intelligence War on Terrorism," *Intelligence and National Security* 29, no. 6 (2014): 841–42. I also discuss the limitations of strategic warning in Erik J. Dahl, *Intelligence and Surprise Attack: Failure and Success from Pearl Harbor to 9/11 and Beyond* (Georgetown University Press, 2013).

62 Michael Morell with Bill Harlow, *The Great War of Our Time: The CIA's Fight against Terrorism—From al Qa'ida to ISIS* (New York: Twelve, 2015), p. 302.

63 Timothy Naftali, *Blind Spot: The Secret History of American Counterterrorism* (New York: Basic Books, 2005), pp. 322–23. Slightly different versions of this story are told elsewhere, such as in Roger Z. George, "The Art and Strategy of Intelligence," in *Analyzing Intelligence: National Security Practitioners' Perspectives*, 2d ed., edited by Roger Z. George and James B. Bruce (Georgetown University Press, 2014), p. 188.

64 Kam, "The Islamic State Surprise," p. 29.

65 Jeffrey A. Friedman and Richard Zeckhauser, "Why Assessing Estimative Accuracy Is Feasible and Desirable," *Intelligence and National Security* 31, no. 2 (2016): 178–200.

66 Speech by Secretary of Defense Robert M. Gates delivered at the United States Military Academy, West Point, N.Y., February 25, 2011 (archive .defense.gov/Speeches/Speech.aspx?SpeechID=1539).

67 Office of the Director of National Intelligence, *The National Intelligence Strategy of the United States of America* (2014), p. 7.

68 Mark Mazzetti, "Delays in Effort to Refocus C.I.A. from Drone War," *New York Times*, April 5, 2014.

69 James R. Clapper, Remarks as Delivered on Current and Future Worldwide Threats to the Senate Armed Services Committee, February 11, 2014.

70 Nicole Gaouette, "Top US Intelligence Official: I Submitted My Resignation," CNN.com, November 18, 2016 (www.cnn.com/2016/11/17/politics /dni-james-clapper-submitted-his-resignation/).

71 Mark Mazzetti, "C.I.A. to Be Overhauled to Fight Modern Threats," *New York Times*, March 7, 2015.

72 Kam, "The Islamic State Surprise," p. 29.

73 Josh Kerbel, "The U.S. Intelligence Community's Kodak Moment," *National Interest*, May 15, 2014.

74 Jane Harman, "Disrupting the Intelligence Community," *Foreign Affairs*, March/April 2015, p. 100.

75 Jeff Stein, "U.S. Spies May Be Back in Action against ISIS," *Newsweek*, December 1, 2015; David Ignatius, "The U.S.'s Big Intelligence Problem," *Washington Post*, May 28, 2015.

76 Siobhan Gorman and Julian E. Barnes, "U.S. Spying on Syria Yields Bonus: Intelligence on Islamic State," *Wall Street Journal*, October 31, 2014.

77 Joe Gould, "Dunford: Better Intel Improving Counter-ISIS Airstrikes," DefenseNews.com, March 29, 2016 (www.defensenews.com/story/defense /2016/03/29/dunford-better-intel-improving-counter-isis-airstrikes /82382726/); Kristina Wong, "U.S. Commander: Lack of Intelligence Assets Slowing Down ISIS War," *The Hill*, June 7, 2016.

78 Michael T. Flynn, Matt Pottinger, and Paul D. Batchelor, *Fixing Intel: A Blueprint for Making Intelligence Relevant in Afghanistan* (Washington: Center for a New American Security, January 2010), p. 7. Flynn served later as director of the Defense Intelligence Agency and briefly as national security adviser for President Donald Trump.

79 Damian Paletta, "CIA Reorganizes to Target Islamic State," *Wall Street Journal*, June 15, 2015.

80 National Research Council, *Intelligence Analysis for Tomorrow: Advances from the Behavioral and Social Sciences* (Washington: National Academies Press, 2011), p. 12.

81 Kam, "The Islamic State Surprise," p. 30.

82 On the need for more work in the area of net assessment, see chapter 4 of this volume, and also Erik J. Dahl, "A Homeland Security Net Assessment Needed Now!" *Strategic Studies Quarterly* 9 (Winter 2015): 62–86.

83 *The National Intelligence Strategy of the United States of America 2014* (www.dni.gov/files/documents/2014_NIS_Publication.pdf).

84 Office of the Director of National Intelligence, *National Intelligence Estimate: The Terrorist Threat to the US Homeland*, July 2007, unclassified excerpts (nsarchive.gwu.edu/nukevault/ebb270/18.pdf).

4

When Do You Give It a Name?

Theoretical Observations about the ISIS Intelligence Failure

James J. Wirtz

Intelligence failures can take many forms and can have many causes. When using the term "intelligence failure," however, it is important to be specific about what intelligence analysts and organizations have failed to do or to predict. Indeed, intelligence failure usually refers to the absence of a timely warning about the occurrence of a discrete event. In other words, if intelligence analysts fail to estimate what is about to occur, where and when it will occur, and why it is occurring, and to provide that estimate to policymakers in time for them to take appropriate action, then the label "intelligence failure" is likely to be used to characterize recent events.

Without comprehensive data, it is impossible to judge definitively how well intelligence agencies actually succeed at this demanding task; the literature on intelligence failure selects on the dependent variable, so to speak. Failures rather than successes gain the lion's share of attention from scholars, practitioners, officials, and the public alike. Nevertheless, intelligence analysts sometimes get it right. On the eve of the Battle of Midway

in 1942, naval intelligence analysts and officers accurately estimated that
Midway would be the target of a Japanese attack and positioned the U.S.
fleet to launch a devastating carrier air strike against the Japanese force
nearing Midway.[1] In October 1962, U.S. intelligence analysts, after first
predicting such an eventuality was unlikely,[2] detected the Soviet deployment of medium-range and intermediate-range ballistic missiles in Cuba,
providing the John F. Kennedy administration with enough warning to
take constructive action. Such "moments of splendid," to use Sherman
Kent's phrase, are admittedly rare, but they do occur.[3]

By contrast, general warnings of deteriorating conditions that are not
accompanied by discrete event predictions are not enough to prevent
analysts from being accused of responsibility for an "intelligence failure."
In the weeks leading up to Pearl Harbor, for example, the Franklin D.
Roosevelt administration was aware that Japanese-American relations
had reached a nadir. Naval officers and intelligence analysts actually expected some sort of Japanese military action in the Far East and had even
expressed profound misgivings about forward deploying the U.S. fleet to
Pearl Harbor, a move that they believed left the fleet vulnerable and badly
positioned to respond to the outbreak of hostilities in the Pacific.[4] Similarly, in the days before the September 11, 2001, terrorist attacks on the
World Trade Center and the Pentagon, the U.S. intelligence community
delivered a strategic warning to the White House. The highly classified
and communitywide product, the President's Daily Brief (PDB), stated
that al Qaeda had expressed interest in hijacking commercial airliners.
Excerpts from the August 6, 2001, PDB, published in the 9/11 Commission report, also made it clear that al Qaeda operatives were quite active
in the United States.[5] Nevertheless, despite the fact that the system was
indeed "blinking red" in December 1941 and September 2001, Pearl Harbor and 9/11 are today synonymous with the term "intelligence failure"
in the annals of the intelligence studies literature.

So what exactly is meant by labeling the U.S. intelligence community's response to the rise of Islamic State in Iraq and Syria (ISIS) in 2013
and early 2014 an intelligence failure? This chapter posits that the so-
called ISIS intelligence failure indeed has much in common with the
events leading up to both Pearl Harbor and the 9/11 attacks. On the one

hand, both intelligence and press reports provided accurate and timely warning of a deteriorating security situation within Iraq produced by what was believed to be a resurgence of al Qaeda. On the other hand, the intelligence community, and the press for that matter, failed to anticipate the political-military shock that placed ISIS at the forefront of U.S. domestic politics and international diplomacy, the June 2014 fall of Mosul and the collapse of the Iraqi Army. This was an especially alarming turn of events: approximately 1,500 ISIS fighters prevailed over a 30,000-man Iraqi force that simply disintegrated after years of U.S. training and material support. In other words, the intelligence community managed to issue some strategic warnings about the deteriorating military situation in Iraq, but it failed to provide a compelling estimate of the true nature of the emerging threat or to warn policymakers about how it would likely manifest. Not surprisingly, the term "intelligence failure" now surrounds the rise of ISIS.

Nevertheless, if one explores this so-called intelligence failure, one can begin to understand the hurdles faced by the intelligence community in developing an accurate and timely estimate of ISIS and a nuanced reassessment of exactly what the intelligence community failed to understand about the rise of the Islamic State. To offer this reassessment, the chapter first suggests that there were several unique elements about ISIS that represented a departure from the "al Qaeda model" of international terrorism. It also focuses on the structural constraints inherent in the U.S. intelligence community that made ISIS a difficult target. The chapter then offers some concluding observations about the so-called ISIS intelligence failure and how it might constitute a harbinger of things to come.

The ISIS Estimate

Today both experts and average citizens have a detailed and horrifying image of ISIS, whose rank and file routinely and gleefully commit and digitize unmentionable atrocities against Shia, "sheikists," Christians, Yazidis, apostates, prisoners of war, and even their own members suspected of disloyalty. In 2014, for instance, *Newsweek* magazine provided an impressive and rather strange list of ISIS's opponents: Salafis; Arab oil sheiks; Shiites; the governments and militaries of the United States, Iran, Iraq, Syria, and Turkey; Hamas; Hezbollah; and al Qaeda.[6] Indeed, the list of ISIS's opponents continues to grow and now includes the Lebanese Army, the Kurdistan Workers' Party, the Islamic Front (rebel groups in Syria allied with al Qaeda), and the Free Syrian Army. Nevertheless, it is important not to allow hindsight to guide one's judgments about the intelligence community's assessments of ISIS. Various aspects of ISIS were unique on the world stage, combing to create what amounts to a new type of nonstate actor. The elements that made ISIS unique also made it a difficult target for the U.S. intelligence community.

The Lack of Net Assessment
The origins of ISIS can be traced to the chaos and anarchy that gripped Iraq in the aftermath of the Second Gulf War and the fall of the Baathist regime in Baghdad. Coalition Provisional Authority (CPA) Proclamations 1 and 2, which banned the Baath Party and dismantled the Iraqi Army in May 2003, left about the top 1 percent of the personnel in the Iraqi government and military outside the new Iraqi government (approximately 20,000 individuals). CPA Proclamations 1 and 2 did not destabilize the situation on the ground in Iraq, but their impact was amplified by the fact that the Iraqi Army literally "self-demobilized" rather than face the brunt of the international coalition arrayed against it during the Second Gulf War. Iraq's defeat and the initial decisions made by the CPA abruptly changed the political balance in Iraq. Specifically, Saddam Hussein's government and officer corps was dominated by Sunnis, and in the aftermath of the war this leadership was left adrift in a country now dominated by a Shia majority. L. Paul Bremer, the top civilian administrator of the CPA, noted that the U.S. government had little real choice in the matter of "de-Baathification," noting:

> 80% of the population, the Kurds and the Shia, were very clear about the likely results of our recalling the army. Each had heard rumors that some American soldiers favored recalling Saddam's

army. The Kurdish leaders—Masoud Barzani and Jalal Talabani—told me if you recall the army, we Kurds will secede from Iraq. The secession of the Kurds from Iraq then or today or in the future will, in my view, bring on a major regional war. It will start civil war in Iraq. But it would also likely bring on a major regional war because neither the Iranians nor the Turks could tolerate an independent Kurdistan. The Shia leaders said they interpreted these rumors as showing our intention to install "Saddamism without Saddam." The Shias had been cooperating with the Coalition following guidance from Grand Ayatollah Ali-al Sistani. So the political arguments against recalling the army were even stronger than the practical arguments.[7]

Bremer notes that the U.S. response to this dilemma was to create a new Iraqi Army; it was politically impossible, and as events would show, not realistic, to remobilize Baathist Iraqi units.[8]

Although Bremer is correct to note that de-Baathification was limited in scope, the political and security impact of postwar policies greatly curtailed the ability of Sunni personnel to participate in Iraq's new government and security forces. In 2003, for instance, the CPA formed the Iraqi Governing Council, whose membership was allocated along sectarian lines. The decision, according to Isaac Kfir, "heightened sectarianism, as representation was based on quotas that only reinforced the simmering age-old divisions, instead of being meritocratic."[9] In hindsight, it is clear that these disenfranchised individuals constituted a disgruntled group that would be politically and ethnically attracted to a Sunni-centric, anti-Shia ideology—the kind of ideology advanced by ISIS. What is not clear in hindsight, however, is the hurdle the U.S. intelligence community would have to overcome to make the connection between de-Baathification and the rise of ISIS. The community would have had to engage in a "net assessment" to identify the second- and third-order risks created by de-Baathification. In other words, they would have had to make a deliberate estimate of how U.S. policy was producing unintended and unwanted consequences. Organizational culture, however, leaves the U.S. intelligence community incapable of conducting this type of assessment.

Two normative theories, reflected in the culture of analysts, make it difficult to conduct a net assessment as a routine part of the analytical process. One, most closely associated with the work of Sherman Kent, focuses on ensuring the independence of intelligence analysts in providing information to policymakers. Kent's thinking, which shaped the formation and early evolution of the U.S. intelligence community, identifies the importance of political and policy detachment in producing relevant and effective finished intelligence. The strength of Kent's approach is that it preserves the independence of analysts by separating the intelligence community from the overt pressure or organizational and interpersonal incentives that can shape intelligence to conform to current policy or the personal and political biases of policymakers.[10] Yet, by creating a strong barrier against politicization, Kent's prescriptions can separate intelligence too completely from policymakers; in this framework, policy assessment is beyond the scope of the intelligence community. The other operational framework, most closely associated with the reforms instituted in the mid-1980s by then director of Central Intelligence Robert M. Gates, focuses on providing "actionable" intelligence, information of immediate and direct use to policymakers. To produce actionable intelligence, analysts have to maintain close working relationships with policymakers, literally looking at officials' in-boxes to make sure finished intelligence addresses important policy issues of the day.[11] Nevertheless, following the Gates model too closely can create its own set of problems. There is a possibility that policymakers will pose biased questions to the intelligence community to guarantee that analysis favorable to their positions will emerge, or that they will fail to pose the correct questions, leading to an incomplete understanding of the challenges they face. By following the Gates model, the only way that the U.S. intelligence community would have linked the growth of ISIS to de-Baathification is if they were directly asked that question by senior officials. It defies credulity to believe that, barring some extremely dire set of circumstances, policymakers would deliberately task the U.S. intelligence community with assessing the role of U.S. postwar policy in the rise of sectarian violence in Iraq.

ISIS was a particularly difficult target for the U.S. intelligence community because an accurate estimate of the origins of the movement would have needed to recognize the impetus it received from U.S. policy. An accurate assessment, ceteris paribus, would have amounted to a critique of a decade's worth of American policy toward Iraq. In terms of organizational culture, this sort of assessment is largely beyond the capability of the U.S. intelligence community. Indeed, other weak or misleading assessments produced by the U.S. intelligence community have been tied to the absence of a net assessment—that is, a failure to account for the impact of U.S policy on an unfolding situation. The failure of the Central Intelligence Agency to foresee the fall of the Shah or the fact that U.S. policy had stymied Saddam Hussein's efforts to acquire weapons of mass destruction are cases in point.[12] In any event, without this net assessment, it was impossible to develop an accurate estimate of the potential scope and appeal of ISIS. U.S. policy made ISIS appealing to more than true radicals; it made it appealing to Sunnis who were politically disenfranchised following the Second Gulf War.

An Ideological Twist: ISIS Is Not al Qaeda

As Erik Dahl's contribution to the volume makes clear, beginning in the middle of 2013 the intelligence community repeatedly sounded the tocsin warning of deteriorating conditions in Iraq. These estimates, however, focused primarily on the growing strength and activity of al Qaeda in Iraq (AQI), a Sunni-based organization inspired by the exploits of Osama bin Laden, which would eventually morph into ISIS. In hindsight, it is clear that ISIS and al Qaeda embraced different political agendas; indeed, they are completely different animals. ISIS and al Qaeda are different organizations with different goals that operate in different ways and pose different threats. As a result, just warning about an increasing "al Qaeda-like" threat in Iraq mischaracterized the real danger posed by the nascent ISIS. And, as Dahl's commentary demonstrates, there was nothing in the intelligence reporting that suggested that something fundamentally different from al Qaeda was about to emerge out of the chaos of the Syrian civil war and political unrest in Iraq. Dahl demonstrates that the intelligence community did notice that things were heating up in Syria and Iraq; what they failed to note was that the very nature of the threat was changing.

Admittedly, experts debate the finer points about al Qaeda's objectives and operational style, but it is possible to characterize the organization and its objectives in a general way to highlight some important differences between al Qaeda and ISIS. Al Qaeda was ultimately about influencing events within the Muslim world, especially Saudi Arabia. Nevertheless, by 1997 bin Laden turned his attention toward non-Muslim states in an effort to drive Western influence from the Middle East, leaving targeted regimes unable to resist the "internal jihad" that would follow. To undertake this strategy, al Qaeda employed a centrally controlled, hierarchical organization that specialized in finely crafted operations mostly directed against transportation targets.[13] The organization employed the Internet to communicate to operatives and to disseminate its message to a global audience, but it was cautious when it came to vetting recruits and disseminating operationally sensitive information. It used trained and apparently "cleared" operatives who evidenced relatively sophisticated tradecraft. Al Qaeda also operated a sort of "franchise system," lending its stamp of approval to local and regional organizations, but apparently only after the new franchisees agreed to take a degree of guidance from al Qaeda central.[14] And, as Bruce Hoffman has noted, bin Laden remained engaged in all facets of the al Qaeda operation until his demise in 2011, despite reports suggesting he was "out of sync" or disengaged from al Qaeda and its affiliates around the world.[15]

Before his death, bin Laden had crafted a strategy for al Qaeda central and its affiliates. According to U.S. military intelligence, bin Laden had apparently articulated a strategy for al Qaeda to continue to maintain its traditional goals while taking steps to preserve itself in the face of U.S. pressure:

- attriting and enervating America so that a weakened United States would be forced out of Muslim lands and therefore have neither the will nor the capability to intervene;

- taking over and controlling territory, creating the physical sanctuaries and safe havens that are Al-Qaeda's lifeblood;

- declaring "emirates" in these liberated lands that would be safe from U.S. and Western intervention because of their collective enfeeblement.[16]

In a remarkably prescient analysis, Hoffman identifies what in hindsight are the origins of ISIS, which emerged when AQI applied bin Laden's strategy to the deteriorating security situations in Iraq and Syria:

Syria has . . . long been an Al Qaeda *idée fixe*. . . . That country has even more of the characteristics of the same type of perfect *jihadi* storm than Afghanistan possessed three decades ago: widespread support among the Arab world, the provision of financial assistance from wealthy Gulf supporters, a popular cause that readily attracts foreign volunteers, and a contiguous border facilitating the movements of these fighters into and out of the declared battle space.[17]

Syria also offers a base in the Arab heartland, and offered AQI an opportunity to do battle with the "hated Shi'a apostate Alawite minority" in the country.[18]

In hindsight, this "perfect jihadi storm" began to build by the middle of 2012. First, with the death of bin Laden, al Qaeda's efforts to centrally direct its franchisees seem to have lost traction, freeing affiliates to act more independently. Second, as AQI and other al Qaeda allies (such as the Syrian rebel organization Jabhat al- Nusra li-Ahl al Sham) attempted to exploit conditions in Syria, they escalated their operations and began to enjoy success. Third, to better exploit these opportunities, a new organization, ISIS, began to displace AQI and to embrace different objectives and strategies. ISIS embraced a patently sectarian strategy that captured disaffected Sunnis and directed them against Shia and Alawites. Fourth, ISIS also shifted to "internal Jihad," by at least initially focusing on the establishment of its own safe haven in territory formerly controlled by Syria and Iraq. Fifth, ISIS began to recruit disenfranchised, disillusioned, and marginalized youth, not just from Arab countries but from the entire world. In other words, unlike al Qaeda central, ISIS did not focus on developing trained and vetted operatives for complex operations, but instead welcomed all sorts of fellow travelers and adventure seekers to fill its emerging army. ISIS reportedly even set up training camps for youth in Ninevah Governorate in Iraq and in Aleppo and Raqqah in Syria to bolster its ranks with children taken from captured territory.[19] Needless to say, al Qaeda central never resorted to this sort of tactic to increase the number of its operatives.

Viewed in this manner, ISIS again posed a very difficult target for the U.S. intelligence community. An accurate estimate of the threat posed by ISIS involved more than just an assessment of the growing number of fighters or its growing combat capability (that is, the ability to deploy crew-served weapons or to field relatively large military units). An accurate estimate would have needed to account for the opportunities presented by the death of bin Laden and the chaos of the Syrian civil war and the impact of a shift to internal jihad, a sectarian strategy, and a change in recruiting preferences. The real intelligence challenge did not involve recognizing that the potential for death and destruction was increasing; the intelligence community actually sounded that warning. Instead, it was to understand that AQI was being displaced by ISIS and that these organizations were fundamentally different entities. And, once again, the U.S. intelligence community would have benefited from a net assessment that focused on the externalities created by the death of Osama bin Laden.[20]

These issues were in fact acknowledged by an intelligence scholar/practitioner working in the Office of the Director of National Intelligence. When asked if the rise of ISIS represented a failure on the part of the U.S. intelligence community, he responded with the question, "When do you give it a name?"[21] In other words, ISIS represented a departure among violent nonstate actors. It was difficult to anticipate because its whole was greater than the sum of its contributing parts and enabling factors. It was new and different, making it difficult to define until it actually existed.

ISIS Is Not a "Normal" Clandestine Actor

In the years immediately following the 9/11 terrorist attacks, scholars became particularly interested in searching for clandestine links between different types of nonstate actors. There was a fear that criminal networks, black marketeers and money-laundering operations, smugglers, grassroots political or ethnic movements, proliferation entrepreneurs, or terrorist groups might somehow collaborate by sharing services, networks, or personnel for mutual advantage.[22] This type of collaboration was neither unknown nor unprecedented. In 1993, for instance, a Chinese narcotics organization in New York City linked up with a human trafficking operation and branched into smuggling illegal immigrants into California by transferring paying clients from oceangoing vessels to smaller fishing boats near San Francisco and Moss Landing.[23] What was of special concern was the use of similar drug smuggling networks to move terrorists and weapons of mass destruction across international borders. In other words, there was a fear that multifaceted organizations would emerge when different types of nonstate actors pooled resources, communications, and logistical networks.

ISIS is different in this regard. It is a multifaceted, entrepreneurial enterprise that exploits opportunities by pursuing a variety of objectives simultaneously. It is not a network of different nonstate actors (the traditional fear); instead it is a nonstate actor that undertakes multiple activities that in the past required specialized entities. For instance, it can be characterized as a political movement to create its own state. Alternatively, it can be characterized as a commercial operation that exploits black market trade, especially by selling the oil produced under its control. It also can be characterized as a sectarian movement, exploiting Sunni hostility toward Shia and other minority groups (Christians, Yazidis, and others) in areas under its control. Sometimes, it appears to be a way for disenfranchised Baathists to gain political control over local areas. More recently, it has branched out into a global terrorist network that uses operatives or self-radicalized individuals to carry our relatively unsophisticated, albeit deadly, attacks on Western targets in revenge for Western kinetic operations against its forces in the areas that it controls. It could even be characterized as a youth movement, reaching out to disaffected adolescents who seek liberation from local constraints (that is, their parents).

ISIS is also an especially dangerous threat because it is the first terrorist organization to exploit Internet-enabled social media for its own nefarious purposes. Al Qaeda central rode the rails of the information revolution and globalization to undertake precision strikes at intercontinental ranges, but ISIS used social media like Twitter and Facebook, platforms that both emerged around 2006, to communicate highly personalized messages to young people around the world. These messages were framed to appeal to young people and speak a language that young people relate to. They offered the prospect of adventure, romance, and escape from the constraints of overbearing parents—the type of message that has a universal appeal to its key demographic. German intelligence officials, for example, have reported that almost 700 people left Germany to join ISIS, many of whom were characterized as "normal teens."[24] ISIS uses a host of new media that incorporate audio and visual messaging that is easy for teenagers to understand but often incomprehensible to most adults. Indeed, many adults are completely unfamiliar with the "apps" used to communicate to young people. According to Kathleen Bouzis:

> The group utilizes numerous communication platforms including Snapchat, Kik, Twitter, ASK.fm, Facebook, YouTube, WhatsApp, and others. Its multiplatform social media messaging targets a broad recruitment audience in at least 23 languages and is part of the reason for ISIS's estimated 31,500 fighters. ISIL has also reached out to computer-savvy youth hacking networks that have conducted pro-ISIL attacks on over two hundred websites. These hacks included banners that read "I love you ISIS" and are targeted at seemingly arbitrary websites such as the University of New Brunswick Student Union.[25]

For individuals whose significant reality exists in cyberspace, not in the physical reality of everyday life, social media take on a special importance that displaces family, friends, school, and the workplace. In other words, ISIS's appeal is to the young and impressionable audience that "lives" in cyberspace, an appeal that has more to with the discontent of adolescence than with the exigencies of jihad. Social media provide the group with an especially potent recruiting tool. This audience and this tool simply did not exist in the years preceding the 9/11 attacks. At least in its international manifestation, ISIS might in fact be best characterized as a youth movement, a sort of pied piper to restless adolescents everywhere.

An accurate estimate of the threat posed by ISIS would have required an assessment of how a new technology, "social media," could be employed in an innovative manner by a nonstate actor to open new communication and recruitment strategies and broaden its base of international support. ISIS can thus be seen as a form of technological surprise in the sense that it pioneered an innovative application of an emerging technology. Although the political use of social media—tweets, false news stories, and personalized political messages delivered by anyone with access to a Facebook account—was unheard of before 2007, in the aftermath of the 2016 U.S. presidential election it is now a fixture in our social reality. ISIS pioneered the use of these new media to increase its appeal to a global youth audience.

Theoretical Musings

In a volume on the impact of intelligence organizations since 1945, Paul Maddrell and his coauthors offer an important observation about the ability of intelligence organizations to warn policymakers about untoward events.[26] Intelligence organizations and the policymakers they serve tend to operate with a common view of the world that channels analysis along a relatively narrow path. If unfolding events fit within the scope of this analytical and policy consensus, then intelligence agencies often provide useful and relevant analysis to policymakers. If unfolding developments are beyond this shared consensus, however, then it is unlikely that intelligence analysts will be able to provide timely warnings to policymakers. Failures of omission and commission lie behind this observation. Questions that need to be addressed might never be raised by analysts or policymakers because they seem irrelevant given the shared consensus. And if discordant analysis somehow manages to emerge from intelligence agencies, it is likely to be altered to fit the shared consensus or ignored as an irrelevant outlier. An intelligence culture, shaped by bureaucratic, social, and political preferences, bounds the realm of the possible when it comes to the capabilities of national intelligence agencies. When something emerges outside this realm, it is difficult to recognize. ISIS emerged in a way that was outside the realm of the U.S. intelligence consensus.

The preceding analysis suggests several factors that made ISIS a difficult target for the U.S. intelligence community. First, a net assessment would have greatly facilitated an accurate estimate of the threat posed by ISIS, but the U.S. government, not to mention the U.S. intelligence community, lacks a formal mechanism not only to evaluate the success or failure of U.S. policy but also to determine if U.S. policy is producing externalities that are leading to a deteriorating international situation. Admittedly, the impact of de-Baathification on the security situation in Iraq remains a hotly debated topic. Nevertheless, it would appear that the U.S. intelligence community did not directly address how disenfranchising thousands of Sunnis might bolster AQI and inflame sectarian tensions in Iraq. Ironically, the "fundamental attribution error" (that is, "we had no choice") echoes in the explanations offered by policymakers for the possible link between the rise of AQI/ISIS and de-Baathification. Similarly, the death of Osama bin Laden in 2011 was touted as a great success for U.S. counterterrorism policy. Nevertheless, questions about unintended consequences—such as the impact on al Qaeda franchisees—never seemed to be entertained. *Everyone* seems to have forgotten that no government policy is universally good or bad, but instead represents a mix of positive and negative effects. The idea that the U.S. government would have undertaken a net assessment to better understand the externalities created by the death of Osama bin Laden, even in hindsight, appears far-fetched. The question itself was beyond the intelligence consensus, and the intelligence community rarely conducts this type of net assessment. In other words, if a net assessment was critical to the ISIS estimate, the occurrence of an "intelligence failure" appears to be overdetermined.

Second, as contributors to the Maddrell volume note, the rise of ISIS contained a theological and religious component, which is difficult to detect and assess within the U.S. intelligence consensus. The separation of church and state in the American political context runs deep, restricting the ability of the U.S. intelligence community to monitor the way theological differences influence Islamic fundamentalists. Mark Stout, for instance, has noted that this failure to understand the interaction between Islam and terrorism slowed an accurate appreciation of al Qaeda:

This prejudice against religion manifested itself in the IC no less than in the rest of the government. Lt. Gen. James Clapper, who had led the DIA [Defense Intelligence Agency] from 1991 to 1996, recalls no discussion of religion whatsoever during that time. For its part the CIA [Central Intelligence Agency] veered toward "hard fact" reporting (names, dates, places and the like) creating an environment in which consideration of the divine did not fit comfortably. The result was that analysts tended to address terrorism either through ethnic or national lenses (despite the fact that this enemy explicitly denigrated such distinctions) or simply focused on the tactical mechanics of the problem. In essence, the IC projected its self-image onto the enemy.[27]

Because an accurate estimate of the menace posed by ISIS required a nuanced appreciation of theological or ideological differences between ISIS and al Qaeda, developing this estimate did not easily fit within U.S. intelligence culture. As Stout notes, stark assessments of the interaction between Islam and terrorism, which were admittedly not particularly nuanced, were injected into intelligence debates by outsiders four years after the September 11, 2001, terror attacks.[28] Because its operational style and agenda are rooted in theological differences with other Islamic fundamentalists, ISIS posed a difficult target for those operating within the U.S. intelligence consensus.

Third, although Americans launched the information revolution, rushing to exploit the opportunities created by the impact of Moore's Law on everyday life, they take both a technical and rather utopian view of the impact of emerging technology on the human condition. In the view of the creators of the information revolution, new technologies are supposed to drive a steady improvement in the human condition as they increase productivity, disseminate best practices, and empower individuals at the expense of bureaucracies and governments.[29] Outside of this positive-sum view of technology, however, Americans, along with other proponents of the information revolution, are slow to focus on the externalities created by the information revolution or to envision the social, political, and strategic impact of the new information technologies.[30] Other strategic and intelligence cultures appear far more adept at estimating the broad societal and political impact of the information revolution and are more adept at exploiting the new possibilities created by the emergence of cyberspace.[31] In other words, grasping that social media could have a profound impact on politics and society is not the forte of the U.S. intelligence community. Recognition that there is an "information revolution 2.0" under way is now entering our collective consciousness, but only after other groups—ISIS in particular—recognized the true political and social opportunities created by these new information technologies. Although the argument appears counterintuitive, the intelligence failure related to ISIS might be based on a failure to properly assess the impact of technology on society.

Conclusion

There is an old saying among analysts that comes to mind when one offers judgments about the performance of the U.S. intelligence community against ISIS: "There is no such thing as a policy failure, only an intelligence failure." In other words, regardless of the performance of intelligence analysts, they will be blamed when policymakers encounter a policy setback. With that said, it really is impossible to tell what, if anything, went wrong inside the U.S. intelligence community until a complete accounting is made of the classified warnings and estimates that accompanied the rise of ISIS. It is possible that the U.S. intelligence community issued detailed and profound warnings about the nature and implications of the rise of ISIS without having any discernible impact on U.S. policymakers. This sort of situation is not unprecedented. Before the Nazi invasion of the Soviet Union in World War II, national intelligence agencies, diplomats, and even foreign governments provided a string of detailed and compelling warnings to the Soviet government with no real effect. Sometimes policy is impervious to intelligence.

More realistically, however, the rise of ISIS constituted a very modern and maddening conundrum for the U.S. intelligence community. It emerged from a complex interaction among theological debate, sectarianism, opportunism, and technological innovation that produced a new type of nonstate actor on the world stage. It represented an abrupt and dangerous departure from conventional wisdom, from policy expectations, from what was considered to be socially, politically, and strategically possible. ISIS constituted an abrupt change. In fact it was the speed of this change, not necessarily the transformation of AQI into ISIS, that made the ISIS estimate so difficult. And because the pace of change in international affairs continues to accelerate, the ISIS "intelligence failure" might be a harbinger of things to come.

Notes

1 Gordon W. Prange with Donald M. Goldstein and Katherine V. Dillon, *Miracle at Midway* (New York: Penguin Books, 1982).

2 The Central Intelligence Agency Special National Intelligence Estimate 85-3-62 dated September 19, 1962, stated that the Soviet Union was unlikely to deploy ballistic missiles to Cuba because such a move would be deemed too risky by the Kremlin. See James J. Wirtz, "Organizing for Crisis Intelligence: Lessons from the Cuban Missile Crisis," in *Intelligence and the Cuban Missile Crisis*, edited by James G. Blight and David A. Welch (London: Frank Cass, 1998), pp. 120–49; and Peter S. Usowski, "John McCone and the Cuban Missile Crisis: A Persistent Approach to the Intelligence-Policy Relationship," *International Journal of Intelligence and Counterintelligence* 2 (Winter 1988): 547–76.

3 Sherman Kent, a longtime CIA analyst and later Yale professor, said that collecting photographic evidence of Soviet efforts to deploy missiles in Cuba was a "moment of splendid"; Kent is quoted in Loch Johnson, *National Security Intelligence* (Cambridge: Polity, 2012), p. 50.

4 Navy officers wanted the Pacific fleet to return to the West Coast to prepare for war and believed that the lack of facilities at Pearl Harbor made forward deployment a hollow deterrent that only served to give the American public a false sense of confidence in U.S. defenses in the Pacific. When its commander, Admiral J. O. Richardson, failed to persuade his superiors to reposition the fleet in California, he penned a message to President Franklin D. Roosevelt that led to his relief: "The senior officers of the Navy do not have the trust and confidence in the civilian leadership of this country that is essential for a successful prosecution of a war in the Pacific"; see George W. Baer, *One Hundred Years of Sea Power: The U.S. Navy, 1890–1990* (Stanford University Press, 1994), p. 151.

5 *9/11 Commission Report*, pp. 261–62 (https://9-11commision.gov/report /911Report.pdf).

6 Kurt Eichenwald, "ISIS's Enemy List: 10 Reasons the Islamic State Is Doomed," *Newsweek*, September 8, 2014.

7 Interview with L. Paul Bremer, "De-Baathification and Dismantling the Iraqi Army," Association for Diplomatic Studies and Training (http://adst .org/2016/01/de-baathification-and-dismantling-the-iraqi-army/).

8 Bremer retells a story that demonstrates that it indeed might have been impossible to reconstitute the Iraqi Army: "In the spring of 2004, the Marines were trying to subdue violence in the western city of Fallujah. The commanding general of the Marines decided, apparently on his own, to recall a brigade of the old Iraqi Army there. . . . The recall of this single brigade caused a political crisis in Baghdad and among Iraqis everywhere. Several Iraqi ministers resigned or threatened to resign. Several members of the Governing Council tendered their resignations. . . . Worse, when the recalled brigade was sent by the Marines into Fallujah, instead of helping to restore order, the entire unit went over to the enemy itself and had to be disbanded." Ibid.

9 Isaac Kfir, "Social Identity Group and Human (In)Security: The Case of Islamic State in Iraq and the Levant (ISIL)," *Studies in Conflict and Terrorism* 38, no. 1 (2015): 238.

10 Sherman Kent, *Strategic Intelligence for American World Policy* (Princeton University Press, 1946).

11 H. Bradford Westerfield, "Inside Ivory Bunkers: CIA Analysts Resist Mangers' 'Pandering'—Part II," *International Journal of Intelligence and Counterintelligence* 10 (Spring 1997): 19–54; Richard K. Betts, "Politicization of Intelligence: Costs and Benefits," in *Paradoxes of Strategic Intelligence*, edited by Richard K. Betts and Thomas Mahnken (London: Frank Cass, 2003), pp. 59–79.

12 James J. Wirtz, "The Art of the Intelligence Autopsy," *Intelligence and National Security* 29, no. 1 (2014): 1–8.

13 Rohan Gunaratna and Aviv Oreg, "Al Qaeda's Organization Structure and Its Evolution," *Studies in Conflict and Terrorism* 33 no. 12 (2010): 1043–78.

14 Under pressure from the international coalition arrayed against it, al Qaeda central, according to Isaac Kfir, "came to promote franchises aimed at instill[ing] its ideology and agenda." It became "more identified with an ideology rather than operating as a traditional, hierarchical, terrorist organization, committing acts of terror." Kfir, "Social Identity Group," p. 233.

15 Bruce Hoffman, "Al Qaeda's Uncertain Future," *Studies in Conflict and Terrorism* 36, no. 8 (2013): 639.

16 U.S. Special Operations Command 2012 Intelligence Estimate quoted by Hoffman in "Al Qaeda's Uncertain Future," pp. 640–41.

17 Ibid., p. 644.

18 Ed Husain, "Syria; Why al Qaeda Is Winning," *National Review Online*, August 23, 2012 (www.nationalreview.com/articles/314685/syria-why-al Qaeda-winning-ed-husain).

19 Kathleen Bouzis, "Countering the Islamic State: U.S. Counterterrorism Measures," *Studies in Conflict and Terrorism* 38, no. 10 (2015): 887.

20 This was the issue that set Bruce Hoffman's pen to paper in early 2013: the possibility that al Qaeda central, to say nothing of its franchisees, might have not been terminally damaged by bin Laden's death; see Hoffman, "Al Qaeda's Uncertain Future."

21 Author's interview with a member of the intelligence community, September 20, 2016.

22 James Russell and James Wirtz, eds., *Globalization and WMD Proliferation: Terrorism, Transnational Networks and International Security* (New York: Routledge, 2007).

23 Richard C. Paddock and Katherine Edwards, "300 Illegal Chinese Immigrants Arrested: Smuggling Boats Try to Take Refugees Ashore South of San Francisco," *Los Angeles Times*, June 3, 1993.

24 Florian Flade, Carolin George, and Per Hinrichs, "Why 2 'Normal' Teens Joined ISIS," OZY.com (www.ozy.com/true-story/why-2-normal-teens -joined-isis/61629).

25 Bouzis, "Countering the Islamic State," p. 888.

26 Paul Maddrell, ed., *The Image of the Enemy: Intelligence Analysis of Adversaries since 1945* (Georgetown University Press, 2015).

27 Mark Stout, "American Intelligence Assessments of the Jihadists, 1989– 2011," in *The Image of the Enemy*, edited by Maddrell, p. 263.

28 Ibid., p. 264.

29 Bill Gates, *The Road Ahead* (New York: Penguin, 1996); Mark Tovey, ed., *Collective Intelligence: Creating a Prosperous World at Peace* (Oakton, Va.: Earth Intelligence Network, 2008).

30 James J. Wirtz, "Blogging in the World Cafe," *International Journal of Intelligence and Counterintelligence* 22 (Summer 2009): 357–59.

31 Dima Adamsky, *The Culture of Military Innovation: The Impact of Cultural Factors on the Revolution in Military Affairs in Russia, the U.S. and Israel* (Stanford University Press, 2010); and James J. Wirtz, "The Russian Integration of Cyber Power into Grand Strategy," in *Cyber War in Perspective: Russian Aggression against Ukraine*, edited by Kenneth Geers (Tallinn: NATO Cooperative Cyber Defence Centre of Excellence, 2015), pp. 29–38.

PART III

Local Actors

5

Syria and Iraq

ISIS and Other Actors in Historical Context

Kevin W. Martin

Despite all the media attention devoted to ISIS and the context in which it emerged and thrived, the study of these phenomena presents numerous dilemmas for the social scientist and the policymaker. The rapid pace of events, the complexity of a multisided conflict featuring shifting alliances, and the paucity of independently verifiable information greatly complicate attempts to draw reliable conclusions and formulate effective responses. That said, after surveying the massive body of journalism, policy analysis, and scholarship, it is possible to place the ISIS phenomenon in historical context and thereby identify certain issues that clarify past events, suggest the course of future developments, and offer lessons for observers of the region.

First, the histories of ISIS, of the conflicts in which it has been enmeshed, and of its relationships with other local actors in these conflicts display multiple continuities with Syrian, Iraqi, and regional history. In other words, ISIS, its fellow jihadist groups, and the deeply intertwined Syrian and Iraqi conflicts did not appear ex nihilo. They are thoroughly explicable—although not inevitable—outcomes of familiar historical processes and experiences. As such, they cannot be successfully addressed, intellectually or instrumentally, without reference to that history. In this macrohistorical context, ISIS, all other groups attempting to overthrow existing regimes, and the various popular movements designated by the term "Arab Spring" are manifestations of a broad, deep, transgenerational dissatisfaction with the Middle East's political system.

Second, the Syrian and Iraqi conflicts that provided the site and context for ISIS's emergence have transformed, perhaps permanently, the region, the parties to these conflicts, their victims, and the relationships between all of them. The terms of the post–World War I settlement that produced the Middle East have been destabilized. Despite recent "victories" over ISIS and other violent opposition groups, it remains unclear whether Syria and Iraq can survive as sovereign, unitary states within their current borders.

Third, once an isolated pariah state, Iran has emerged as a regional superpower, enjoying the status of hegemon in Baghdad, a nearly comparable position in Damascus, and increasing weight in Turkey, Lebanon, Yemen, and the "Arabian Gulf." In addition, Russia's forceful intervention in support of the Assad regime has compelled strategic recalculations in Ankara, Amman, and elsewhere.

Fourth, despotic government has returned to Iraq and been reinvigorated in Syria. The populations of these countries have been "mobilized" in every sense of that overused term: terrorized into exile or submission, militarized, "radicalized" into embracing one or another totalitarian vision of the future, or exterminated. And whether motivated by sincerely held notions of doctrinal purity or by cynical pragmatism, all parties responsible have adopted practices deemed war crimes and crimes against humanity by the United Nations and the International Court of Justice. In addition to the mass murder of civilians, human trafficking, the denial of food and medical services, and the destruction and pillaging of both countries' cultural heritage, the most common (and potentially consequential) set of illegal practices constitutes the Orwellian neologism "demographic reengineering," or the manipulation of population settlement patterns for political purposes, an ongoing process that historian Joshua Landis has dubbed "the great sorting out."[1]

Owing to the transnational status of ISIS and the interstate reach of several local and regional actors, disentangling events in Syria and Iraq is empirically unsustainable. But for clarity's sake I treat the two states separately, their governments serving as axes around which networks of allies and opponents are arrayed. While well aware of arguments to the contrary, I also treat ISIS as a "real" (rather than "so-called") state, as it has clearly displayed the characteristics of the Weberian and most other social science definitions of such entities.[2]

Syrian Government Armed Forces

The Syrian Armed Forces (SAF) are divided into four branches: Army, Navy, Air Force, and Air Defense Forces. The SAF experienced a number of defections and performed poorly in the early stages of the rebellion. As a result, by late 2014 its numbers had been reduced to 150,000–178,000 active-duty troops, or less than half its pre-uprising contingent.[3] The government has thus expended considerable effort on expanding and upgrading reserves and auxiliaries. In 2013 most of these forces were reorganized and institutionalized as the National Defense Forces (NDF). Trained and equipped (and some observers maintain, led) by the Iranian Revolutionary Guards and Lebanese Hezbollah, these 90,000–100,000 "volunteers" have played an increasingly significant role in the conflict.[4]

Yet the SAF and NDF have been used sparingly against the most formidable armed opposition groups—the Salafist and Kurdish-led groups operating in northeastern Syria. The regime has instead focused most of its destructive power on Free Syrian Army units and other more "moderate Islamist" groups, a tendency also displayed by its Iranian and Russian allies.[5]

This selective use of military power is in keeping with long-term policy. Since before the uprising, Bashar al Assad repeatedly declared that Syria (and by extension, the world) had three alternatives: himself, jihadi terrorists bent on waging genocide against religious minorities, or the dismemberment of the state, a process that would destabilize the entire region for decades to come.[6] Many of Assad's subsequent actions appear designed to make this assertion a reality.[7] In response to the peaceful protests of spring 2011, he promulgated a "reform" program that included amnesty for political prisoners. Yet the overwhelming majority of those released were "violent Islamists" who subsequently joined ISIS, Jabhat Fatah al-Sham (Front for the Conquest of Syria), and other Salafist militias.[8]

The effect of these selective releases was, of course, to enable extremist domination of the insurgency. Early in the conflict, the practice was so pervasive and so central to regime policy that some observers have argued that Assad and ISIS were codependent, "exploit[ing] each other's existence in pursuit of a common goal—the wholesale destruction of any and all credible alternatives to themselves."[9] Such a conclusion is supported by the fact that the Assad regime long provided utilities to the former "capital" of the Islamic State at Raqqah, while ISIS sold electricity to "the Syrian government through third parties."[10]

Another regime practice with significant long-term consequences is the aforementioned "demographic reengineering," in this case preventing the return of populations to areas from which they were displaced by the conflict in order to punish perceived disloyalty, and to "ensure that rebellious communities do not re-establish themselves."[11]

Domestic Allies of the Syrian Government

The Assad regime is also supported by a number of "irregular" armed groups that serve as "home guards" for their own communities and as security guards at government installations, checkpoints, and other sensitive sites; they also provide logistical support to the SAF and NDF. According to some sources, they have also been used as cannon fodder during major assaults. Among the more significant such groups are the Liwa Abu al-Fadl al-Abbas (Abbas Brigade), Liwa Asad Allah al-Ghalib fi al-Iraq wa al-Sham (Conquering Lion of God Brigade in Iraq and the Levant), Fouj al-Mughawayr al-Bahir (Marines Regiment), Jaysh al-Muwahideen (Army of Monotheists), Liwa Suqur al-Sahara (Desert Hawks Brigade), Al-Haras al-Qawmi al-Arabi (Arab Nationalist Guard), and Al-Muqawama al-Suriyya (Syrian Resistance).[12]

Like elements of the NDF, many of these organizations have received foreign equipment and training. Several operate on both sides of the Syrian-Iraqi border and include "foreign fighters" in their ranks. And many are organized on a sectarian or ethnic basis. Thus their existence and proliferation since 2013 signify several critical developments: (1) the internationalization of the Syrian conflict; (2) the breadth and depth of support for the Assad regime in some minority communities; and (3) the eroding distinction between Syria and Iraq as theaters of war.

Regional Allies of the Syrian Government

The Islamic Republic of Iran is by far the most significant regional ally of the Assad regime. Building on a long-term strategic partnership, Iran has provided considerable financial assistance, as well as various forms of technical and logistical support to the Syrian government.[13] In addition to the training, equipping, and guiding of militias, Iran's Revolutionary Guard Corps has done the same for two wholly foreign Shia militias fighting in Syria, Liwa al-Fatimiyyun (Fatimid Brigade), and Liwa Zainebiyyun (Zaynabid Brigade).[14] The Guard Corps also provides advisers to the SAF, and members of its Quds Force provide intelligence and participate in important combat missions. In fact, the critical, ever-expanding role of the Quds Force has prompted some to argue that its leader, Major General Qasem Soleimani, "controls, directly or indirectly, most of the al-Assad regime's security establishment and attendant war machine."[15]

Another long-term strategic ally of the regime is the Lebanese "state within a state," Hezbollah. It has provided logistical support and combat troops since late 2011, operating primarily along the Lebanese border, in the Orontes River Valley, the outlying areas of Damascus, and more recently Aleppo. At any given time approximately 10,000 combat forces are present in Syria, and they have played a significant role in several regime victories. In the process they have suffered hundreds of casualties, including the loss of Mustafa Badreddine and numerous other senior commanders.[16]

The story of Iraq's involvement in the Syrian civil war is more complex and ambiguous. Seeking to deter U.S. intervention in Syria and "to divert Islamists' attention away from his regime," from 2003 to late 2009 Bashar al-Assad made support for the Sunni insurgency in Iraq a core policy.[17] During this period Assad's director of military intelligence (and brother-in-law), the late Assef Shawkat, provided sanctuary and support to former Saddamists and leaders of the insurgency Izzat Ibrahim al-Douri and Mohammed Younis al-Ahmed. By such means, Syrian intelligence "facilitated and suborned al-Qaeda terrorism" in Iraq, including deadly attacks against Iraqi police and bureaucrats in August 2009.[18] Since the uprising against Assad's regime, however, the two governments, both allies of Iran, have found common ground, and Iraq has provided financial and logistical support—for example, air and land transshipment of Iranian weapons, supplies, and personnel.

Opponents of the Syrian Government and Their Allies

The armed opposition to the Syrian government presents the most difficult challenges for scholars and policymakers. An astonishing number and variety of organizations have taken up arms against the regime since 2011.[19] Although they share the stated purpose of effacing the old political order in Syria, little else unites them. Most have defied the efforts of exiled opposition leaders and other external actors to impose some measure of unified command and control. And most have proved incapable of establishing stable cooperative arrangements amongst themselves. Small and medium-sized units frequently "defect" from one larger group to join another, change their names, or disband altogether, only to reappear in another guise. In short, with a few notable exceptions, Syria's armed opposition groups have been fluid, ephemeral, and in the absence of continuous external support, unsustainable.

Furthermore, the terms Western observers have employed to classify these groups are descriptively imprecise and bear little analytical utility. What, for example, does the term "moderate opposition" denote when describing participants in an armed uprising that seeks the violent overthrow of an existing government? Conversely, how does the term "Islamist" serve as an antonym for "moderate" or "secular" when so many groups thus designated advocate a political system based on sharia? In the absence of a more elegant and precise taxonomy, I have adopted "Salaf-ist" for those groups whose ideologies and practices are more extreme than those of other local actors and have retained "moderate" (always in quotation marks) for the remainder.

The Political Opposition

The Syrian opposition's political leadership has been singularly ineffec-tive at achieving its stated aim, the removal of Bashar al-Assad from power. Divided, exiled, and isolated from events on the ground in Syria, these figures have proved incapable of establishing meaningful constituencies among the population, imposing centralized command and control on the armed opposition, or wielding influence with foreign governments.

The oldest and most prominent organization is the Syrian National Council, which was founded under Turkish auspices in August 2011. The council claims to represent 60 percent of the opposition and has been granted official "recognition" by the European Union, the Arab League, and several UN-member states, and is affiliated with the Free Syrian Army. Owing to its many splits and defections, and its perceived domi-nation by members of the Muslim Brotherhood, the council has steadily lost influence since 2013.[20] In November 2012 the council joined a larger umbrella group, the newly formed National Coalition for Syrian Revo-lutionary and Opposition Forces, popularly known as the Syrian National Coalition.[21] Another significant opposition organization is the Syrian Democratic Council, founded in December 2015. It is the political face of the Syrian Democratic Forces (SDF), a militia about which I say much more in the following sections. The council is unique among such um-brella organizations in that it is closely integrated with a disciplined and capable armed force, it was founded with and possesses a real constitu-ency inside Syria, and its political program, which calls for a secular, democratic, and federalist Syria, is appealing to governments and public opinion in the West.

The "Moderate" Armed Opposition

Most observers date the militarization of the Syrian uprising to July 29, 2011, when Colonel Riad al-Asaad announced the formation of the Free Syrian Army (FSA). Initially at the core of the armed revolt, the FSA has faded in significance. Never a coherent military force, since 2015 the FSA has become little more than a brand name used episodically by disparate groups throughout Syria. Underfunded and lightly armed (overt American support has been restricted to nonlethal aid), most FSA units have been unable to hold captured territory when subjected to air power, heavy weapons, or well-executed ground attacks. As a result, mass defections to Jabhat Fatah al-Sham, ISIS, the SDF, and other organizations have been common.

The FSA's close identification with the Turkish government (many Syrians consider it a creation of Turkish military intelligence) and the corrupt practices and human rights abuses of many units using the FSA label have undermined the organization's standing among civilians.[22] Furthermore, the presence within the FSA of fighters expressing jihadist rhetoric, along with senior commanders' demonstrated inability to establish a coherent system of command and control, has caused the ardor of many Western supporters to cool. Finally, Turkey's policy adjustments in light of Russian intervention render doubtful the FSA's longevity.

An organization of more recent vintage, the Syrian Democratic Forces, presents a very different picture. Founded in October 2015, the SDF is the armed wing of the aforementioned Syrian Democratic Council, and comprises nineteen militias of predominantly Kurdish, Arab, Assyrian, Armenian, Turkmen, or Circassian ethnicity, people of mixed ethnicity, and several tribal militias operating in northern and northeastern Syria.[23] The SDF is the official defense force of the SDC's Rojava [West Kurdistan] Revolution, whose goal is the creation of an autonomous region within the context of a secular, democratic, and federal Syrian Republic.

The largest and most formidable of the SDF militias are those fighting under the banner of the People's Protection Units (YPG), the armed units of the Kurdish Democratic Union Party (PYD). As of late 2015, the YPG had become the U.S. Central Command's favored proxy in the fight against ISIS.[24] It has also received various forms of support from Kurdish militias based in Iraq, and air support from British, Canadian, and French forces. Boasting of several victories, the YPG is widely acknowledged to be the most experienced, motivated, and effective force confronting ISIS in northern Syria. Yet its parent organization's affiliation with the Kurdish Workers' Party (PKK), the PYD's March 2016 declaration of self-governance within an imagined federal Syria, and the PYD's de facto creation of an autonomous polity along much of the Syrian-Turkish border have made them anathema to Ankara, a fact that bodes ill for the future of U.S. support and thus for the SDF's very existence.[25]

As noted, Syrian government forces have largely refrained from attacking YPG units and PYD institutions. In fact Assad began to withdraw his military and security personnel from predominantly Kurdish areas in 2013.[26] This was a cunning rebuke to the Turkish government, which had been the first meaningful supporter of armed resistance to the Assad regime and fears nothing more than the establishment of a PKK-allied entity on its southern border.

The most significant development affecting non-Salafist opposition groups is the emergence of *ghurfat amaliyat* (operations rooms). Not fixed, physical installations, these began as ad hoc intelligence-sharing and planning units providing support for a specific military operation. Unconfirmed media reports and leaks from within opposition groups maintain that operation rooms' member groups receive funding, communications gear, advice, logistical support, and sometimes weapons and training from the United States and its regional allies. For this purpose they are reportedly linked to one of the Joint Military Operations Centers (MOCs) that the United States has established in Jordan and Turkey. After repeatedly failing to engender a broad-based political coalition or coherent military command, the operations rooms appeared to be the Obama administration's Plan B for influencing events in the Syrian civil war. Dozens of such "rooms" have appeared since early 2014, and a few—for example, the Southern Front and the Euphrates Volcano—have evolved into semi-stable alliances of armed groups. Given the impact of Russian intervention, however, and the potential consequences of the unfolding Turkish-Russian rapprochement, the future of the operations rooms is uncertain.

The "Salafist" Armed Opposition

One thing is clear: Salafism is not a novel phenomenon in Syria. It has deep historical roots. In the generic meaning of religious, social, and political reform with reference to *al-salaf al-salih*, or "the pious ancestors," it can be traced to clerics and other pious intellectuals of the mid-nineteenth century.[27] As a coherent political ideology that aspires to replace the existing political order with an "Islamic State," it appeared in the 1940s as a central tenet of the Syrian Muslim Brotherhood's program.[28]

In addition, the current conflict in Syria is in many ways a reprise, albeit on a much larger scale, of the 1976–1982 Muslim Brotherhood–led armed uprising against Hafez al-Assad. All the Syrian leaders of Salafist groups engaged in the current uprising draw their ideological inspiration from the leaders of the previous one, particularly Marwan Hadid, the founder of al-Talia al-Muqatila (Fighting Vanguard), the Brotherhood's armed wing.[29]

Furthermore, today's Salafist groups display other continuities with modern Syrian history. The Salafist project seeks to efface the boundaries created by the post–World War I settlement.[30] This goal was foundational for the Arab Nationalist Movement of George Habash, the Arab Baath Socialist Party, Antun Saada's Syrian Social Nationalist Party, and numerous other nationalist, leftist, and ostensibly secular movements that professed the necessity of violence from the 1930s to the 1970s.

Finally, while ruthlessly suppressed, the 1976–82 uprising prompted Hafez al-Assad to seek a rapprochement with the Sunni merchant class of Syria's cities. As a result, Assad facilitated the creation of numerous Islamic charitable foundations that constructed schools, hospitals, and mosques. This "strategic alliance" created institutional spaces and relationships within which ideological opponents of both Assad regimes could organize and profess Salafist doctrine to the masses.[31]

Many of the most significant groups that have emerged from this historical process to take up arms against Bashar al-Assad's rule were organized into a sizable Saudi-backed coalition (an estimated 45,000 fighters), al-Jabhat al-Islamiyya (Islamic Front). Its members include Jaysh al-Islam (Army of Islam); Harakat Ahrar al-Sham al-Islamiyya (Islamic Movement of the Free People of the Levant, popularly known as Ahrar al-Sham); and Kitaib Ansar al-Sham (Supporters of the Levant Brigades, popularly known as Ansar al-Sham). While these groups are explicitly opposed to ISIS, they sometimes operate in alliance with Jabhat Fatah al-Sham. Another sizable (est. 7,000–10,000) such alliance is Tahaluf al-Muhajirin wal-Ansar (Alliance of Emigrants and Helpers), which includes Jund al-Aqsa (Soldiers of Aqsa) and other groups with direct connections to al Qaeda. Just to complicate the picture further, as part of a general trend of consolidation since 2015, some of these groups have, at various times, joined or left the large Saudi-sponsored operations room Jaysh al-Fatah (Army of Conquest).

Yet the Salafist groups that have played the most significant role in the Syrian conflict are ISIS and Jabhat Fatah al-Sham. The latter group originated in August 2011 as a delegation from the amir of the Islamic State of Iraq, Abu Bakr al-Baghdadi, to Salafist groups fighting the Assad regime in Sunni-majority areas of northern Syria. After extensive discussions, the formation of Jabhat al-Nusra li Ahl al-Sham (Front for Support of the People of Syria) was announced in January 2012.[32]

Soon hundreds of Syrians with experience fighting in Iraq flocked to Jabhat al-Nusra's banner. Thus it quickly earned a reputation as one of the most skilled, disciplined, and effective forces in the insurgency.[33] Its amir, Abu Muhammad al-Julani (real name Ahmed Hussein al-Shara), was initially careful to cultivate positive relations with other Sunni groups and leaders of local communities and to refrain from the sectarian excesses and depredations of his parent organization.[34] For all of these reasons, for its perceived "Syrian" pedigree, its efforts to maintain law and order, and its attempts to provide "state services" to the populations under its control, the organization enjoyed popular support in its areas of operation.[35]

Although al-Jolani was formally Abu Bakr al-Baghdadi's deputy, and he received arms and funding and from the Islamic State of Iraq (ISI), his group operated autonomously and often contrary to al-Baghdadi's stated policies. In April 2013, after several (sometimes violent) disagreements, al-Baghdadi attempted to reassert control by announcing the merger of Jabhat al-Nusra and ISI to form a new organization, al-Dawla al-Islamiyya fi al-Iraq wa al-Sham (Islamic State in Iraq and the Levant, ISIL).[36] Al-Jolani swiftly announced his rejection of the union, declaring that he had not been consulted about the merger. He then renewed his personal (and his organization's) pledge of fealty to al Qaeda leader Ayman al-Zawahiri.[37]

From 2013 to 2016, al-Nusra experienced many "successes" in battlefield, terrorist, and kidnapping and ransom operations. Yet these activities invited air strikes by Syrian government, Russian, and American forces. Conflict also erupted between al-Nusra and former allies among Salafist groups and FSA units. As a result, al-Nusra's position was weakened.

In July 2016, al-Jolani announced that al-Nusra was severing its ties with al Qaeda and changing its name to Jabhat Fatah al-Sham. Many Western observers disputed the sincerity of this secession, characterizing it as a ploy to garner more funding from al-Nusra's reputed sponsor Qatar and other wealthy Gulf donors.[38] Given the group's terrorist operations, assassinations, forced conversions of non-Sunnis, and many other human rights abuses, even a genuine break with al Qaeda is unlikely to change attitudes toward the group outside the region's "Salafist community."

Regional Actors and the Syrian Opposition
The Turkish Republic has been a major player in the Syrian conflict since its inception. Initially, this took the form of fostering the creation of the Free Syrian Army by providing refuge, funding, equipment, and training to SAF defectors. Soon thereafter, journalists and senior state officials in the region, Europe, and the United States began presenting evidence that Turkey's National Intelligence Organization (MIT) was providing comparable support to Salafist groups, permitting their fighters to cross the Turkish-Syrian border at will, facilitating the safe passage of foreign recruits between Turkey, Syria, and Europe, partnering in smuggling and other illicit forms of commerce that benefited ISIS, and even participating in terrorist operations inside Syria.[39]

Turkey's 2011 decision to actively support the armed rebellion against the Assad regime represents a dramatic shift from its posture of the previous decade. But one facet of its policy during the uprising displays perfect consistency with its strategic vision since the foundation of the republic. If one disposition unites President Recep Tayyip Erdoğan's ruling Justice and Development Party (AKP), its "enemies" in the movement of Fethullah Gülen, and its secular, nationalist predecessors in the People's Republican Party, it is the absolute refusal to countenance the establishment of a Kurdish-ruled state on its southern border.

This continuity in policy explains Turkey's willingness to "get in bed" with any and all opponents of the People's Protection Units of the SDF, including ISIS and other Salafist groups otherwise hostile to the Ankara government: "When it came to the war in Syria, NATO's second-largest member state would rather hamper the Kurds than defeat ISIS."[40] Thus Turkey delayed granting the United States, other NATO members, and regional allies permission to use Incirlik Air Base for bombing missions against ISIS targets; and it implacably opposes U.S. assistance to, or co-operation with, the YPG. Turkey mounted Operation Euphrates Shield (August 2016–March 2017) with allied forces in northern Syria to create a "safe zone" by clearing SDF forces up to the west bank of the Euphrates River, and to clear ISIS from towns adjacent to the Turkish border. While Turkey's official pronouncements have routinely equated the SDF and ISIS as "terrorist" organizations, the state's air power was, until October 2016, almost exclusively targeting the Kurdish militia's positions.[41]

A 2016 policy shift in Ankara could have momentous consequences for the outcome and aftermath of the conflict. I refer here to the ongoing rapprochement with Russia. While seemingly irreconcilable policy differences remain—Turkey continues to call for the removal of Assad, and the Russians are reported to have established closer ties with the SDF—these contradictions could be resolved via a quid pro quo agreement—that is, Turkey's acceptance of Assad remaining in charge of a unitary (rather than federal) state, and Russia's abjuring support for the all-too-frequently abandoned Kurds.

Jordan's role in the Syrian conflict has been less obvious or significant. Abu Musab al-Zarqawi, the founder of Tanzim Qaidat al-Jihad fi Bilad al-Rafidayn (Organization for the Jihad's Base in Mesopotamia), more commonly called al Qaeda in Iraq (AQI), was a Jordanian criminal who was "radicalized" by his studies at the al-Hussein Bin Ali Mosque in Amman and his experience waging jihad in Afghanistan.[42] An implacable enemy of Jordan's King Abdullah, al-Zarqawi sought to destabilize and destroy the Hashemite monarchy by mounting assassinations and spectacular terrorist operations in Amman.[43] Jordan subsequently participated in the 2014 bombing campaign against ISIS in Syria, only to "quietly deescalate" after the group's horrific murder of captured Air Force lieutenant Muath al-Kasasbeh.[44] Since late 2015, Jordanian involvement appears to have been focused on intelligence cooperation with "U.S.,

European, and regional intelligence services" through the aforementioned Military Operations Command in Amman and hosting forward deployments of U.S. Central Command equipment and personnel.[45]

Saudi Arabia has also played a significant role in the conflict, serving since 2013 as the single largest provider of weapons (transshipped through Turkey and Jordan) and funds to the armed opposition. This is unsurprising given the Saudi government's deep pockets and its perception of the conflict as a proxy war with its existential foe, the Islamic Republic of Iran. Since 2015, Saudi Arabia has funneled most such support to members of the Jaysh al-Fatah (Army of Conquest) operations room, but reports persist that it has dispensed similar largesse to ISIS and any other "Islamist" group deemed capable of inflicting pain on Assad's Iranian allies.

Despite its differences with the Saudis and other Gulf Cooperation Council (GCC) members, Qatar has played a similar role, providing arms and cash to rebel groups across the political spectrum and offering generous aid packages to a small number of Syrian refugees. Since 2014 it has also operated (in cooperation with the United States) a small-unit training facility. It is reputed to favor Jaysh al-Fatah and (covertly) Jabhat Fatah al-Sham, and it has permitted the Syrian National Coalition to operate an embassy in Doha since 2013.

Another country that has played a significant, though largely covert, role in the Syrian conflict is Israel, which conducted numerous well-publicized air strikes against Syrian and/or Hezbollah military installations and convoys and exchanged artillery and small arms fire with Syrian government and rebel forces between 2013 and 2016. Less well documented are reports of Israel's provision of ambulance and other medical services to Druze rebels operating near the Golan Heights and its participation in operations rooms in Jordan, Turkey, and Syria.

The Iraqi Government, Its Allies, and Its Opponents

Its transnational aspirations notwithstanding, ISIS is very much the product of Iraq-specific historical experiences. Decades of personalized authoritarian rule, "revolutionary" indoctrination, militarism, war, sectarian propaganda, state attempts to co-opt Islamist and tribal groups, and foreign intervention produced the attitudes, skills, and institutional memories informing the emergence of ISIS's precursors and their evolution to date. Thus the Islamic State should be a thoroughly "familiar foe" to those seeking its elimination.[46] In what follows, I refer to the historical context as necessary, but focus primarily on events subsequent to the 2013 declaration of ISIS, or the period of the "Second Iraq War."

Iraqi Government Armed Forces
Iraq's conventional armed forces comprise the Iraqi Army (including Special Operations Forces), the Iraqi Air Force, the Iraqi Navy (including Marines), the Iraqi Air Defense Forces, and various Interior Ministry troops, together totaling approximately 800,000 active-duty personnel as of late 2017. The United States lavished enormous resources on building the "New Iraqi Army" between 2003 and 2012.[47] Nevertheless, Iraq's conventional armed forces have not performed well against ISIS or other manifestations of Sunni rebellion.

Domestic Allies of the Iraqi Government
Thus Iraq, like Syria, has been compelled to draw on the resources of irregular forces and regional allies. In June 2014 the government announced the formation of al-Hashd al-Shaabi (Popular Mobilization Forces, PMF) an umbrella organization consisting of sixteen major—and dozens of lesser—militias, totaling approximately 110,000 armed men.[48] Some of the PMF's most significant components are the Badr Organization (formerly the Badr Brigades), Asaib Ahl al-Haqq (League of the Righteous), Saraya al-Salam (Peace Brigades), Kataib Hezbollah (Hezbollah Brigades), and Kitaib al-Imam Ali (Imam Ali Brigades).[49] Most of these militias, several of which have been the beneficiaries of U.S. training and air support, have engaged in "demographic reengineering" and other war crimes.[50]

The PMF report to the Iraqi prime minister, but many observers assert that they actually take their orders from Tehran via Iranian Revolutionary Guard Corps commander Qasem Soleimani, who is reputed to wield even greater power in Iraq than he does in Syria.[51]

Consensus holds that the Iraqi government would have failed to halt ISIS's 2014 expansion southward, let alone retake much of the seized territory, without the intervention of the PMF and Guard Corps. There is also general agreement that, by ceding such critical state security functions to its neighbor, Baghdad has further diluted its sovereignty.[52]

Another formidable military force occupies an ambiguous space between the Iraqi Armed Forces, its allies, and its opponents: the Kurdish militias collectively known as the Peshmerga. Reliable figures are unavailable, but estimates range from 150,000 to 200,000 armed personnel. Though nominally allied with the Iraqi central government in the fight against ISIS, the Peshmerga take their orders from one or another institution of the autonomous self-governing Kurdistan Regional Government (KRG), not from Baghdad.[53]

Since 2014 Peshmerga offensives have expelled ISIS from allegedly Kurdish-majority regions of four provinces and in the process have taken control of land formally under the authority of the central government. The KRG reportedly plans to use these territories as bargaining chips in future negotiations with Baghdad, a process rendered more contentious by the KRG independence referendum of September 2017.[54] Furthermore, Amnesty International and others have accused the Peshmerga of "demographic engineering" in these territories: destroying homes in Arab villages, blocking former residents from returning, and effectively annexing oil-rich areas to the Kurdistan Regional Government.[55] These actions presage difficult relations between the central government and the KRG, if and when both parties deem the ISIS threat eliminated.

Another armed group with potential future significance is the Irak Türkmen Cephesi (Iraqi Turkmen Front, ITF), which claims to protect Turkmen rights in Kirkuk, Mosul, and areas in the Diyala Governorate with substantial Turkmen populations. With the apparent consent of Baghdad and the KRG, they have received training and equipment from Turkish Special Forces and have participated in offensives against ISIS. The central government has announced plans to incorporate the ITF into the Iraqi Armed Forces after ISIS is defeated.

Regional Allies of the Iraqi Government

Since 2011, improved relations between Damascus and Baghdad have led to intelligence sharing, coordination of some military operations, and a limited number of Syrian air strikes against ISIS targets in Iraq. Continued cooperation, however, is dependent on the influence of Iran, which is by far Baghdad's most significant regional ally in the fight against ISIS. This should be no surprise, given the two states' proximity and the two governments' numerous political and religious affinities. In addition, many of Iraq's current political elite—members of the Islamic Dawa or Islamic Supreme Council of Iraq (ISCI) Parties—spent many years in exile in the Islamic Republic, where they cooperated with that country's intelligence services in attempts to overthrow Saddam Hussein.[56]

Iran has provided financial, technical, and logistical support to the governments of Nuri al-Maliki and Haider al-Abadi. In addition to funding, training, and equipping the People's Mobilization Units (PMUs), Iran has assisted in the planning of offensives and provided weapons and ammunition to the Kurdish Peshmerga.[57] Despite repeated claims to the contrary, since summer 2014 Tehran has also intervened in the conflict directly, mounting air strikes against ISIS targets and deploying armor and infantry in coordination with Peshmerga, PMUs, and Iraqi Army troops. In the process, IRGC forces have sustained numerous casualties, including the death of several senior officers.[58]

Armed Opposition to the Iraqi Government

At first glance, the story of armed opposition to the Iraqi government is as complex and confusing as that in Syria. Groups have changed names, alliances, and apparent purpose with dizzying frequency. Furthermore, in the absence of verifiable information, it is often difficult to determine whether some smaller units are currently affiliated with one larger umbrella group or another, or if some groups remain active. In addition, observers can't agree on the orientation of many groups, alternately describing the same organization as "Baathist," "tribal," or "Islamist."

Yet, upon closer examination, several significant facts become clear. First, as in Syria, the insurgency features numerous continuities with past events and actors. For example, key institutions, ideologies, policies, and officials of Saddam Hussein's regime featured in the post-2003 insurgency and have shaped its continuing existence.

Second, many manifestations of the ongoing insurgency were utterly preventable. In other words, the actions of the Maliki government produced, in some measure, the resumption of broad-based conflict and frequently hampered efforts to defeat ISIS. Many groups that participated in the uprisings against U.S. forces ceased hostilities, demobilized, and/or changed their mode of opposition after the implementation of the 2011 Status of Forces Agreement (SOFA) that led to the withdrawal of U.S. combat troops. The Maliki government's violation of previous agreements to incorporate Sunni insurgents into Iraqi government forces, its manipulation of national elections to deny office to Sunni candidates, and its violent suppression of peaceful demonstrations have prompted many to take up arms again.[59] Furthermore, several Sunni insurgent leaders, though avowed enemies of ISIS, have often refused to attack its positions until these and other grievances against the central government are addressed.

In addition, many of ISIS's most stunning military successes in Iraq can be attributed to former prime minister Nuri al-Maliki's efforts to "coup proof" Iraq's armed forces, replacing more competent professionals with loyal cronies who were often inexperienced, corrupt, and prone to abandon the soldiers and civilians under their command upon the first threat of insurgent attack.[60] Finally, although Iran's robust participation in the campaign against ISIS appears to have temporarily rescued Baghdad from itself, its perceived domination of Iraq virtually guarantees the persistence of a Sunni insurgency into the foreseeable future.

Because these issues defy classification, I have not attempted to place the major armed opposition groups into neat categories. Instead, I simply treat them in turn, indicating in each case the various ways they have been characterized given their origins, their stated goals, and their postures toward ISIS and the Iraqi government. ISIS is treated last.

Al-Qiyada al-Aliyya lil-Jihad wal-Tahrir (Supreme Command for Jihad and Liberation, SCJL), is a coalition of twenty-three armed groups operating throughout much of Iraq. Founded in 2007, most of its constituent members took up arms against the United States in 2003. The

SCJL ceased attacking Iraqi government targets after the 2011 SOFA implementation, only to resume hostilities with Baghdad in January 2014. The SCJL describes itself as "Islamist" and "Arab nationalist," but because it is led by former Iraqi vice president Izaat Ibrahim al-Douri, many observers have characterized it as Baathist. The largest and most formidable of its components is Jaysh Rijal al-Tariqa al-Naqshbandiyya (Army of the Men of the Naqshbandi [Sufi] Order), which is also led by al-Douri. SCJL is implacably opposed to the current Iraqi government and its Iranian patron. Thus, though not formally allied with ISIS, it has praised some of the group's actions and partnered with it during the 2014 "Northern Offensive" that captured Mosul and other Iraqi cities.

Al-Majlis al-Askari al-Amm li Thuwwar al-Iraq (General Military Council for Iraqi Revolutionaries, GMCIR) was founded in January 2014 by former bureaucrats and military officers of the Saddam Hussein regime, reportedly in response to the Maliki regime's killing of unarmed Sunni protestors in 2012 and 2103. The GMCIR, sometimes characterized as "tribal," describes itself as democratic and nonsectarian and claims to command 75,000 armed fighters in Anbar and four other governorates. Like the SCJL, it is an opponent of Iranian influence in Iraq and cooperated with ISIS in the 2014 Northern Offensive.

Al-Majlis al-Askari li Thuwwar Al-Ashair (Military Council of Tribal Revolutionaries), popularly known as the Anbar Tribes Revolutionary Council, is the most recent incarnation of Anbar Governorate–centered tribal militias that participated in the 2003–07 insurgency as well as the anti–al Qaeda "Awakening." Formerly led by Sheikh Ali Hatem al-Suleiman, they once boasted of 60,000 (mostly Dulaim) tribesmen at arms. The council also attempted, post-SOFA, to engage in peaceful electoral politics. As the Maliki government suppressed these efforts, the council returned to armed resistance, participating in the 2014 Northern Offensive. Unlike many other insurgent groups, the council does not demand the dissolution of the current Iraqi government. But it has refused to attack ISIS forces until government troops are withdrawn from Anbar and other governorates and other demands are met.

Al-Majlis al-Siyasi lil-Muqawamat al-Iraqiyya (Political Council for the Iraqi Resistance, PCIR) is a coalition of several insurgent groups that also demobilized in 2011 and attempted to participate in the political process. The most significant of its members are Hamas al-Iraq (Hamas of Iraq), Al-Jabha al-Islamiyya lil-Muqawama al-Iraqiyya–Jama (Islamic Front for the Iraqi Resistance), and al-Jaysh al-Islami fi al-Iraq (Islamic Army in Iraq, IAI). The IAI was one of the largest and most effective groups participating in the 2003–07 anti-U.S. insurgency, in the Awakening against AQI, *and* in the ISIS-led campaign that captured Mosul.[61]

By the summer of 2010, the Islamic State of Iraq was on the verge of extinction.[62] U.S., Iraqi government, and Sunni Awakening forces had killed its top leadership, severely depleted its ranks, and driven it from most cities. Two sets of events transformed its fortunes: The onset of the Syrian civil war and the actions of the Maliki government. The withdrawal of Syrian armed forces and security services from the Sunni-majority regions along the country's eastern border created another theater of operations, enabling ISI's new leader, Abu Bakr al-Baghdadi, to transform al-Zarqawi's Iraq-centered project into a truly transnational enterprise.[63] And the Maliki government's refusal to pay the salaries of former Awakening fighters now on the Iraqi government payroll sent experienced, vengeful insurgents flooding back into ISI's ranks.

This transfusion of manpower and expertise also threw yet another continuity into sharp relief: the ideological affinities and intertwined histories of ISIS and Iraqi Baathism. When named ISI's new amir, al-Baghdadi immediately began to expand on al-Zarqawi's policy of enlisting as many of Saddam's former military and security personnel as possible. Many became midlevel and senior military commanders.[64] And ISIS's reorganized intelligence and security agencies—al-Amniyyat—were designed, staffed, and managed by former officers of Saddam's feared Mukhabarat.[65] Furthermore, as of late 2015, all of Abu Bakr al-Baghdadi's senior advisers and governors of Iraqi governorates were former officers in the pre-2003 army, ostensibly secular Baathists closely associated with Saddam Hussein's notorious eldest son, Uday.[66]

In fact, al-Baghdadi's personal history is replete with Baathist associations. He was a member of "Saddam's Youth," in which he absorbed sectarian bigotry and the normalization of authoritarian government.[67] He received his BA, MA, and PhD at the Saddam University for Islamic

Studies, entry to which, scholars have argued, was impossible without references from senior party members.[68] Finally, rumors persist that close relatives of al-Baghdadi were employees of Saddam's intelligence services.[69] All of these connections have prompted some observers to declare that ISIS was "born out of the failure of the Baath" and to characterize the organization as "a spectral holdover of . . . 'secular' Baathism."[70] Indeed, in many ways, the murderous, fiercely intolerant founders and leaders of ISIS are truly "Saddam's children."[71]

Conclusion: The Future of the Islamic State and of Nation-States

Unsurprisingly, the United States and its allies have failed to formulate and implement a policy that could achieve several contradictory objectives: the destruction of ISIS, the preservation of the Iranian-allied Iraqi regime, the elimination of the Iranian-allied Syrian regime, the preservation and enhancement of Western influence in the region, and the shaping of NATO member Turkey's behavior.

As a result, Iran has adroitly exploited violence and instability to transform itself into a regional superpower, and Russia's forceful intervention on behalf of the Assad regime has altered the calculus of regional actors. Specifically, Ankara has entered an awkward embrace with Moscow and Tehran, apparently abandoning its goal of displacing Bashar al-Assad. Turkey has instead "refocused on curbing Kurdish expansion" in northern Syria.[72] Thus the trajectory of events seems clear. The Iranian-allied regimes in Damascus and Baghdad will remain in power, the U.S.-allied Kurds' aspirations for autonomy in northern Syria will be thwarted, and Western influence in the region will be further diminished.

Yet, owing to the Syrian and Iraqi regimes' incompetence, corruption, and brutality, "victories" like those in Aleppo, Mosul, and Raqqah will not herald the imminent return to stability. Neither do they suggest that either regime can successfully govern these "liberated" territories.[73] ISIS, under this or another name, will almost certainly retain the capacity to wage guerrilla warfare and mount spectacular terrorist operations.[74]

Even an absolute military victory over the Islamic State would not mean an end to conflict, for, as Andrew Bacevich has noted, the "conditions that had given rise to ISIS would persist."[75]

In Syria, although the Assad regime has used propaganda effectively to convince a sizable segment of the population that it alone can engender a return to "normal life," economic realities will almost certainly prevent the emergence of anything resembling that state.[76] And, in the absence of fundamental changes to what is widely perceived as a police state of profound sectarian complexion, "deep divisions in the polity" will endure and fester.[77]

In Iraq many Sunnis appear to believe that the establishment of Iranian hegemony in their country was the opening gambit in a global conspiracy contrived to "disinherit" "1.3 billion Sunni Muslims."[78] Unless the Abadi regime or its successors sincerely attempt to address the legitimate grievances of Iraq's Sunni citizens, the number of those who currently see violent resistance à la ISIS as their "only option" is almost certain to increase.[79]

In brief, if regional actors seek to reduce support for ISIS and similarly violent expressions of opposition to the existing political order, they should promote the establishment of better governance. Otherwise, vicious conflict will emerge once more, featuring protagonists whose destabilizing potential meets or exceeds that of ISIS.

Notes

1 I encountered this term in an article by Elizabeth Tsurkov and Hasan al-Homsi, "Seven Months after 'Liberating' Palmyra, Residents Still Cannot Return," Atlantic Council, October 13, 2016 (www.atlanticcouncil.org /blogs/syriasource/seven-months-after-liberating-palmyra-residents-still -cannot-return). Perhaps a more evocative euphemism is "denominational cleansing," found in Michael Weiss and Hassan Hassan's *ISIS: Inside the Army of Terror* (New York: Regan Arts, 2016), p. 142. Examples of these practices abound. On ISIS's forced conversion of the Druze in northern Syria, see Aymen Jawad Al-Tamimi, "Dar al-Qada Statement in Jabal al-Summaq: Translation & Analysis," Atlantic Council, November 18, 2016

(www.atlanticcouncil.org/blogs/syriasource/dar-al-qada-statement-in
-jabal-al-summaq-translation-analysis). On the Assad regime's eviction of
perceived opponents in Darayya, see Hosam Al-Jablawi, "Assad Ends 'Damascus Reconciliations' and Makes Stopping the Bombing Conditional on
the Opposition's Departure," Atlantic Council, October 19, 2016 (www
.atlanticcouncil.org/blogs/syriasource/assad-ends-damascus-reconciliations
-and-makes-stopping-the-bombing-conditional-on-the-opposition-s
-departure). On the Kurdish People's Defense Units looting, burning, and
evicting Arabs in the Jazira, see Haid Haid, "The Impact of the Kurdish-
Led Campaign to Isolate Raqqa," *SyriaSource*, November 15, 2016 (www
.atlanticcouncil.org/blogs/syriasource/the-impact-of-the-kurdish-led
-campaign-to-isolate-raqqa). On ISIS's slaughter of Shia soldiers in Tikrit,
see Weiss and Hassan, *ISIS*, p. 30. On ISIS slaughtering, expelling, raping,
and enslaving the Yazidi people of Mt. Sinjar, see Sami Moubayed, *Under the
Black Flag: At the Frontier of the New Jihad* (New York: I. B. Tauris, 2015),
p. 138. On Assad regime-sanctioned massacres in the Orontes River Valley,
see Weiss and Hassan, *ISIS*, p. 168. On Shia militias' multiple war crimes
conducted with U.S. air support in central and western Iraq, see Weiss and
Hassan, *ISIS*, p. xvi. On Sadrists and Iranian-run Special Groups occupying
army checkpoints to identify, lead away, and execute Sunnis, see Moubayed,
Under the Black Flag, p. 138. On the National Defense Force carrying out
"anti-Sunni pogroms," see Weiss and Hassan, *ISIS*, p. 132. On Iraqi military
and police units under the direct authority of Prime Minister Maliki engaging in the murder and abduction of Sunnis, see Weiss and Hassan, *ISIS*, p. 64.
On the "great sorting out," see "Joshua Landis on ISIS, Syria & the 'Great
Sorting Out' in the Middle East—Interview with Danny Postel," *SyriaCom-
ment,* October 17, 2014 (www.joshualandis.com/blog/joshua-landis-isis
-syria-great-sorting-middle-east-interview-danny-postel).

2 In the territories under their control, ISIS assumed the trappings of a "real"
state, establishing dependable revenue streams, forming numerous intelligence and security agencies, and creating administrative councils, media
outlets, and other structures to oversee public sanitation, public safety, education, health care, and the provision of utilities. It successfully fulfilled
the primary Weberian criterion by establishing a monopoly on the use of
force. Moubayed, *Under the Black Flag*, pp. 75–76. See also Weiss and Hassan, *ISIS*, pp. 169, 211–12, 214. I am aware of, but not convinced by, the
opposing arguments. See, for example, Andrew Bacevich, *America's War for
the Greater Middle East: A Military History* (New York: Random House,
2016), pp. 342–43.

3 "Syria Increasing Efforts to Build Up Military after Substantial Losses,"
South China Morning Post, December 29, 2014 (www.scmp.com/news/world

/article/1670515/syria-increasing-efforts-build-military-after-substantial
-losses).

4 Weiss and Hassan, *ISIS*, p. 131. The predominantly Alawi "Shabiha," or
   "ghost" militias have been folded into the NDF, as have the Kitaib al-Baath,
   or Baath Party Brigades. Weiss and Hassan assert that National Defense
   Force units are "supervised by a Revolutionary Guards Corps officer who
   acts the part of an embedded commissar ensuring ideological discipline."

5 Weiss and Hassan, *ISIS*, pp. 154–58.

6 Ibid., pp. 128, 130, 142.

7 Ibid., p. xiv.

8 Among the most significant of these figures are Abu al-Athir al-Absi, who
   became ISIS governor of Aleppo Province; Abu Khalid al-Suri, who co-
   founded Ahrar al-Sham; and Zahran Alloush, military commander of Jaysh
   al-Islam. Weiss and Hassan, *ISIS*, pp. xiv, 137–39, 148, 165; Moubayed,
   Under the Black Flag, p. 70. The reader will note that I sometimes translate
   the Arabic term al-Sham as "Syria" and sometimes as "the Levant." Depending on context, al-Sham can designate Damascus, Syria, or the larger
   Levant (Bilad al-Sham), I have translated it selectively, according to the purpose, area of operations, and/or public statements of the group using the
   term.

9 Weiss and Hassan, *ISIS*, p. xv.

10 Moubayed, *Under the Black Flag*, p. 144. For ISIS's sale of oil and natural
   gas to the Assad regime, see Weiss and Hassan, *ISIS*, pp. xiv, 212–13, 274.

11 Elizabeth Tsurkov and Hasan al-Homsi, "Seven Months after 'Liberating'
   Palmyra, Residents Still Cannot Return," Atlantic Council, October 13,
   2016 (www.atlanticcouncil.org/blogs/syriasource/seven-months-after
   -liberating-palmyra-residents-still-cannot-return). See also Hosam Al-
   Jablawi, "Increasing Tactics of Forced Displacement in Syria," Atlantic
   Council, October 6, 2016 (www.atlanticcouncil.org/blogs/syriasource
   /increasing-tactics-of-forced-displacement-in-syria).

12 The Abbas Brigade is a Twelver Shia/Alawi militia formed in 2012 to defend Shiite holy sites. Its personnel are a mix of Iraqis and Syrians. The
   Conquering Lion of God Brigade is a spin-off of the Abbas Brigade consisting of Iraqi and Syrian fighters. The Army of Monotheists is a Druze militia
   operating primarily in the Jabal al-Druze and Druze-majority neighborhoods of Deraa and Damascus. The Marines Regiment is Russian trained
   and equipped. The Arab Nationalist Guard is a small, secular, and Arab nationalist militia that includes many fighters from other Arab countries. The
   Syrian Resistance is a Marxist, primarily Alawi, militia of approximately
   2,000 fighters. In addition, the Syrian Social Nationalist Party (SSNP) has
   fielded approximately 7,000—primarily Greek Orthodox and Druze—

fighters in support of the government. Sootoro, a militia/police force of 500–600 Syriac Christians and Armenians operates in the northern city of Qamishli. Members of the Popular Front for the Liberation of Palestine–General Command (PFLP–GC) also took up arms in support of the al-Assad regime in Damascus.

13 Estimates of total expenditures since 2013 range from $6 billion to $15 billion annually. Eli Lake, "Iran Spends Billions to Prop Up Assad," *Bloomberg View,* June 9, 2015 (www.bloomberg.com/view/articles/2015-06-09/iran-spends-billions-to-prop-up-assad).

14 The former is recruited from Afghan Shia and the latter from Pakistani Shia.

15 Weiss and Hassan, *ISIS,* p. 358.

16 The figure of 10,000 is provided by Moubayed in *Under the Black Flag,* p. 164. The regime victory in al-Qausayr has been declared to be "almost single-handedly" the work of Hezbollah fighters. Weiss and Hassan, *ISIS,* p. 135.

17 Ibid., pp. 100, 98.

18 Ibid., pp. xiv, 91, 104, 107. Another element of this policy was the protection of Mahmud al-Aghasi, aka Abu al-Qaqa, the fiery mosque preacher and founder of the foreign jihadi militia Ghuraba al-Sham. Moubayed, *Under the Black Flag,* pp. 62–63.

19 As of October 2015, 227 such groups were identified by name, purpose, and area(s) of operation. Jennifer Cafarella and Genevieve Casagrande, "Syrian Opposition Guide," Institute for the Study of War, October 7, 2015 (www.understandingwar.org/backgrounder/syrian-opposition-guide).

20 Syrian Patriotic Group (Haitham al-Maleh). Hassan Hassan, "How the Muslim Brotherhood Hijacked Syria's Revolution," *Foreign Policy,* March 13, 2013 (www.foreignpolicy.com/2013/03/13/how-the-muslim-brotherhood-hijacked-syrias-revolution/).

21 Syria's Tomorrow Movement, formed in Cairo by former coalition president Ahmad Jarba in March 2016, is also a coalition member.

22 Weiss and Hassan, *ISIS,* p. 203.

23 Jabbat Thuwwar al-Raqqa (Raqqah Revolutionaries Front), itself the merger of two groups—Liwa' Thuwwar al-Raqqa and the Tribes Army—joined the SDF in November 2015.

24 American, British, and French Special Forces have provided training, weapons, and support services to the YPG and their Syrian Arab Coalition colleagues. Hassan Mneimneh, "Turkey's Role in Iraq: Too Little, Too Late," Middle East Institute, October 12, 2016 (www.mei.edu/content/article/turkey-s-role-iraq-too-little-too-late).

25 Ibid.

26 Weiss and Hassan, *ISIS,* p. 260.

27 The authoritative account of this phenomenon in Damascus remains David Dean Commins, *Islamic Reform: Politics and Social Change in Late-Ottoman Syria* (Oxford University Press, 1990).

28 Moubayed, *Under the Black Flag*, p. 22.

29 For a detailed account of Hadid's impact on the previous and current conflicts, see ibid., pp. 26–34.

30 ISIS's public statements have often cited the overturning of the Sykes-Picot Agreement as one of its central tenets. Weiss and Hassan, *ISIS*, pp. 40, 148. The secret 1916 agreement between France and Britain became the basis of the post–World War I order in the region, as the two empires divided the "Arab lands" of the now defunct Ottoman Empire between themselves. The modern nation-states of the region—Iraq, Syria, Lebanon, Jordan, and Palestine/Israel—can trace their origins to this agreement.

31 The role of Chamber of Commerce president Badreddine al-Challah is well documented, but the details and consequences of this rapprochement remains largely unexplored. The characterization of this postconflict relationship as a "strategic alliance" appears, with a somewhat different interpretation, in ibid., p. 98.

32 Moubayed, *Under the Black Flag*, p. 67. Six months later, the group published its "founding charter" on the Internet. The document revealed numerous ideological continuities with "the Muslim Brotherhood in the 1940s." Idem, p. 69.

33 Ibid., p. 67.

34 Weiss and Hassan, *ISIS*, p. 141.

35 Moubayed, *Under the Black Flag*, pp. 87, 115.

36 Weiss and Hassan, *ISIS*, pp. 183–84. See also, Moubayed, *Under the Black Flag*, pp. 116–18.

37 Ibid., pp. 184.

38 Sharif Nashashibi, "The Ramifications of the Nusra's split from al-Qaeda," *Al Jazeera,* August 7, 2016 (www.aljazeera.com/indepth/opinion/2016/08/ramifications-nusra-split-al-qaeda-160807080125157.html).

39 On the systematic pillaging of Syria's cultural heritage, see Moubayed, *Under the Black Flag*, p. 145.

40 Weiss and Hassan, *ISIS*, p. 226.

41 Haid Haid, "The Impact of the Kurdish-Led Campaign to Isolate Raqqa," *SyriaSource*, November 15, 2016 (www.atlanticcouncil.org/blogs/syriasource/the-impact-of-the-kurdish-led-campaign-to-isolate-raqqa). See also Haid Haid, "Challenges Facing the Turkish-led Offensive on al-Bab," Atlantic Council, October 28, 2016 (www.atlanticcouncil.org/blogs/syriasource/challenges-facing-the-turkish-led-offensive-on-al-bab).

42 Moubayed, *Under the Black Flag*, p. 88.

43 The assassination of senior U.S. AID official Laurence Foley and the November 2005 hotel bombings that killed sixty were attributed to Zarqawi. Ibid., p. 90.

44 Weiss and Hassan, *ISIS*, p. 238.

45 Ibid., p. 275.

46 Ibid., p. xiii.

47 The U.S.-Iraq Status of Forces Agreement was implemented on December 31, 2011.

48 Some experts believe there are over 200 such (predominantly Shia) militias operating in Iraq. Weiss and Hassan, *ISIS*, p. 239.

49 The Kataib al-Imam Ali armed and trained a subunit of Syriac Christians from the Mosul area bearing the name Kitaib Ruh Allah Isa, Ibn Maryam (Spirit of God, Jesus, Son of Mary Brigades). Aymenn Jawad al-Tamimi, "Sample Concepts of a Christian-Shi'a Alliance in Iraq," *Syria Comment*, December 31, 2014 (www.joshualandis.com/blog/sample-concepts-christian-shia-alliance-iraq/).

50 Weiss and Hassan, *ISIS*, pp. 58, 242–44.

51 Ibid., p. 240.

52 Mneimneh, "Turkey's Role in Iraq."

53 As recently as January 2015 approximately two-thirds of Peshmerga units were under the command of one of the region's political parties, and the remaining one-third answered to the KRG. Fazel Hawramy, "Kurdish Peshmerga Divisions Hamper War Effort," *Al-Monitor*, January 13, 2015 (www.al-monitor.com/pulse/originals/2015/01/iraq-kurdish-peshmerga-division-islamic-state.html).

54 Ben Kesling, "Iraqi Kurds Seize State-Held Land, Bolstering Leverage for the Future," *Wall Street Journal*, September 14, 2016 (www.wsj.com/articles/iraqi-kurds-seize-islamic-state-held-land-bolstering-leverage-for-future-1473903162).

55 Reuters, "Iraqi Kurds' Destruction of Arab Villages Could Be a War Crime: HRW," November 13, 2016 (www.reuters.com/article/us-mideast-crisis-iraq-kurds/iraqi-kurds-destruction-of-arab-villages-could-be-war-crime-hrw-idUSKBN13803V). Amnesty International, "Northern Iraq: Satellite Images Back Up Evidence of Deliberate Mass Destruction in Peshmerga-Controlled Arab Villages," Amnesty International, January 20, 2016 (www.amnesty.org/en/latest/news/2016/01/northern-iraq-satellite-images-back-up-evidence-of-deliberate-mass-destruction-in-peshmerga-controlled-arab-villages/).

56 Weiss and Hassan, *ISIS*, p. 54.

57 Isabel Coles, "Iran Supplied Weapons to Iraqi Kurds; Baghdad Bomb Kills 12," Reuters, August 24, 2014 (www.reuters.com/article/us-iraq-security

-kurds/iran-supplied-weapons-to-iraqi-kurds-baghdad-bomb-kills-12
-idUSKBN0GQ11P20140826).

58 "Death of a General," *The Economist,* January 3, 2015 (www.economist.com
/news/middle-east-and-africa/21637416-wars-syria-and-iraq-are-sucking
-iran-ever-more-tangled-conflicts-death).

59 Weiss and Hassan, *ISIS*, pp. 89–91.

60 Moubayed, *Under the Black Flag*, pp. 113–14.

61 Weiss and Hassan, *ISIS*, p. 78. Other potentially significant groups are Al-
Jaysh al-Mujahidiin (Mujahidiin Army), Kitaib Thawra al-Ashriin (1920
Revolution Brigade), and al-Jaish al-Iraqi al-Hurr (Free Iraqi Army).

62 Moubayed, *Under the Black Flag,* pp. 95–96.

63 Al-Baghdadi was "elected" to office on May 16, 2010. Moubayed, *Under the
Black Flag*, p. 97.

64 Among the most prominent and effective were Abdul Karim Mutaa Khei-
rallah, Air Force Intelligence Colonel Samir al-Khlifawi, Intelligence and
Republican Guard Lieutenant Colonel Fadel Ahmad Abdullah al-Hyali,
and infantry officer Adnan Ismail Najm. Moubayed, *Under the Black Flag*,
pp. 104, 106–09. For more on former Saddamists who have achieved high
office in ISIS, see Weiss and Hassan, *ISIS*, pp. 116–20, 149.

65 Ibid., p. 210.

66 Moubayed, *Under the Black Flag*, pp. 110–11. See also, Weiss and Hassan,
ISIS, p. 119.

67 Moubayed, *Under the Black Flag*, pp. 99–100.

68 Ibid., p. 102. See also Weiss and Hassan, *ISIS*, pp. 112–14.

69 Weiss and Hassan, *ISIS*, p. 117.

70 Moubayed, *Under the Black Flag*, p. 211; Weiss and Hassan, *ISIS*, p. xviii.

71 I refer here to Jillian Becker's *Hitler's Children: The Story of the Baader-Meinhof
Terrorist Gang* (Philadelphia: Lippincott, 1977), which argues that this "Revolutionary Marxist" organization was an obvious product of the ideological and cultural atmosphere of the Third Reich.

72 Faysal Itani, "Aleppo's Fate Is No Surprise," Atlantic Council, November 29, 2016 (http://www.atlanticcouncil.org/blogs/syriasource/aleppo-s
-fate-is-no-surprise).

73 Anthony H. Cordesman, "Raqqa, Mosul, and the Long War," Center for
Strategic and International Studies, November 9, 2016 (www.csis.org
/analysis/raqqa-mosul-and-long-war).

74 Mona Alami, "What the Loss of Mosul Will Mean for ISIS," Atlantic
Council, November 8, 2016 (www.atlanticcouncil.org/blogs/menasource
/what-the-loss-of-mosul-will-mean-for-isis). Corky Siemaszko, NBC News,
"The Battle for Mosul Won't End with the Ouster of ISIS," October 18,
2016 (www.nbcnews.com/storyline/iraq-turmoil/battle-mosul-won-t

-end-ouster-isis-n668166). Maher Chmaytelli, Reuters, "Islamic State Claims Suicide Attacks as Mosul Campaign Makes Slow Progress," November 14, 2016 (www.reuters.com/article/us-mideast-crisis-iraq/islamic -state-claims-suicide-attacks-as-mosul-campaign-makes-slow-progress -idUSKBN1392AF); Feras Hanoush, "ISIS' Next Stop," Atlantic Council, October 13, 2016 (www.atlanticcouncil.org/blogs/syriasource/isis -next-stop).

75 Bacevich, *America's War for the Greater Middle East*, p. 356.

76 Annia Ciezadlo, "Analysis: Why Assad's Propaganda Isn't as Crazy as It Seems," *Syria Deeply,* October 3, 2016 (www.newsdeeply.com/syria/articles /2016/10/03/analysis-why-assads-propaganda-isnt-as-crazy-as-it-seems). All national indicators are catastrophic: electricity is at less than half previous capacity; 40–50 percent of the health care infrastructure and expertise is absent; 65 percent of housing stock is damaged or destroyed; foreign reserves are almost nonexistent; approximately 50 percent of the remaining population is unemployed. Mona Alami, "Assad Wants to Rule Syria, but Economics Say Otherwise," Atlantic Council, October 29, 2016 (www .atlanticcouncil.org/blogs/syriasource/assad-wants-to-rule-syria-but -economics-say-otherwise).

77 Heiko Wimmen, "Syria's Path from Civic Uprising to Civil War," Carnegie Endowment for International Peace, November 22, 2016 (http:// carnegieendowment.org/2016/11/22/syria-s-path-from-civic-uprising -to-civil-war-pub-66171).

78 Weiss and Hassan, *ISIS*, p. 39; for details, see pp. xviii, 59, 241, 259.

79 Ibid., p. 168.

6

Islamic State–Khurasan Province

Amin Tarzi

The international threat assessments and strategies to counter the group referring to itself as the Islamic State (IS) have been focused on Iraq and Syria, where IS has emerged as a serious threat to international security and from 2014 to 2017 held large swaths of territory in those two countries.[1] Although the territoriality of IS in Iraq and Syria has diminished significantly, the group's ideology and affinity are spreading into regional groups as well, expanding IS's potential reach and regional destabilizing ability. Affiliates and supporters of IS in other parts of the world, such as Afghanistan, Algeria, Egypt, Libya, Nigeria, Pakistan, Saudi Arabia, and Yemen—in which there is a proclaimed IS province (*wilayah*)—have received varying degrees of international attention depending on the scale and type of threat they pose to broader international security.[2] The availability of assets by the United States and/or other IS-countering states in the aforementioned countries also influences the range of strategies available to respond to these groups' activities and territorial aspirations. One such group is the Islamic State–Khurasan Province (ISKP), active in Afghanistan and Pakistan.[3] ISKP proclaims to represent an area covering Central Asia, most of India, and parts of Iran. This chapter examines ISKP from its formal emergence in early 2015 and explores

ISKP's use of historic and imaginary Khurasan in identity formation and its relationship with established Islamist organizations, particularly the Taliban, active in the area. The chapter reviews some aspects of the conflict between the two groups and how this conflict is affecting the strategies and interests of regional and local governments as well as the United States to counter ISKP. The chapter concludes with a discussion of how to incorporate lessons learned from this situation into broader international counterterrorism strategies.

Black Flags Unfurl in Afghanistan

In 2014 individuals and small groups of disgruntled Islamists in Afghanistan and Pakistan began pledging allegiance to IS in Iraq and its leader, Abu Bakr al-Baghdadi. The sources of discontent were numerous and a combination of various factors. Some began distancing themselves from the policies and theological leanings of their existing groups.[4] Others had personal disputes with their leadership. A number were awed by the successes of IS in Iraq and later Syria, and some were mere opportunists looking for better compensation or adventure. Whatever their grievance or motivation, they found individual reasons to align themselves with this newly emerging pan-Islamist group.[5]

In early 2014, IS expansion grew beyond individual pockets of discontent, as a dozen mostly Pakistani militants pledged their allegiance to IS, beginning the very dynamic and often misinterpreted formation of what has become ISKP. The principal cadre of IS influence in Afghanistan and the Federally Administered Tribal Areas (FATA) in Pakistan had links to a number of militant organizations, including more established jihadist organizations such as al Qaeda, Lashkar-e Taiba, Harakat al-Mujahdin, and Tahrik-e Taliban Pakistan (TTP) and smaller newly emerged outfits like Tahrik-e Khilafat wa Jihad (later renamed Ansar al-Khilafat wal-Jihad) and Jundullah (both the Pakistan-based and the mostly Uzbek, Afghanistan-based organizations).[6] In the fall the commander (amir) of the Islamic Movement of Uzbekistan (IMU), Osman Ghazi (aka Adil/Odil Osman), issued a statement aligning IMU with IS and breaking its longstanding alliances with al Qaeda and the Taliban. Ghazi did not, however, pledge allegiance to al-Baghdadi.[7] With IMU coming alongside, a locally grown IS presence grew in the region.

Central Asian Connections
The rationale behind IMU's decision is curious and remains understudied. The move by IMU may have represented an ideological shift by the militant organization or its leader. Instead of seeking to depose the governments of Central Asian states and institute the sharia, maybe the idea of establishing a pan-Islamist global caliphate resonated with Ghazi. Upon declaring the intention of his group to join ranks with IS, Ghani praised the organization's disregard for state boundaries and expressed hope that IS would take control of Palestine, Mecca, and Medina.[8] While this was the ideology followed by another Uzbek-dominated group, Hizb al-Tahrir al-Islami, this message was unfamiliar to the majority of IMU's core constituents.[9] It also could have been related to more practical concerns associated with IMU's areas of operation and alliances rather than with an ideological shift. In June 2014, Pakistan launched military operations code-named Zarb-e Azb to curtail militant presence and activities in FATA, whose principal targets were TTP, its local affiliates, and IMU.[10] As a result, IMU's maneuverability was considerably restricted and its security threatened. Meanwhile, IMU's longstanding alliance with the Afghan Taliban was weakening as the latter gained more political acceptance and was increasingly tolerated by both China and Russia. These two countries regard the Uzbek group as a serious threat to the security and stability of trans-Oxus Central Asia and Xingjian. IMU potentially saw an opportunity to reshape its alliances to ensure survivability and relevance in the region. What the proclamation did for IS, in theory if not in practice, was enable it to lay claim to adherents in Transoxiana.

Birth of ISKP
Initial reports of an organized group calling itself ISKP emerged in January 2015 in two locations in Afghanistan: in the eastern Afghan province of Nangarhar close to the border with FATA, and in the Kajaki district of the southern Afghan province of Helmand. The group seemed an

amalgamation of the individualized IS adherents, al Qaeda discontents, and IMU, rebranded under one name proclaiming itself to be IS in Khurasan. By late January, IS spokesman Abu Muhammad al-Adnani officially announced the expansion of his group's authority to Khurasan, a region he identified as encompassing Afghanistan, Pakistan, and other adjacent territories. Adnani called on all in Khurasan who professed the unity of God or Unitarians (*muwahhidun*) to abandon disunity and factionalism by joining the caliphate (IS). Use of the term "muwahhidun" by Adnani reached back to early Islamic radical monotheism and iconoclasm in Hijaz.[11]

Muwahhidun, originally theologized by Taqi al-Din ibn Taymiyyah (d. 1328), later became the self-designated name for the forces under Muhammad ibn Abd al-Wahhab (d. 1792).[12] The term in modern Salafist thought is a rejection of the Shiis, Islamic mysticism (Sufism), the customs of veneration of saints and statuary, and any action or object that in their view brings an association with the absoluteness of the unity of God. Evoking Afghan history, Adnani referred to his audience as the progeny of those who had fought against British and Russian oppression and called on them to join the new fight against the Americans and to enforce monotheism (*tawid*) and vanquish polytheism (*shirk*). The IS spokesman identified Hafiz Sayyid Khan, formerly commander of TTP in the Orakzai Agency within FATA, as the governor (*wali*) of Khurasan Province and Shaykh Abd al-Rauf Khadim Abu Talhah as his deputy.[13]

Initially, ISKP had limited success in recruiting. It had gained several hundred active recruits and a larger number of sympathizers in FATA as well as in the Afghan provinces of Nangarhar, Helmand, Kunar, Logar, and possibly Farah, Zabul, and Ghazni, though some of the early activities attributed to ISKP were later discredited or revealed to be exaggerated. In February, ISKP suffered a considerable setback when Khadim was killed in an air strike in Kajaki, reducing the group's territorial presence to only a few districts of Nangarhar where they had entrenched themselves.[14]

ISKP under Assault

By summer 2015, according to General John F. Campbell, commander of U.S. Forces in Afghanistan (USFOR-A), ISKP had become "operationally emergent in Afghanistan," leading to the authorization in December for the U.S. forces to target ISKP fighters by affiliation, regardless of whether they posed a direct threat to U.S. or allied forces.[15] In 2016 the joint U.S. and Afghan counterterrorism operation Green Sword killed one-third of ISKP's members, including its leader, Hafiz Sayyid Khan, and reduced the territory the group held by two-thirds. This effort was augmented by Taliban attacks, which reduced ISKP to fewer than 3,000 fighters.[16] By some estimates, ISKP fighters had been reduced to 1,200–1,300 in September 2016, and even as low as 700 by April 2017.[17] By this time, ISKP's territorial hold was reduced to three districts in Nangarhar.

Although any rapid territorial expansion of ISKP inside Afghanistan or Pakistan seems highly improbable, there are opportunities for ISKP to gain territory—both politically and literally—as Afghanistan's political situation remains unstable and its relations with the Pakistanis ebb and flow between conflict and cooperation. Further disenchantment within the Taliban about their peacemaking deals and accommodating policies both inside Afghanistan and with regional countries also could create a vacuum for ISKP to fill, despite the group's weak position and the fact that its message is alien to the majority of Afghans and Pakistanis.

Working to prevent the growth of ISKP requires more than kinetic action. An understanding of the narrative employed by ISKP and operationalizing the inconsistencies inherent therein would be a major step in preventing the group from expanding beyond the limited number of hardcore Salafists, castaways, and opportunists waving the IS black banner.

Whither Khurasan?

The story of Khurasan is part myth, part theology, and part geography, intermingled with the story of the expansion of Islam among non-Arabs in the lands formerly under the rule of the Sasanian Empire. Khurasan continues to symbolize and mean different things to pan-Islamists, Iranians, and Afghans. The majority of reports and analyses on ISKP take the group's understanding of Khurasan to be geographically framed as an area encompassing Afghanistan and Pakistan, the Central Asian republics, and parts of eastern (or all of) Iran and western (or all of) India, while some have identified the area as simply meaning Afghanistan and Pakistan; few have questioned the historicity of ISKP's understanding of the term.[18] What does the word Khurasan symbolize?

The use of myths is a natural part of any political organization's quest to claim legitimacy and garner support, especially those trying to link their aims and campaigns to historical periods of grandeur—real or perceived—to achieve greater glory. In its use of myths and fables as well as religious allegories, IS joins a long list of organizations trying to change the status quo with extreme violence while offering an idealized future for those who follow its dictates and vision. In counterterrorism, understanding how myths are operationalized by an organization such as IS can be instrumental to countering its broader narrative and appeal to the intended audience of these accounts.

Khurasan in the Global Jihadist and Local Lexicons

For the Islamists who seek to establish a global caliphate by force, Khurasan's significance is related to a saying attributed by some Sunni Muslims to the Prophet Muhammad that an army carrying black flags originating from Khurasan will include the Mahdi (Messiah) among them. The chain of transmission of this prophetic tradition remains very weak, and there are different versions of this saying, one of which is that the deliverance of Muhammad's own family from suffering will come from the east.[19] The messianic version, whether evoked by a fringe al Qaeda group in Syria in September 2014 or by ISKP, has an amplified symbolism denoting the ultimate apocalyptic battle between Islam and its enemies.[20] However, for Iranian and later Afghan historical understanding, the significance of Khurasan—including the black banners—is tied to the enigmatic historical figure and the later legends of Abd al-Rahman bin Muslim (d.755), better known as Abu Muslim al-Khurasani.[21] Abu Muslim and his followers wore black clothing and carried a black flag when leading the revolt from Khurasan against the Arab-dominated Umayyad Caliphate, bringing to power the joint Persian-Arab Abbasid dynasty and ushering in what is considered to be the zenith of Islamic power. Abu Muslim was instrumental in the resurgence of the Iranian peoples within the Arab-dominated Muslim empire and in the revival of Iranian cultural and linguistic heritage. This resurgence began in Khurasan, where Abu Muslim became the overlord before being killed on the order of the very dynasty he had helped bring to power.[22] Historically, in the Iranian, Turkic, and later Afghan worlds, Abu Muslim is associated with the rise of local forces in the face of Arab domination as well as, in some cases, with the beginnings of activist Shiism.[23] In fact, the national flag of Afghanistan until 1927 was all black with a white seal in its center.

In addition to the starkly divergent meanings associated with Khurasan and the black flags by those living in the region and the Islamist propaganda from outside the region, there are contradictions in how the two groups define the geographical limits of Khurasan as well. Since the conquest of the eastern flank of the Sasanian Empire by the Arabs in the mid-seventh century, the province of Khurasan has existed on maps and covers a geographic space roughly corresponding to modern-day northeastern Iran, southern Turkmenistan, southern Uzbekistan, all of Tajikistan, and most of Afghanistan, with the exception of the eastern and southern strip of the country bordering present-day Pakistan. In no historical or later rendition has Khurasan included Pakistan, India, or beyond.[24] Today, in Iran, Khurasan appears in the names of three northeastern Iranian provinces.

For Afghanistan, the term has a much more political appeal in that country's ongoing national identity struggles and formulations. Since the 1930s, as part of Afghanistan's nation-building process, the country's history has been linked to pre-Islamic Aryana and to Khurasan in Islamic tradition. In this constructed narrative, Afghanistan, since 1747, is positioned as the successor state to Khurasan, sharing in its glories and resistance, including against the domination of the Arab Umayyads. Abu Muslim's birthplace, which commonly is accepted as Merv in modern-day Turkmenistan, has been shifted to the northern Afghan city of Maymana in the Afghan narrative, and he has been elevated to the status of an Afghan hero.[25] Since the Soviet invasion and through the Taliban period, people mobilized around ethnic identities, and battles, whether against the communists or the Taliban, were fought largely along ethnic lines. Khurasan serves as a counterbalance to the Pashtun domination of the country, providing a more inclusive national construct. The word Afghanistan means the land of the Afghans, another name for Pashtuns. Non-Pashtun citizens of Afghanistan have been using Khurasan as their preferred name for the country, signifying its non-Pashtun and, thus, inclusive past.

Operationalization of the Term Khurasan

The use of the term Khurasan by ISKP allows the group to signal to followers and to enemies that it is now in a position to initiate the final battle for Islamic domination of the world and the arrival of the Mahdi. The Afghan analyst Borhan Osman writes that the substitution of Khurasan for Afghanistan and Pakistan allows IS to avoid the recognition of nation-states, a construct that the pan-Islamists reject.[26] This argument would have had more currency if IS had not pointedly included in its own name the word "state" (*al-dawlah*), which was a late inclusion in Islamic terminology through the Ottomans and is subtly different than the notion of a caliphate.[27] The IS strategy, which falls outside the scope of this chapter, seems more a geopolitical reorganization of existing nation-states than an effort to eliminate them.

However, Osman's suggestion reveals another, perhaps unintended, consequence, which if not countered may provide future currency for the ISKP model. Improving Afghan-Pakistani relations remains a critical aspect of enhancing security and stability, not only in Afghanistan but also increasingly in Pakistan and indeed in the region as a whole. The long-standing border dispute between the two neighbors has led to decades of both states denying the full legitimacy of the other and presents an ever-present obstacle to building trust between the neighbors. On the one hand, the mistrust and conflict have led Islamabad to meddle in internal Afghan politics, including through the use of proxies. On the other hand, Kabul has blamed its neighbor for all its ills while maintaining territorial ambitions on Pakistani territory. Each side has, at times, harbored and nurtured elements that could and do threaten and seek to destabilize the other. The emergence of the Taliban phenomenon in the

1990s and its survival after 2001 are widely regarded as manifestations of this.[28] If Afghan-Pakistani relations do not witness a fundamental change whereby the two countries establish a genuine strategic understanding, future groups like ISKP that espouse a territorially unbound, antinational system of an Islamic state or caliphate might find room for greater maneuverability in the region and be used by one or the other side or by elements within each government to impose that government's interests on the other. Again, the emergence of the initial Taliban movement in the Afghan political scene in the mid-1990s should be a vivid reminder of such a potentiality.[29]

Since the Khurasan narrative and symbols used by ISKP contradict what the majority of the local populations believe about Khurasan, a deeper operationalization of this discrepancy, using local, historical, and national symbols—particularly in the case of Afghanistan—might further diminish any potential appeal that this organization may have beyond the circle of dedicated pan-Islamists. The debunking of ISKP's "Khurasan" claim, both historically and geographically, could also lessen the appeal of joining up for future fringe elements who might be attracted to the organization for its claim to a history and territory that, for these elements, evoke a historical struggle, be it anti-Pashtun in the case of Afghanistan or Islamist pan-Turkic in the case of Central Asia.

Islamic State versus Islamic Emirate

Although Afghanistan did not give birth to IS, the country was pivotal in the upbringing of its "founding father," Abu Musab al-Zarqawi. The links between the leadership of what has become IS and Afghanistan go back to the 1980s Islamist-nationalist resistance groups against the Soviets (commonly referred to as the Mujahidiin) and the government they supported in Kabul and continued with the emergence of the Taliban and their rule over most of that country from the mid-1990s to 2001.[30] The current leader of IS, al-Baghdadi, is alleged to have lived for some time in Kabul under the Taliban in the 1990s. He was affiliated with al Qaeda while Zarqawi first fought against the leftist Afghan government and later returned in 2000 with al Qaeda's support to run a jihadist training camp in the western Afghan city of Herat. These spaces outside of the Afghan government's control served as an "incubator" for individuals who later became the core leadership of IS.[31]

The Islamic Emirate of Afghanistan

Almost two decades before al-Baghdadi's declaration of the Islamic State and his assumption of the title of caliph, the Taliban Movement of Afghanistan in September 1996 declared their leader Mullah Muhammad Omar Mujahid to be the commander of the faithful (amir al-muminin) in Qandahar and announced the formation of the Islamic Emirate of Afghanistan.[32] From the outset, unlike IS, the Taliban sought international legitimacy, but only managed to secure formal recognition by three countries—Pakistan, Saudi Arabia, and the United Arab Emirates. The initial proclamations of the Taliban's Islamic Emirate were mostly Afghan-centric. However, with the cementing of their ties with al Qaeda, their outlook became more pan-Islamist. Retrospectively, the strategies of the Taliban and those of al Qaeda differed fundamentally, as the former wanted to become a national movement and be recognized by the international community as such, while the latter wanted to keep Afghanistan in a perpetual state of anarchy, using it as a base for waging global jihad. The current, or neo-, Taliban have mostly returned to the founding Afghanistan-centric principles of the movement with an arguably less religiously zealous message, calling on Muslims to avoid extremism in the religion with the goal of becoming a legitimate force in the political arena of the country.[33] Of course, the Taliban remain a violent insurgency and are very keen not only on retaining their monopoly over this violence but also on controlling and managing it.[34]

Under the Islamic Emirate, the Taliban hosted Osama bin Laden and his al Qaeda organization, a policy that ultimately led to its political demise in the aftermath of the 2001 terror attacks in the United States. However, while al Qaeda remained more of an idea than an organization or a political entity, the Taliban quickly organized themselves into a governing organization and administrative system.[35] An argument can be made that one of the weaknesses of the Taliban message was the lack of a cohesive ideology other than trying to enforce a southern Afghan "village identity" on the entire country.[36] One idea that has remained a guiding principle of the Taliban from the outset has been that of localism, with little regard beyond the occasional verbal support for causes such as the Palestinian issue and some of the al Qaeda–inspired messaging. In the early days of the Islamic Emirate, the localism of the Taliban did not extend beyond their own greater Qandahar region. Ayman al-Zawahiri, then al Qaeda's deputy leader, reportedly warned Zarqawi before he left for Iraq not to repeat the mistake of the Taliban whose power base hinged mostly on southern Afghanistan and the Qandahari elements therein.[37] Perhaps learning from their initial mistakes, the re-emerged Taliban have tried to speak for all of Afghanistan, including providing assurances that they will respect the rights of the Shiites and other minorities within the country.

The emergence of ISKP occurred in a highly sensitive period for the Taliban, who had lost their elusive but unifying founding leader sometime in spring 2013. Although the movement managed to keep a lid on Mullah Omar's demise until it was officially revealed two years later by the Afghan government, the Taliban had to deal with internal fractures due to the absence of their undisputed leader in a time when major decisions needed to be made about whether and how to make peace with the Afghan government, to open dialogue with foreign countries, and to shape relations with Pakistan, in addition to decisions on military matters and expanding their areas of operation. Following the confirmation of Mullah Omar's death, the head of the Taliban leadership council, Mullah Akhtar Muhammad Mansur, became the new amir al-muminin and secured the allegiance of Zawahiri, among others, but disagreements remained among top members of the movement over leadership positions.[38] The Taliban leadership took another hit when in May 2016 the United States conducted an air strike, killing Mansur, who was replaced by Mawlawi Haibatullah Akhundzada.[39] Compounding the Taliban's loss of personnel is the increased pressure being put on them by their "hitherto largely friendly host, Pakistan." As a result, they are looking to move to more remote and unstable regions of Afghanistan, which brings the potential of conflict with ISKP.[40]

Challenge to the Islamic Emirate

Taking advantage of the discontent over internal leadership struggles, ISKP began recruiting among the Taliban members, meeting with limited success. ISKP used the absence of and later the confirmation of the demise of Mullah Omar in their propaganda, courting disgruntled members of the Taliban and arguing that he no longer was the legitimate leader of the Islamic community or emirate. They argued that these former Taliban should pledge their loyalty to al-Baghdadi, the legitimate Islamic leader. The most significant switching of sides occurred in the heartland of the Taliban, when Khadim set up a cell with a few hundred fighters in the Kajaki district of Helmand Province. He was a former commander of the Taliban who, according to Osman, after being released from the U.S. detention facility at Guantanamo Bay, Cuba, in 2007, rose to prominence, becoming the second in command within the movement's military establishment. He later fell from grace because of the Salafist views he acquired while in detention, which contradicted the Taliban's steadfast adherence to local interpretations of Islam—an admixture of the Hanafi school of jurisprudence and local Pashtun customary codes. For the core IS leadership, Khadim exemplified an ideal representative in the region of Afghanistan and Pakistan. He followed their Islamist worldview based on forceful propagation and enforcement of strict monotheism to the exclusion of the Shiites, Sufis, and local customs such as veneration of Muslim saints and visiting of shrines, adhered to their interpretation of the sharia, and rejected national boundaries. In addition, he had direct communication with IS leadership in Iraq and Syria while based in the heartland of the Taliban. What Khadim did not possess was the taste for brutality that had become the signature of IS operatives. In a trend that seems to have been the case for a majority of ISKP recruits, the rationale for Khadim's association with the new organization was "pragmatic rather than based on convergence with the aims and methods of the IS."[41] Three years after his triumphant return to the Taliban ranks, Khadim was marginalized from the Taliban leadership council, which had become dominated by Mullah Mansur following Mullah Omar's illness and ultimate demise. While Khadim's Salafist tendencies might have been the cause for his marginalization, there are also reports of intertribal conflicts that were complicating his commitment to the emerging Taliban leadership. The cell formed by Khadim posed a danger to the Taliban as ISKP expanded beyond Khadim's native Kajaki to neighboring districts of Musa Qala, Nawzad, and Baghran. Within weeks of Khadim's appointment as the deputy governor of ISKP, he was killed in an airstrike, to the Taliban's relief. Since Khadim's death, no one of his stature has switched sides from the Taliban to ISKP.[42]

Despite tactical cooperation of convenience, on a strategic level ISKP continues to delegitimize and seek ways to weaken the Taliban. ISKP has tried to portray the Taliban as puppets of Pakistan and has criticized them for not committing to implement sharia-specified punishment and for tolerating the drug trade in the areas under its control. They have also leveraged the perceived softening of the Taliban on the Shiite and other minorities to exploit ethnic divides by inserting indirect messaging of exclusion—for example, Adnani addressing his announcement of the formation of ISKP specifically to the "muwahhidin in Khurasan," which, of course, excludes the Shiites and other non-Salafists.[43]

The Emirate Strikes Back

In June 2015, ISKP reportedly killed three Taliban shadow district governors in Nangarhar, ushering in full and open hostility between the Islamic Emirate and the Islamic State.[44] In response to this attack, Mullah Mansur, then acting as the head of the Taliban leadership council, dispatched an open letter to al-Baghdadi, warning that, if ISKP did not cease the formation of parallel jihadist fronts, the Taliban "[would] be forced to defend" their achievements. Mansur also cautioned IS leadership to distrust those "who were either disappointed with the Taliban because of various reasons or thrown out of their organization for committing crimes."[45] The letter revealed not only the threat that ISKP posed to the Taliban's near monopoly of the Islamist resistance in Afghanistan and the fractures among its membership "for various reasons," but also the Taliban's positioning itself as the defender, the legitimate insurgent in this fight. Mansur's letter failed to persuade IS leadership to curtail ISKP's activities.[46] In fact, the two jihadist organizations began targeting each other more vigorously and with increased violence. Signature IS brutalities such as broadcasting beheadings and blowing up Taliban sympathizers began appearing in Afghanistan. This escalation of violence by ISKP provoked the Taliban ulama to issue a fatwa in June, allowing the Talibs to wage a "defensive" campaign to counter ISKP in Nangarhar that resulted in significant territorial losses for ISKP in the southern districts of the province. By early January 2016 the Taliban ulama broadened their defensive edict to include an added obligation to wage an offensive jihad against ISKP.[47]

In late 2015 the Taliban also started going after ISKP affiliates and supporters beyond Nangarhar. In November the Taliban scored a decisive victory in the southern Afghan province of Zabul against the IMU—ISKP's main Uzbek affiliate, killing its leader, Osman Ghazi. The Taliban also began opposing the mainly Uzbek Jundullah, an IMU splinter group operating in northeastern Afghanistan in proximity to Tajikistan.[48] Commenting on the IMU's conclusive defeat, an IS supporter posted this statement: "The Taliban achieved in 24 hours what the Americans were unable to do in 14 years."[49] These victories were a two-pronged blessing for the Taliban. First, the Taliban stopped a major local rival from gaining a foothold in Afghanistan, isolating the IMU even more after their displacement from FATA, and reversed the brief territorial gains made by Jundullah. Second, they were propaganda boons for the Taliban in Central Asian, Chinese, and Russian circles.

Struggles over Ownership of Battlespace and Violence
The Taliban's goal is to preserve the insurgency inside Afghanistan as its exclusive prerogative, and it has worked since ISKP's formation to maintain the upper hand. Tensions are escalating between the two groups as ISKP seeks to insert itself into the Afghan political and military battlespace. In April 2016 a suicide attack at a bank in Jalalabad, the provincial capital of Nangarhar, resulted in over thirty deaths and many injuries. Another attack close by, on the same day, targeted a Sufi saint's shrine. The Taliban denied and condemned both attacks. According to Kate Clark, a reporter and analyst covering Afghanistan since 1999, the first bore the hallmarks of Taliban tactics; the second did not. In an unverified social media posting, Shahidullah Shahid, formerly a spokesman for TTP,

claimed responsibility for both attacks in the name of ISKP. The international news outlets and the Afghan government took his claim as factual; thus the first IS attack in Afghanistan was recorded.[50] The denial of the attacks by the Taliban illustrated their movement's responsiveness and sensitivity to local and perhaps even international attitudes toward them. However, in attacks in June that targeted foreigners such as the Gurkha guards employed by the Canadian embassy in Kabul and an attack on Mawlana Ataullah Faizani, a member of the Kabul provincial council, both the Taliban and ISKP claimed responsibility. In this case, according to a member of the Taliban speaking in private, his group claimed to have carried out the attacks, despite not having done so, to deflect attention away from ISKP, fearing their presence and activities would prolong the presence of foreign forces in Afghanistan. The removal of foreign forces from the country is the Taliban's paramount demand for accepting a peaceful resolution of their insurgency.[51]

The battle lines are drawn between the two Islamist organizations. One the one hand, ISKP presents ideological and operational challenges for the Taliban, the defection of key Taliban leaders to ISKP being a significant one, as that opens for ISKP the front door to the mind-set and strategies of the Taliban. On the other hand, overall the emergence of the new organization has also had a positive impact on the Taliban's quest for broader acceptance both inside and outside of Afghanistan, as they seek to be a local Islamist solution to Afghanistan's instability.

The wild card in this pursuit is Pakistan, the longtime backer and host of the Taliban. As echoed in early 2017 by the new commander of US-FOR-A, General John W. Nicholson, "The insurgents cannot be defeated while they enjoy external sanctuary and support . . . in Pakistan."[52] As the Taliban gain more acceptability with regional countries mainly because of their opposition to ISKP, their submissiveness to Islamabad's directives should be expected to decrease. The question to consider is whether a united Taliban with more freedom of political decisionmaking will emerge to seriously engage in peace negotiations with the Afghan government or whether ISKP will morph into a savvier spoiler role and create new alternatives to the Taliban, prolonging the instability in Afghanistan and the region.

Afghan Government Begins Counter-ISKP Operations
Early in 2016 ISKP's activities started to attract attention from others besides its local Islamist competitor. Before that, other interested parties for the most part allowed the two groups to battle it out between themselves. As ISKP was establishing itself in Nangarhar, the message to the local population and the Afghan National Defense and Security Forces (ANDSF) was conciliatory. They did not harass government institutions and employees but claimed, according to one report, that they were in Nangarhar to counter the "ISI Emirate"—linking the Taliban with Pakistan's Inter-Services Intelligence.[53] With ISKP's mid-January attack on the Pakistani consulate in Jalalabad, that all changed. Until then, ANDSF had mostly been on the sidelines, engaging in limited campaigns against ISKP. After that they went on full offensive against the group, supported by the Special Operations Joint Task Force–Afghanistan, the counterterrorism force within the U.S. Operation Freedom's Sentinel. Another group making a difference in the fight against ISKP in Nangarhar are the local fighters, who in contrast to the Afghan military "have made a name for being effective, aggressive against the enemy and, unlike other places, not particularly abusive of the population."[54] The U.S. Department of State also designated ISKP as a foreign terrorist organization, a label that rings true with the local militias who see the fight against ISKP as "an existential fight and the ISKP as a foreign force which has behaved with unparalleled brutality towards civilians."[55]

The impact on ISKP has been significant. Since the middle of 2016 the operations carried out by the Taliban, ANDSF, and the United States have severely disrupted ISKP's territorial hold. During this time, ISKP reverted to its former modus operandi and reignited attacks on sectarian targets. Whether this is because of their failure to mount a successful campaign to capture territory in either Afghanistan or Pakistan or for some other reason is not known.

ISKP Reintroduces Sectarian Violence to the Afghan Conflict
The first manifestation of their resurrected strategy was in July 2016. ISKP claimed responsibility for an attack on a predominately Shiite demonstration that resulted in the death of eighty individuals and demonstrated

their reach into Kabul. In response to Taliban condemnation, ISKP issued a fatwa claiming that the Shiites were indisputably infidels, adding that any Sunni religious scholar who rejects this understanding and ISKP's right to kill them is himself an apostate. In October two attackers targeted a popular shrine during Ashura—the commemoration of the death of Husayn, a grandson of the Prophet Muhammad, who is the third imam for the Shiites—killing nineteen people.[56]

The Taliban's response shows how the group has evolved since its emergence in the 1990s. The Taliban condemned ISKP's attacks, referring to the Shiites as their "brothers."[57] In its initial campaign to gain control of Afghanistan in the 1990s, the Taliban at times targeted Shiites because of their religious affiliation, not just because of their refusal to submit to Taliban rule. As the movement gained more authority, its antisectarian tendencies diminished. The neo-Taliban, in spite of its alliances with militant jihadist outfits with antisectarian doctrines, has largely stayed away from sectarianism and has called on the Shiites to join the Taliban movement as an Islamic—rather than just Sunni—national liberation front. There are no credible statistics on the number of Shiites among the Taliban ranks, but the numbers are likely small given the low level of support for the Taliban in the predominantly Shiite regions of Afghanistan. The overarching policy of the movement has been to remain aloof on sectarian issues.

Overall, from the early days of the Afghan anticommunist resistance to the ensuing civil war and through the Taliban period, despite clear splits in groups based on sectarian identities, the level of Sunni-Shiite open confrontation in Afghanistan has been very low. In comparison with the levels of sectarian conflict in post-2003 Iraq and in Syria, the levels in Afghanistan have been almost negligible. Political grievances in Afghanistan are usually not based on sectarian issues. However, lack of open confrontation should not be regarded as an indication of lack of sectarian discord. There is tension, perhaps less because of theological issues (as in the case of the Salafist groups) and more because of ethnohistorical questions of social justice and representation. Indeed, the preferred name for the country by many of Afghanistan's non-Pashtun political activists is Khurasan, while some nationalist Hazarahs prefer the regional construct of "Hazaristan" as their homeland. According to sociologist Anand Gopal, the Taliban have been unable to put into practice their nationalist vision, and although the "Taliban is not a 'Pashtun movement', it is a movement comprised predominantly of Pashtuns."[58]

And this tension could be exploited. The majority of Afghans, including the Taliban, thus far have tried to show a unified front against ISKP attacks, specifically those targeting the Shiites. In addition, part of the Taliban's current sectarian policies can be traced to their warming relationship with the Islamic Republic of Iran, an entity anathema to IS and its goals.

What Role Will Iran Play?

According to some reports, the Taliban have drawn a red line on direct sectarian-driven operations, turning down financial incentives from Arab Gulf states to engage in anti-Iran and anti-Shiite operations.[59] In preparation for the December 2016 conference of the Iran-based World Forum for Proximity of Islamic Schools of Thought, according to its Secretary General Ayatollah Mohsen Araki, invitations were extended to some "figures in the Taliban movement who believe in the unity of Muslims."[60] The strengthening bonds with Shiite Iran challenges ISKP and the broader Arab-dominated IS community. With the potential growth of discontent by non-Afghans and Afghan Salafists within ISKP's ranks with current Taliban leadership's Shiite-tolerant or Shiite-friendly policies, there are dangers that the hallmark antisectarianism of IS could be mobilized to further push Afghanistan's war toward a more sectarian conflict. Such a move could potentially reignite the regional proxy war in Afghanistan with realigned alliances and newcomers and increase the threat to global security emanating from regions of Afghanistan that fall outside of the government's control. Moreover, if the Afghan government's control over its territory deteriorates further, Iran could come to see the Taliban as its least threatening option, which would bring the complicating Iranian voice—regardless of Tehran's direct participation—into the on-again, off-again peace negotiations with the Taliban. The United States has publicly acknowledged Tehran's backing of the Taliban, as well as Iran's multidimensional relationship with the Afghan government.[61] It is also important to keep in mind that since 2001 the number of madrassas in Afghanistan quadrupled, mostly funded by Iran and Saudi Arabia.[62] If the sectarian divide in the country is politicized as it has been in Iraq and Syria, the graduates of these schools most likely will follow groups such as ISKP or even harsher versions of it and their Shiite equivalents. Furthermore, since IS territorial losses in Iraq and Syria, its supporters in the Afghanistan-Pakistan region could provide any number of its ranks a refuge and space to regroup and merge into an array of militant groups formerly based in Pakistan.[63]

Reemergence of Russia on the Afghan Scene
Another player in this complex security environment not to be ignored is Russia. In their operations against IMU and their overall opposition to IS-inspired or -backed groups, the Taliban have found a sympathetic ear in Moscow, potentially inducing the reinternationalization of the Afghan conflict. Taliban successes prompted Zamir Kabulov, Russia's special envoy to Afghanistan, to state that "Taliban interests objectively coincide with ours."[64] The potential is reminiscent of the 1990s proxy wars supported by India, Iran, and Russia on one side and Pakistan, Saudi Arabia, and, to a certain point, the United States on the other. To the discomfort of Kabul and New Delhi, the Russians with Iranian and Chinese support have opened a dialogue with the Taliban. Russia, along with China and Pakistan—but without the participation of Afghanistan and India—held a meeting in Moscow in November 2016 to discuss countermeasures to the threats posed by ISKP. After complaints by Afghanistan and India, another meeting in Moscow was organized two months later that included representatives from Afghanistan and India. Although specific information about what the Moscow talks entailed is not available, the maneuverings are eerily reminiscent of the political jockeying before and after the formation of the Taliban.[65] According to General Nicholson, "Russia has overtly lent legitimacy to the Taliban," and he added that Moscow, with a position based "not on facts," believes the Taliban are only engaged against ISKP and not against the Afghan government.[66] Nicholson went even further in his accusations in April 2017 when he declined to refute reports that "they [the Russians] are sending weapons

to the Taliban" to counter ISKP—these weapons having surfaced in the Helmand Province.[67]

The multiplicity of groups and policies engaged in Afghanistan once again could undermine peace and stability in Afghanistan. There is a risk to the continued legitimacy of the Afghan government and an incentive for the Taliban ranks to split to accommodate or take advantage of one or another group of potential supporters. Such a scenario would also open more opportunities for ISKP or its future incarnations, not only inside Afghanistan and Pakistan but also in Central Asia and in India—Kashmir in particular. In 2008, while serving as his country's ambassador to Afghanistan, Kabulov is reported to have said that the United States and its allies have repeated all of the Soviets' mistakes, adding, "Now they are making mistakes of their own, ones for which we do not own the copyright."[68] It would be interesting to ask Ambassador Kabulov whether Russia's reemergence onto the Afghan scene would be regarded as a new mistake or a solution.

A Way Forward

By the start of 2018, ISKP had yet to recover any significant territory and had fewer than 2,000 followers with some estimates as low as 700.[69] ISKP has thus far been unable to align its call for an apocalyptic fight to establish a largely undefined vision of an Islamic state (or caliphate) with the aspirations of the majority of Afghan or Pakistani Islamists who are more inclined to focus on establishing their own national or regional versions of Islamist polities. The message of ISKP has thus far alienated the majority of rural Afghans and Pakistanis. However, there is a danger that they might attract followers among urban university students in both countries who are dissatisfied with the existing governments and opposition groups, and the group's potential to morph into another manifestation of militant Islam in either country should not be overlooked.[70]

In Afghanistan, the Taliban remain an undeniable opposition force and as such have become a political and military reality among the regional states and beyond. They have had local success garnering support and in military operations, having gained control over most of the country in the 1990s. They have experience employing both brutal violence and nonviolent measures and have used both to maintain that support and control and to gain political legitimacy. They have also faced defeat, tactically before 2001 and strategically when their leadership was ousted from Afghanistan altogether as a result of the U.S.-led campaign Operation Enduring Freedom. Despite those losses, they have maintained a significant presence in the country, denying the Afghan government control in over 36 percent of the country's districts. The Afghan government has been denied control despite the support of the United States, NATO, and the international coalition and having more funds at its disposal than were allocated under the Marshall Plan—the U.S. aid program that, between 1948 and 1952, helped sixteen Western European countries recover after World War II.[71] More recent nongovernmental reports indicate that the Taliban threaten 70 percent of Afghanistan, while being in full control of fourteen districts.[72]

Notwithstanding their internal leadership problems and difficulties with Pakistan over policy issues such as the modalities of reconciliation strategies with the Afghan government, the Taliban are still viable opponents. The advent of ISKP has challenged the Taliban's monopoly over the insurgency and has opened an opportunity for ISKP to grow its ranks by attracting members of the movement who are dissatisfied with the Taliban leadership's decisions. ISKP also has attracted former Taliban allies such as TTP and IMU since the Taliban does not condone attacks inside Pakistan or in any of Transoxiana states.

Of the ninety-eight U.S.-designated terrorist groups, twenty operate in the Afghanistan-Pakistan region, and three violent extremist organizations—including the Taliban—are active in the region.[73] The advent of ISKP—an organization inspired and supported by the only militant jihadist group that has managed to control large swaths of territory—within this region can only delay even more the prospects for peace and security, not only in the region but also beyond. While ISKP is still in its infancy and in a relatively weak state of organization and proliferation, two factors could mitigate its potential empowerment in the region and weaken the pan-Islamist message overall.

The first and obvious factor is the relationship between Afghanistan and Pakistan. Similar to the beginnings of IS in Iraq and Syria, ISKP germinated in areas where governmental authority was weak or nonexistent. These groups fill vacuums; they seldom create them. The area known today as FATA is a by-product of late-nineteenth-century political calculations by the British to ensure the safety of its imperial domains in India. Unlike the vacuums created as result of the war in Iraq, FATA is a land without central governance by colonial design. The Afghan ruler of the late nineteenth century wanted to incorporate the area he referred to as Yaghistan—the land of the unruly or hostile—into his emirate and impose the rule of governance therein; however, in the final agreement it remained a part of British India. In the case of Afghanistan and Pakistan, as I have argued elsewhere, both countries' refusal to accept the viability of the other as a state with full sovereignty within their existing internationally accepted borders has been at the core of their inability to build a durable trusting relationship.[74] The vacuum of authority in FATA partially stems from the Afghan-Pakistani border disagreement, which allows militants and terrorists to establish roots. In addition, both sides at times have used such groups to put pressure on the other side. There were reports in 2017 of an impending decision by Pakistan to incorporate FATA—an area similar in size to Belgium—into the province of Khyber Pakhtunkhwa; this would be a positive step toward bringing governance to this region.[75] However, governance needs to be coupled with prospects for economic prosperity, which can be best achieved with an inclusive package deal between Afghanistan and Pakistan. Such a deal would need the backing of their international partners, which include those who regard ISKP as a direct threat to their own security. The idea is not new, but its implementation has always taken a back seat to more immediate concerns. However, failure to address this underlying cause of many of the immediate concerns is tantamount to treating the symptoms and not the disease. This disease is not only cross-contaminating Afghanistan and Pakistan but also spreading regionally and, through IS-style groups, into the youth pools across the globe. In 2017 Pakistan began the construction of a 2,500-kilometer (1,500-mile) chain-link fence along the Durand Line, hoping to prevent militants from passing into and out of Afghanistan. However, Afghanistan has vehemently protested the establishment of such a barrier since it would delineate the border.[76]

Bringing Kabul and Islamabad into a trusting relationship is a multifaceted project with many players and wild cards. A more immediate measure that could reduce ISKP's ability to expand its information operations and serve as a countermeasure to the pan-Islamist message being put forth by IS would be to focus on the major contradictions and discrepancies inherent in their claims to Khurasan and use them to weaken the group's ability to recruit. Their Khurasan narrative, including its historical and geographic constructs, contains factual flaws and contradicts local understandings of the term. By repeating that Khurasan includes Pakistan, analysts and reporters inadvertently lend credence to an obscure allegory of Islam's final victory and also support the incorporation of the Indian subcontinent into the calculations of the jihadists such as ISKP. A deeper analysis of the term and its history can illustrate the inaccuracies of ISKP's historical and cultural understanding of their own message. In a battle for minds, symbolic details such as these offer powerful tools.

At a time when ISKP is in retreat, it is time to focus on undermining its message and find ways to fill the political vacuums it seeks.

Notes

The opinions and conclusions expressed herein are those of the individual author and do not necessarily represent the views of either the Marine Corps University or any other U.S. government agency. References to this chapter should include the foregoing statement.

1 The Islamic State is also known by the group's earlier name, the Islamic State of Iraq and the Levant, ISIL/ISIS, or DA'ISH (Daesh), the Arabic acronym for ISIL. Until late in the Obama administration the U.S. Department of Defense referred to the group as ISIL; in the Trump administration the preferred term is ISIS. In this chapter I use IS to acknowledge this group's territorial ambitions, as well as its assault on the notion of state in comparison with other terrorist organizations with global reach such as al Qaeda. Acknowledging the group's territoriality can be an asset for countering its message now and in the future when IS losses its territorial rule.

2 See, for example, Christopher M. Blanchard and Carla E. Humud, "The Islamic State and U.S. Policy," Congressional Research Service, February 2, 2017; Katherine Bauer, ed., "Beyond Syria and Iraq: Examining Islamic State Provinces," Policy Focus 149, Washington Institute for Near East Policy, 2016; Bardia Rahmani and Andrea Tanco, "ISIS's Growing Caliphate: Profiles and Affiliates," Wilson Center, February 19, 2016 (www.wilsoncenter .org/article/isiss-growing-caliphate-profiles-affiliates).

3 ISKP is also known as the Islamic State of Iraq and the Levant-Khorasan, ISIL-K.

4 Amin Tarzi, "Iran, Russia, and the Taliban: Reassessing the Future of the Afghan State," Foreign Policy Research Institute, June 14, 2017 (www.fpri .org/article/2017/06/iran-russia-taliban-reassessing-future-afghan-state/).

5 On the emergence of IS affiliates in Afghanistan and Pakistan, see, for example, Borhan Osman, "The Shadows of 'Islamic State' in Afghanistan: What Threat Does It Hold?," Afghanistan Analysts Network, February 12, 2015 (www.afghanistan-analysts.org/the-shadows-of-islamic -state-in-afghanistan-what-threat-does-it-hold/); and Dan Rassler, "Situating the Emergence of the Islamic State of Khorasan," *CTC Sentinel* 8 (March 2015): 7–11.

6 Rassler, "Islamic State of Khorasan"; Obaid Ali, "The 2016 Insurgency in the North: Raising the Daesh Flag (although Not for Long)," Afghanistan Analysts Network, July 15, 2016 (www.afghanistan-analysts.org/the -2016-insurgency-in-the-north-raising-the-daesh-flag-although-not-for -long/). There are no reports of ideological or operational links between the Jundullah operating in northern Afghanistan and the mainly Baluch Jundullah operating against the Iranian state and championing the cause of the Baluch minority in Iran.

7 Hannah Byrne, John Krzyzaniak, and Qasim Khan, "The Death of Mullah Omar and the Rise of ISIS in Afghanistan," Institute for the Study of War, August 17, 2015 (www.understandingwar.org); Rassler, "Islamic State of Khurasan"; Ali, "2016 Insurgency."

8 "Uzbek Militants Declare Support for Islamic State," *Dawn*, October 6, 2014 (www.dawn.com/news/1136578/uzbek-militants-declare-support-for -islamic-state/print).

9 For more on IMU, see, for example, Ahmed Rashid, *Jihad: The Rise of Militant Islam in Central Asia* (Yale University Press, 2002), pp. 137–86; and Alisher Ilkhamov, "Uzbek Islamism: Imported Ideology or Grassroots Movement?," *Middle East Report* (Winter 2001): 40–46.

10 Borhan Osman, "Descent into Chaos: Why Did Nangarhar Turn Into an IS Hub?," Afghanistan Analysts Network, September 27, 2016 (www .afghanistan-analysts.org/descent-into-chaos-why-did-nangarhar-turn -into-an-is-hub/).

11 Abu Muhammad al-Adnani "Say, Die in Your Rage!" Speech, January 25, 2015 (https://archive.org/details/SayDieInYourRage); Osman, "Descent into Chaos." For a survey on the dynamic nature of Pakistan-based militant organizations, a number of which morphed into TTP, see Muhammad Amir Rana, *A to Z of Jehadi Organizations in Pakistan*, translated by Saba Ansari (Lahore: Mashal, 2006), pp. 382–84.

12 John L. Esposito, *Islam and Politics* (Syracuse University Press, 1984), pp. 31–35.

13 Adnani, "Say, Die in Your Rage!"

14 Casey Garret Johnson, "The Rise and Stall of the Islamic State in Afghanistan," Special Report 395, United States Institute of Peace, November 2016; Borhan Osman, "The Islamic State in 'Khorasan': How It Began and Where It Stands Now in Nangarhar," Afghanistan Analysts Network, July 27, 2016 (https://www.afghanistan-analysts.org/the-islamic-state-in-khorasan-how-it-began-and-where-it-stands-now-in-nangarhar/).

15 Statement of General John F. Campbell, Commander, U.S. Forces—Afghanistan, before the U.S. Senate Armed Services Committee, Washington, October 6, 2015.

16 Statement for the Record by General John W. Nicholson, Commander, U.S. Forces—Afghanistan, before the Senate Armed Services Committee on the Situation in Afghanistan, Washington, February 9, 2017.

17 Kenneth Katzman and Clayton Thomas, "Afghanistan: Post-Taliban Governance, Security, and U.S. Policy," Congressional Research Service, August 22, 2017 (https://fas.org/sgp/crs/row/RL30588.pdf).

18 See, for example, Rassler, "Islamic State of Khorasan"; Harleen Gambhir, "ISIS in Afghanistan," Backgrounder (Washington: Institute for the Study of War, December 3, 2015) (www.understandingwar.org); Lauren McNally and others, "The Islamic State in Afghanistan: Examining Its Threat to Stability," Policy Focus Series (Washington: Middle East Institute, May 2016). For a source questioning ISKP's understanding of Khurasan, see Osman, "The Islamic State."

19 Khalil 'Athamina, "The Black Banners and the Socio-Political Significance of Flags and Slogans in Medieval Islam," *Arabica* 36 (November 1989): 307–26 (www.jstor.org/stable /4057220).

20 Adam Taylor, "The Strange Story behind the 'Khorasan' Group's Name," *Washington Post*, September 25, 2014.

21 Jacob Lessner, "Abū Muslim al-Khurāsāni: The Emergence of a Secret Agent from Khurāsān, Irāq, or Was It Işfahān?," *Journal of the American Oriental Society* 104, no. 1 (January–March, 1984): 165–75.

22 G. H. Yusofi, "Abu Muslim 'Abd-al-Rahman b. Moslem Korasani," in *Encyclopædia Iranica*, edited by Ehsan Yarshater, Vol. 1 (New York: Encyclopædia Iranica Foundation, 2009), pp. 341–44.

23 For an account of the Khurasani revolution as a non-Arab event and the black flag symbolism, see Saleh Said Agha, "The Agents and Forces that Toppled the Umayyad Caliphate" (PhD diss., University of Toronto, 1993), pp. iii–iv, 81–85, accessed via ProQuest.

24 Mark David Luce, "Frontier as Process: Umayyad Khurāsān" (PhD diss., University of Chicago, 2009), pp. 8–51.

25 Mir Ghualm Muhammad Ghubar and others, *Tarikh-i Afghanistan*, Vol. 3 (Kabul: AH 1336 [1957]), pp. 63–73; Mir Muhammad Siddiq Farhang, *Afghanistan dar panj qarn-i akhir*, Vol. 1 (Qom: AH 1271 [1992]), pp. 17–32.

26 Osman, "Shadows."

27 Hamid Enayat, *Modern Islamic Political Thought* (University of Texas Press, 1988), pp. 69–83.

28 Amin Tarzi, "Political Struggles over the Afghanistan-Pakistan Borderlands," in *Under the Drones: Modern Lives in the Afghanistan-Pakistan Borderlands*, edited by Shahzad Bashir and Robert D. Crews (Harvard University Press, 2012), pp. 17–29.

29 See, for example, Ahmed Rashid, *Taliban: Militant Islam, Oil and Fundamentalism in Central Asia* (Yale University Press, 2000); Wahid Muzhda, *Afghānistān wa panj sāl sultā-ye Tālibān* (Tehran: Nashreney, 2003); and Peter Tomsen, *The Wars of Afghanistan: Messianic Terrorism, Tribal Conflicts, and the Failures of Great Powers* (New York: Public Affairs, 2011).

30 Michael Weiss and Hassan Hassan, *ISIS: Inside the Army of Terror* (New York: Regan Arts, 2015), pp. 2–16.

31 Johnson, "The Rise and Stall," p. 6.

32 Amin Tarzi, "Taliban in Afghanistan," in *Encyclopedia of Islam and the Muslim World*, 2nd ed., Vol. 2., edited by Richard C. Martin (Farmington Hills, Mich.: Gale, 2016), pp. 1140–43.

33 Amin Tarzi, "The Neo-Taliban," in *The Taliban and the Crisis of Afghanistan*, edited by Robert D. Crews and Amin Tarzi (Harvard University Press, 2008), pp. 304–05; Abdel Bari Atwan, *Islamic State: The Digital Caliphate* (University of California Press, 2015), pp. 12, 77.

34 Vanda Felbab-Brown, "Blood and Faith in Afghanistan: A June 2016 Update," Brookings Center for 21st Century Security and Intelligence 17 (www.brookings.edu/wp-content/uploads/2016/07/2016-Felbab-Brown-Paper-BLOOD-AND-FAITH-VFB.pdf).

35 Patrick Cockburn, *The Rise of Islamic State: ISIS and the New Sunni Revolution* (New York: Verso, 2015), p. 54.

36 David B. Edwards, *Before the Taliban: Genealogies of the Afghan Jihad* (University of California Press, 2002), p. 294.

37 Weiss and Hassan, *ISI*, p. 61.

38 Byrne and others, "The Death of Mullah Omar."

39 U.S. Department of Defense, "Enhancing Security and Stability in Afghanistan," June 2016, (www.defense.gov/Portals/1/Documents/Enhancing_Security_and_Stability_in_Afghanistan-June_2016.pdf).

40 Borhan Osman and Fazal Muzhary, "Jihadi Commuters: How the Taleban Cross the Durand Line," Afghanistan Analysts Network, October 17, 2017 (www.afghanistan-analysts.org/jihadi-commuters-how-the-taleban-cross-the-durand-line/).

41 Osman, "Shadows."

42 Ibid.

43 Mark D. Luce, "The Effects of Escalating ISIS IO in Wilayat-i Khurasan," a Cultural Intelligence Information Paper (CISOA), prepared for the 4th Military Information Support Group. I am grateful to Dr. Luce for sharing his analysis with me.

44 Johnson, "The Rise and Stall," pp. 11–12; Borhan Osman, "With an Active Cell in Kabul, ISKP Tries to Bring Sectarianism to the Afghan War," Afghanistan Analysts Network, October 19, 2016 (www.afghanistan-analysts.org/with-an-active-cell-in-kabul-iskp-tries-to-bring-sectarianism-to-the-afghan-war/).

45 Abubakar Siddique, "Taliban Warns IS Militants against Opening a New Front in Afghanistan," RFE/RL, June 16, 2015 (http://gandhara.rferl.org/a/afghanistan-taliban-islamic-state/27075631.html).

46 Ibid.

47 Osman, "Active Cell."

48 Ali, "The 2016 Insurgency in the North."

49 Luce, "The Effects."

50 Kate Clark, "First Wave of IS Attacks? Claim and Denial over the Jalalabad Bombs," Afghanistan Analysts Network, April 22, 2015 (www.afghanistan-analysts.org/first-wave-of-is-attacks-claim-and-denial-over-the-jalalabad-bombs/).

51 Osman, "Active Cell."

52 Statement by General Nicholson, p. 11.

53 Osman, "Active Cell."

54 Kate Clark, "More Militias? Part 2: The Proposed Afghan Territorial Army in the Fight against ISKP," Afghanistan Analysts Network, September 23, 2017 (www.afghanistan-analysts.org/more-militias-part-2-the-proposed-afghan-territorial-army-in-the-fight-against-iskp/).

55 Ibid.

56 Johnson, "The Rise and Stall," p. 13; Osman, "Active Cell."

57 Osman, "Active Cell."

58 Anand Gopal, "The Combined and Uneven Development of Afghan Nationalism," *Studies in Ethnicity and Nationalism* 16, no. 3 (2016): 487.

59 Osman, "Active Cell."

60 "Iran Hosts Taliban Leaders at a Conference in Tehran," Al-Arabiya English, December 14, 2016 (http://english.alarabiya.net/en/News/middle -east/2016/12/14/Iran-hosts-Taliban-leaders-at-a-conference-in-Tehran .html); "Ayatollah Araki Warns: KSA Turning to Muslim Dispersion Base," January 5, 2016 (http://www.iuc.taghrib.com/en/news/nf-en-07).

61 Statement by General Nicholson, p. 10.

62 Carlotta Gall, "Saudis Bankroll Taliban, Even as King Officially Supports Afghan Government," *New York Times*, December 6, 2016.

63 Johnson, "The Rise and Stall," p. 14.

64 Javid Ahmad, "Russia and the Taliban Make Amends," *Foreign Affairs*, January 31, 2016 (www.foreignaffairs.com/articles/afghanistan/2016-01-31 /russia-and-taliban-make-amends).

65 Suhasini Haidar, "India to Join Moscow Meet on Afghanistan," *The Hindu*, February 15, 2017 (www.thehindu.com/news/national/India-to-join -Moscow-meet-on-Afghanistan/article17303436.ece); from 1992 to 1993 I served as a diplomat for Afghanistan's UN delegation and from 1993 to 1996 as an adviser to the Saudi Arabian UN delegation, participating in different rounds of talks on Afghanistan. These talks led to the formation of the 6 + 2 formula that included Afghanistan's six immediate neighbors plus Russia and the United States.

66 "DoD press briefing by Gen. Nicholson in the Pentagon Briefing Room," December 2, 2016 (www.defense.gov/DesktopModules/ArticleCS/Print .aspx?PortalId=1&ModuleId=1144&Article=1019029).

67 Katzman and Thomas, "Afghanistan" (https://fas.org/sgp/crs/row/RL30588 .pdf).

68 Tomsen, *The Wars*, p. 201.

69 Katzman and Thomas, "Afghanistan."

70 Luce, "The Effects."

71 Special Inspector General for Afghanistan Reconstruction, "High-Risk List," January 2017 (www.sigar.mil/pdf/spotlight/2017_High-Risk_List.pdf).

72 Shoaib Sharifi and Louise Adamou, "Taliban Threaten 70% of Afghanistan, BBC Finds," BBC World Service, January 21, 2018 (http://www.bbc .com/news/world-asia-42863116).

73 Statement by General Nicholson, p. 2.

74 Tarzi, "Political Struggles," p. 18; for more on historical Yaghistan, see Amin Tarzi, "Islam, Shari'a, and State Building under 'Abd al-Rahman Khan," in *Afghanistan's Islam: From Conversion to the Taliban*, edited by Nile Green (University of California Press, 2017), pp. 129–32.

75 Abubakar Siddique, "Pakistan to Merge Tribal Area into Northwestern Province," Gandahara RFE/RL, January 25, 2017 (http://gandhara.rferl

.org/a/pakistan-fata-pakhtunkhwa-merger/28259457.html); Tarzi, "Political Struggles," p. 28.

76 "Pakistan, Afghanistan in Angry Tangle over Border Fence to Keep Out Militants," *U.S. News*, October 18, 2017 (www.usnews.com/news/world /articles/2017-10-18/pakistan-afghanistan-in-angry-tangle-over-chicken -wire-border-fence-to-keep-out-militants).

PART IV

Joint Action: U.S. and Regional Powers

7

International and Regional Responses

An Appraisal

Hussein Banai

The emergence and expansion of the Islamic State in Iraq and Syria (ISIS, or Daesh in Arabic) in the summer of 2014 shocked and dismayed the international citizenry. In the short span of just a few weeks, ISIS forces inflicted heavy losses on the Iraqi and Syrian armies, Syrian opposition groups, the Kurdish Peshmerga, and every religious or ethnic minority group from Mosul to the outskirts of Aleppo. As part of the group's sophisticated media strategy, mass executions, ritual beheadings of Western and other foreign citizens, and severe punishments handed down to local residents were broadcast and disseminated over various online media outlets. The brazen attacks on Western targets that soon followed suit revealed the transnational breadth of its recruitment and radicalization methods beyond the troubled borders of the Middle East.

Initially, the international and regional responses to these bewildering developments were slow and piecemeal. At a time when news headlines were dominated by negotiations over Iran's nuclear program or the U.S. diplomatic opening toward Cuba, the conspicuous displays of extraordinary brutality mixed with declarations of statehood were baffling, even to many experts.[1] But as the aims and capabilities of ISIS became more apparent, the United States and its NATO allies took the lead in assembling an international coalition to halt ISIS's momentum and reverse its gains. Key regional states such as Saudi Arabia, Iran, Turkey, and Egypt were even slower in developing counter-ISIS strategies. This was less a reflection of their impotence in the face of a transnational jihadist network and more about their competing interests under new geopolitical conditions that favored some over others.

This chapter considers the joint U.S.-led international and regional responses to ISIS's emergence and expansion in Iraq and Syria. In the first section, it provides an overview of the U.S.-led international efforts to counter ISIS's military and political advances according to the declared strategic objectives of the Global Coalition to Counter Daesh. The second part of the chapter lays out the divergent priorities and competing interests that have shaped major regional powers' responses to ISIS. The approach undertaken in this section is necessarily more analytical given the conflicting strategies pursued by countries such as Iran and Saudi Arabia to stabilize their respective zones of influence. Assessing the implications of the contrasting international and regional responses to the seemingly chronic issue of transnational violent jihadism forms the basis for the third section of the chapter. The chapter concludes by making the case for an alternative framework for addressing the permissive conditions that enable the onset of transnational terrorist networks.

U.S.-Led International Response to ISIS

The international response to the rise and spread of ISIS has largely taken shape and been carried out under the auspices of the U.S.-led Global Coalition against Daesh. The coalition, which was formally established in December 2014, is composed of sixty-eight partner nations from several regions. Notable absences from the coalition include Russia, China, Iran, and the embattled government of Bashar al-Assad in Syria, which, as I discuss in the next section, not only account for the coalition's slower-than-anticipated rate of progress but are also significant in determining the outcome in both Syria and Iraq. The core mission of the coalition, as first outlined by President Obama, has been to "degrade, and ultimately destroy, ISIS through a comprehensive and sustained counterterrorism strategy."[2] The broad outlines of the strategy to achieve this mission have evolved somewhat over time, but they center on five "lines of effort": (i) military components; (ii) stopping the recruitment and flow of foreign fighters; (iii) cutting off ISIS's funding and financing; (iv) offering humanitarian assistance and stabilizing affected areas; and (v) countering ISIS propaganda.

On the military front the campaign has been carried out by air, artillery, and ground units, and has been largely led by the United States through Operation Inherent Resolve (OIR). Of these components, air strikes account for a substantial portion of attacks against ISIS targets inside Syria and Iraq. According to figures released by the Pentagon in 2016, of the nearly 16,000 air strikes (in roughly 128,000 sorties) conducted against leadership, facilities, and the supply networks of ISIS, approximately 13,000 were carried out by the United States.[3] Similar proportions hold between American and other coalition partners in terms of artillery support and ground units working in advising and training capacities. As of this writing, OIR has cost the United States more than $10 billion, or a daily cost of about $12.6 million since the start of operations in August 2014. Despite the disproportionate financial and operational military burdens borne by the United States, the absence of any American ground troops has, correspondingly, placed considerable pressure on local partners to exploit ISIS's vulnerabilities on the ground through intensive counterinsurgency tactics designed to "clear, build, and hold" affected areas. Since August 2014 this combination of air, artillery, and ground assaults has, according to coalition figures, resulted in the liberation of 56 and 27 percent of populated areas under ISIS control in Iraq and Syria, respectively.[4] As of this writing, the battle to recapture Mosul in Iraq is well under way and indications are that the combination of Iraqi ground forces (with special help from the elite forces of the Iranian Revolutionary Guard Corps) and air cover by the coalition warplanes will shrink ISIS's foothold in Iraq further still.

The effort to halt the recruitment and flow of foreign fighters has been more evenly dispersed among members of the coalition, in contrast to the military components of the strategy. Owing to improved border security measures, better human and signals intelligence-sharing mechanisms, improved cybersecurity programs, and the waning novelty of ISIS as a revolutionary force capable of upending longstanding zones of authority in the region, the coalition has been most effective in significantly reducing the inflow of fighters and sympathizers into Iraq and Syria. According to the coalition's own 2016 figures, the number of foreign terrorist fighters entering these territories is "down significantly, from approximately 1,000 per month in 2014, to approximately 500 per month in 2015, to a negligible amount today."[5] As for the danger posed by ISIS outside of Iraq and Syria, the effort to effectively combat sleeper cells and would-be sympathizers is decidedly more complex and challenging. The legal framework behind the international response on this front has been United Nations Security Council Resolution 2178 (adopted unanimously in 2014), which calls on all member states to work toward preventing travel and financial support for ISIS sympathizers. Since the passage of the resolution, according to the U.S. Department of State, "58 countries and the United Nations now contribute foreign terrorist fighter profiles to INTERPOL. At least 23 countries have completed national action plans to counter terrorism and violent extremism, and 11 have launched programs to counter radicalization and recruitment of foreign fighters in their countries. Measures include de-radicalization centers and hot-lines."[6]

To combat ISIS's external and internal sources of funding, the coalition has adopted a two-pronged approach.[7] By identifying and tracking ISIS's management and sale of oil and gas resources, internal taxation, patterns of kidnappings for ransom, and illicit sale of drugs and antiquities, the coalition has been able to mount military and international policing campaigns to halt the revenues generated by these resources. This effort has involved precision bombing of oil fields and convoys of trucks carrying oil and gas, as well as reserves of cash, within and outside ISIS-controlled areas. Coalition aircraft have also targeted key infrastructure and installations used by ISIS to transport money and resources.

Intercepting networks of human and material trafficking alongside the Turkish, Jordanian, and Saudi borders has also substantially reduced the occurrence of kidnappings and human smuggling (for slave labor). What remains difficult to retain are the reserves of cash and gold bullion seized by ISIS forces after their capture of major cities such as Mosul in Iraq (up to $429 million, for instance, believed to have been left behind in Mosul's central bank vault at the time of the city's surrender to ISIS forces).[8] External sources of financing from wealthy private donors in Persian Gulf countries—principally Qatar, Kuwait, the United Arab Emirates, and Saudi Arabia—were instrumental in supporting the formation and early expansion of ISIS.[9] Efforts to combat ISIS's flow of external funding are coordinated through the Counter-Daesh Finance Group (CFIG). The CFIG's mandate has been to disrupt ISIS's use of international financial networks "by designating—domestically, regionally and through existing UN Security Council resolutions—Daesh senior leaders, facilitators and financiers, effectively freezing their assets and making it more costly and more difficult for them to do business."[10] However, fulfilling the mandate of CFIG continues to be a challenge given the complex web of unregistered private charities disguised as "humanitarian" organizations and donations through encrypted social media applications that serve as a global financial lifeline for ISIS.

Of course, none of the successes on the battlefield or against ISIS's human and financial resources would be sustainable without longer-term strategies to stabilize and reconstruct newly liberated areas. To this end, a major effort of the coalition has been to support security and stabilization programs designed to restore infrastructure (schools, hospitals, roads, bridges, power plants, and so forth), train local police units, resettle displaced populations, and revitalize local economies after ISIS forces have been pushed out. In Iraq, where nearly all such efforts have been concentrated in light of the ongoing civil war in Syria, coalition members have pledged monetary support to the UN's Funding Facility for Immediate Stabilization ($200 million pledged) and Funding Facility for Expanded Stabilization ($50 million pledged) programs. To date, the results of these programs have been mixed across Iraq. In some cities, such as Tikrit, UN and coalition efforts to resettle internally displaced populations, to remove mines and improvised explosive devices (IEDs), and to retrain new police officers have been somewhat effective. But successes remain mostly circumstantial owing to the fact that very little of the money pledged has actually materialized to carry out major infrastructure programs and create the conditions for sustainable economic stability in affected areas. These problems are further compounded by the rising tide of sectarianism and an already mistrustful relationship between the Shia-led Iraqi central government (and Iranian-backed militias) and local Sunni tribes and authorities that undercut efforts at dispute resolution and postconflict reconciliation.[11]

Last, given the transnational nature and reach of ISIS's following and activities, a major pillar of the coalition's strategy is to counter jihadist propaganda and radicalization efforts inside and outside the war-torn regions in the Middle East and North Africa. ISIS's dynamic online strategy to identify, radicalize, and recruit sympathizers through propaganda videos, publications, and social media engagements set it apart from other jihadist organizations that eschewed such audacious displays of brutality and gore for fear of alienating potential recruits to their cause. In the aftermath of brazen attacks in Paris, Brussels, Nice, Orlando, and San Bernardino, in addition to the almost routine wave of attacks in Iraq, Syria, and Libya, the qualitative difference between ISIS's propaganda machine and those of other jihadist groups became ominously clear. A much-touted slogan by jihadists since ISIS's rise, as a result, is "half of jihad is media."[12] The counterpropaganda effort undertaken by the coalition is aimed at undermining ISIS's message and self-depiction as a successful revolutionary force, while also appealing to potential recruits with an alternative message of moderation and conciliation. The main partners in executing this strategy are the UAE-based Sawab Center, the U.K.-based Coalition Communications Cell, and the U.S. Department of State's Global Engagement Center. It is very difficult to assess the effectiveness of the coalition's efforts in this domain since there is little public information available. There is little doubt that a string of targeted killings of ISIS's top propagandists such as its spokesman, Abu Muhammad al-Adnani, in late-summer 2016, or its British-born executioner, Muhammad Emwazi (also known as Jihadi John) earlier in the same year,

have succeeded in diminishing the aura of invincibility around the organization among potential recruits. Similarly, social media organizations
have developed more sophisticated methods for detecting and shutting
down accounts used to disseminate jihadi propaganda such as ISIS's main
publication, *Dabiq*. At the very least, these efforts have served to elevate
more credible voices of moderation and reflection—such as theological
authority at venerable institutions such as al-Azhar University—in the
same online forums and networks where extremists seek out disaffected
young Muslims and convert them to the cause of violent jihad.

Together, these five lines of effort have made up the coalition's strategy to "degrade, and ultimately destroy," ISIS's version of the caliphate
that, by 2015, had clearly exploited the quasi-sovereign status of central
governments in Syria and Iraq and exposed the impotence of other countries in the region. As of this writing in 2018, it is indisputably clear that
ISIS's territorial possessions, military capabilities, human and financial
resources, recruitment networks, and propaganda outlets have been significantly reduced since the end of 2014. As a militant organization capable of projecting power, ISIS is a degraded force. That much is evident
based on the metrics identified by the coalition. Just as readily apparent,
however, is the fact that the underlying conditions that facilitated the rise
of ISIS in the first place for the most part remain unaffected by the coalition's overall strategy. To complicate matters more, the coalition against
ISIS does not include some key regional and international players such as
Iran, Russia, and China, which have formed parallel coalitions of their
own in pursuit of their narrow interests in the region. Even within the
U.S.-led coalition, countries such as Saudi Arabia and Turkey have at different junctures pursued objectives that are at odds with the stated goals
of the coalition. As a symptom of state collapse, rising sectarianism, political opportunism of adjacent countries, and trenchant regional rivalries, ISIS's destruction will ultimately require a comprehensive political
strategy that credibly mitigates the security dilemma created by these
underlying factors. The deficiencies and pitfalls of the U.S.-led international response to ISIS become apparent when one considers the regional
dynamics that continually undermine efforts to destroy the organization.
It is to this differential regional response that I turn next.

Regional Paradoxes and Rivalries

As alluded to in the previous section, the regional responses to ISIS's rise and transmutation into a quasi-state operation have been at variance with the U.S.-led Global Coalition's aims and strategies. At first glance, this variation may seem puzzling given the ripples of instability caused by ISIS's expansion throughout the region, which have resulted in the mass displacement of peoples across borders, the heightened risk of further conflict due to rising sectarianism, and the direct threat posed to nearly all regimes in the region by a transnational jihadist ideology openly challenging the legitimacy of established orders. Any one of these factors, it would seem, should have been sufficient to trigger a united regional front against ISIS. It is also evident that the lack of a regional coalition to combat ISIS is not due to any deficits in resources or incompetence of the major states in the region. Arab countries such as Saudi Arabia, Qatar, Egypt, and Jordan are more than capable, both militarily and financially, to take on a peripatetic paramilitary outfit, but have instead mostly remained on the sidelines, only selectively intervening to fortify what they see as their own vital interests. As a member of NATO, Turkey, too, is capable of drawing on its considerable military and intelligence resources to effectively destroy ISIS's base of operations and deprive it of supplies of human and military resources (through its shared borders with Syria and Iraq). Iran's Revolutionary Guard Corps, moreover, has provided crucial security and intelligence assistance to the governments in Iraq and Syria through its elite Quds Force; and yet it has been left out of any regional coalition to take on ISIS.

Rather, the reluctance with which many countries in the region have approached the joint effort to combat ISIS is informed by their competing interests and rational calculations of who will ultimately benefit more from the reconstitution of state authority in Syria and Iraq. As the veteran journalist Patrick Cockburn observed ahead of many policy analysts in Western capitals, "The Islamic State's success has been helped not just by its enemies' incompetence but also by the divisions evident between them. John Kerry boasts of having put together a coalition of sixty countries all pledged to oppose ISIS, but from the beginning it was clear that many important members weren't too concerned about the ISIS threat."[13] Indeed, as Cockburn and others have recounted since, the ISIS threat, often menacingly portrayed as an existential issue in Western media, has from the very beginning been regarded by the countries in the region as a cause for alarm and opportunity mostly for what it entails for their geopolitical interests.[14] Whereas Sunni-majority Arab states (led by Saudi Arabia) have conceived of ISIS as largely a check and a buffer (however unpleasant) against a would-be regional hegemon in Iran, the Iranian security establishment and its Shia Arab allies in Iraq, Lebanon, Syria, and Yemen view ISIS as bait by Sunni countries designed to weaken, and eventually end, Iran's influence in the Arab world. For its part, Turkey has had a muddled set of objectives: at once balancing its keen interest in warding off any developments that would strengthen the cause of Kurdish autonomy with facilitating the arming and movement of Syrian rebels in fighting the Assad regime, including material support for jihadi groups such as Jabhat al-Nusra.

In attempting to unpack this seemingly contradictory assortment of strategic interests, however, one must take into account the military and political developments that hastened the unraveling of the status quo ante in the Middle East. In this respect, as the political scientist Curtis Ryan has argued, the regional response to ISIS must be placed in the context of successive historical "jolts" to the longstanding established order in the region: namely, the 2003 invasion of Iraq, the wave of popular uprisings that swept across the Arab world, and the counterrevolutionary authoritarian backlash in response to them.[15] The 2003 Anglo-American invasion of Iraq left in its wake not only a broken state along sectarian and ethnic lines (despite the best efforts of some leading Iraqi politicians early on to forge a representative republic), but also one beset by terrorism and external meddling by regional powers. It was in this toxic environment, as numerous accounts have shown, that al Qaeda in Iraq (AQI), under the early tutelage of the Jordanian militant Abu Musab al-Zarqawi, transformed itself from a traditional jihadi terror cell into one actively pursuing the establishment of an Islamic State in Iraq (ISI). Upon Zarqawi's death, the leadership of ISI eventually fell to Abu Bakr al-Baghdadi, who took advantage of the mix of increased sectarianism in Iraqi politics and full-blown civil war in Syria to found ISIS. This metamorphosis is covered in greater detail in the early chapters of this volume, but the broad contours of its inception are important to recall here because of what they also reveal about the underlying factors that made them possible. Put simply, in the absence of the fracturing of the Iraqi state—especially along retributively sectarian lines—in the aftermath of the 2003 invasion, the rise of jihadist politics, let alone the transmutation of AQI to ISI to ISIS, would have been impossible.[16]

The aftermath of the invasion was also consequential in propelling the Islamic Republic of Iran to newfound prominence not only as the guardian of Shia interests in the region, but also as a major power player meddling in the internal politics of large and small Arab countries (Bahrain, Iraq, Yemen, Syria, and Lebanon, leaving aside its support for various Shia political movements and militias in major Sunni Arab countries such as Saudi Arabia).[17] Iran played a major role in fortifying Shia political parties and militias in Iraq throughout the postinvasion period. This involvement was especially empowering to Iran's hard-liners and commanders of its Islamic Revolutionary Guard Corps (IRGC), which increasingly operated as a foreign and security establishment parallel to Iran's official government. The significance of IRGC's growing autonomy and power cannot be overstated in the context of increasing sectarianism in the region, for, as "the guardians of the Islamic revolution," the Guards' core mission is the export and safekeeping of Iran's revolutionary ideals throughout the Islamic world.[18] The catastrophic aftermath of the invasion of Iraq provided the IRGC with a renewed sense of mission, a call of duty that they continue to pursue with great zeal from Baghdad to Damascus to Beirut. In Iraq this has meant developing close political, economic, and military ties with Shia parties, commercial entities, and militias, much to the chagrin of Sunni and Kurdish contingents. In Syria the main strategic objective of the Guards, in addition to preserving their longstanding partnership with the Assad regime, is to prevent the emergence of any viable anti-Shia Islamist force among the Syrian opposition should the regime prove too weak to reconstitute its power.[19]

Iran's response to ISIS, therefore, has been largely consistent with its overall strategic objectives in Iraq and Syria. As long as ISIS is contained and weakened to a point where it ceases to pose any serious danger to the status quo in those countries, then neither the Guards nor Iran's political establishment is going to risk getting bogged down in an asymmetric conflict with a jihadist movement.[20] To this end, Iran has been highly selective in its engagement: the IRGC have been more than content to allow Russian and Global Coalition forces to attack ISIS targets in eastern Syria and along the border with Turkey, but in the battle to retake Mosul, IRGC commanders spared no expense and direct military support to the Iraqi central government.

Indeed, the same assessment applies to Russia's actions against ISIS forces. Since its entry into the Syrian conflict, Russia's chief objective has been to fortify the regime of Bashar al-Assad as a bulwark against any encroachments by American and NATO forces into its traditional sphere of influence. The campaign against ISIS, therefore, has provided the Russians a convenient excuse to carry out this strategy under the guise of counterterrorism. In ISIS, Russia also recognizes a familiar enemy it has intermittently fought off in Chechnya (indeed, veterans of the Chechnya conflict can be found among both Russian forces in Syria and ISIS recruits across the region). This familiarity, moreover, has yielded a strategic approach that views such groups as essentially containable and prone to manipulation in service of extraneous strategic interests. Regarding the latter, Russia has been adept at using counter-ISIS measures as a cover for attacking anti-Assad forces and redirecting jihadist attacks against U.S.-backed opposition forces in eastern Syria and along the Turkish border. Much of this, of course, has been carried out in perfect synchrony with the elite units of Iran's IRGC, who share the same objectives.

Iran's ascendance as a regional influencer, in turn, has alarmed much of the Sunni Arab world, especially the member states of the Gulf Cooperation Council (Saudi Arabia, Kuwait, the United Arab Emirates, Qatar, Bahrain, and Oman). In their view (although Oman's position is generally more neutral), Iran's overt support of Shia political parties and social movements in the Arab world, coupled with the expansion of its nuclear and military programs, pose a serious threat to the existing geopolitical order. Since the advent of the Islamic Republic in 1979, the GCC countries have benefited tremendously from an Arab-dominated order in the region. For nearly three decades, GCC countries had reaped hefty domestic and regionwide rewards from close military, intelligence, and economic partnership with the United States. However, the aftermath of the Iraq war and the unexpected wave of Arab uprisings across the region in 2010 and 2011, which led to the de facto collapse of four Arab states (Iraq, Syria, Yemen, and, Libya), effectively resulted in the upending of this order. In addition, the successful negotiation of a nuclear deal between Iran and major world powers has induced major anxiety in Arab capitals about a possible thaw in U.S.-Iran enmity that for so long had worked to their advantage. In response to this remarkable unraveling, leading Gulf states such as Saudi Arabia and Qatar have scrambled financial and military resources to stem the tide of political change in the region (most notably in Egypt and Bahrain) and to counter Iranian influence through sectarian tactics.[21] The most visible aspects of this strategy have been the confrontations with Iran's proxies in Bahrain and Yemen. In each case Saudi Arabia not only swiftly deployed its military forces, but also unleashed a regionwide anti-Shia campaign through its own Salafi jihadist proxies, culminating in the Saudi execution of Sheikh Nimr Baqir al-Nimr, a prominent Shia opposition leader in the kingdom.[22]

The inconsistent and incoherent responses of Arab nations to the emergence and expansion of ISIS, therefore, have to be considered against this backdrop of intense rivalry and sectarianism between Iran and Saudi Arabia. If ISIS could be exploited to diminish Shia and Iranian influence in Arab lands, then Saudi Arabia and its Gulf allies would have little incentive to destroy the group outright. The wild card here, of course, is the extent to which the spread of jihadist militancy could end up destabilizing the pro-Western monarchies themselves. This wariness perhaps accounts for some of the crackdowns on radical preachers and private financial donations to ISIS residing in the GCC countries. In the main, however, forcefully balancing Iran's regional ambitions remains the foremost priority of Saudi Arabia and its Sunni allies. This imperative is evident in the formation of the Saudi-led Islamic Military Alliance to Fight Terrorism (IMAFT) in December 2015, in response to the Iranian government's World Against Violence and Extremism (WAVE) initiative that was launched two years earlier. Notably, IMAFT excludes Iran and its Shia allies, while the aims of the WAVE initiative are almost exclusively focused on Sunni Salafi jihadist movements. Both organizations pay lip service to fighting ISIS, but their respective missions only vaguely refer to the need for combating terror and global extremism.

Last, Turkey's role as the only regional stakeholder with membership in the NATO alliance is also instructive. The onset of civil war in Syria and the subsequent emergence of ISIS as a quasi-state between Iraq and Syria have created a massive humanitarian crisis, with Turkey on its frontlines. As of this writing in 2018, the UN Refugee Agency estimates the number of Syrian refugees in Turkey at 2.8 million, which has added strain to an already depressed economy and heightened security environment. The most burdensome complication for Turkey, however, is the involvement of Syrian and Iraqi Kurdish fighters along its southern border. On the one hand, Turkey cannot be seen as indifferent to the plight of Syrian Kurds bravely holding back an ISIS onslaught; on the other hand, the success of the People's Protection Units (or YPG militias) has alarmed Turkish leaders about the possibility of a revival of separatist sentiments among its own sizable Kurdish community (upwards of 25 percent of its population). As such, the Turkish government has exploited the ISIS threat to ramp up nationalist sentiments against the decades-long insurgency mounted by the Kurdish Workers Party (PKK). Under the cover of the U.S.-led Global Coalition, Turkey has directed a significant portion of its air strikes at PKK camps in northern Iraq.[23] Moreover, as part of the coalition supporting the overthrow of the Assad regime in Syria, Turkey has actively participated in the arming and training of opposition groups such as the Free Syrian Army, and even some jihadist factions like Jabhat al-Nusra. In this effort it has allowed safe passage for jihadist fighters into Syria and Iraq, and according to an EU-commissioned study by Conflict Armament Research has served as a major supply route—whether through lax border control or willful disregard—for bomb-making materials used by ISIS.[24]

In sum, even a cursory look at the regional dynamics would yield a complex, multilayered, intersecting, and contradictory set of security and political priorities for each of the major stakeholders. The mixture of converging anxieties and diverging strategies in the face of the ISIS threat is truly remarkable. Much like the quip about the puzzling longevity of the Ottoman Empire well past its expiration date, ISIS's staying power is ultimately a function of the surrounding states' conflicting interests in the fate of the failed states in which jihadist dystopic visions thrive. The regional malaise can also be blamed on the Global Coalition's strategic goals, which scarcely address the incapacity of state institutions as a result of foreign interventions (Iraq and Libya, for example) and ongoing civil wars (in Syria and Yemen). Without a serious attempt to address the maze of intertwined and conflicting interests of the major powers in the region, efforts at combating ISIS may well succeed in degrading the organization and its displacement from major urban areas, but they will not bring about the end of transnational jihadist terror. This is already evidenced by the ISIS-devised and -inspired attacks carried out against governmental, religious, and civil society targets across the region, most notably in Iran and Egypt.

As with the transmutation of AQI to ISI to ISIS, in the absence of a comprehensive plan to address the regional security dilemma left behind since the invasion of Iraq, as well as myriad crises of political legitimacy in the wake of the Arab Spring, even if ISIS's military capacities are totally degraded, its core ideology and raison d'être will likely survive. The destruction of ISIS can only come about as a result of a synchronized regional and international commitment to achieve lasting peace settlements in Syria and in Yemen, and to embark, then, on a regionwide postwar reconstruction and investment project that would serve as a foundation for joint cooperation and dispute resolution between Sunni- and Shia-majority states. The next section lays out the broad outlines of this alternative framework.

The Path Thus Far Not Taken

The preceding two sections have laid bare the promises and perils of the joint international and regional approaches to tackling the threat posed by ISIS. Although some of the promises of the U.S.-led international response have been fulfilled, such as slowing the progress of ISIS military units and degrading some of its core capacities, the underlying conditions that led to the emergence of the group in the first place remain mostly intact. With the recapture of Mosul in July 2017, and repatriation of most operational bases of ISIS in Iraq nearly complete, it is abundantly clear that dreams of a sprawling Islamic caliphate that redraws the map of the Middle East were just that, a mere chimera. Yet military success against ISIS was never really in dispute. It has no air force or navy; its supplies of weaponry and fighters were paltry even at the height of the group's power; and its leadership and command structure were always built to function as a terrorist entity, not as a state. These fundamental flaws became exposed within days of sustained air attacks against ISIS's leadership, supply routes, and weapons depots. As the previous section made clear, the regional actors never doubted any of these inevitabilities either. Rather, the truly shocking aspect of ISIS's expansion—to these countries and in the view of veteran observers of the Middle East—was what it revealed about the depths of decay and obsolescence of purportedly "robust" and "resilient" authoritarian states in the region. ISIS's rise, arriving on the heels of the Arab Spring, exposed the relative ease with which even the coercive powers of these states could be challenged. What is more, it testified to the general impotence and ineptitude of regional organizations such as the GCC, the Arab League, and the Organization of Islamic Cooperation in the face of a transnational threat to their member countries.

ISIS's emergence and expansion, therefore, must be placed squarely within the context of state failure and institutional ineptitude at the regional level. The internal and external circumstances that led to this permissive environment must be factored into any strategy designed to destroy transnational extremist movements bent on exploiting security vacuums and establishing alternative zones of authority. After all, ISIS is not the only symptom of state failure. In Iraq and Syria, nonjihadist militias (for example, Iran-backed Shia militias such as the Mahdi Army in Iraq or the Defenders of the Shrine in Syria) have also taken advantage of the security vacuum to exact revenge on their enemies and pursue the interests of their foreign state sponsors. It follows, therefore, that efforts to rebuild state security and institutional capacities must be a top priority for any counter-ISIS coalition. Yet little to no mention of such priorities is made in either of the strategic frameworks produced by the U.S.-led Global Coalition or its regional analogues. The omission is not terribly surprising, however. The counter-ISIS coalitions were assembled to merely address the symptom of the reigning disorder, not the permissive environment itself. In this respect, the Global Coalition's mission to "degrade, and ultimately destroy" ISIS and its global affiliates is commensurate with its limited aims of simply neutralizing this particular menace at this particular time.

State-building is an expensive, labor-intensive, and extremely delicate proposition even in times of relative peace and prosperity, so the reluctance of major powers to engage in such projects in a historically volatile region such as the Middle East is understandable. Indeed, many assessments of the international response to the rise of ISIS begin with the obligatory acknowledgment of the utter undesirability of such endeavors. But almost all of these analyses overlook the enormous costs—both human and material—associated with ignoring the permissive environments from which transnational and global jihadist threats have arisen. In the case of ISIS, the costs are almost immeasurable: the genocide of the Yezidi populations in Iraq; mass killings of captured Shia communities in Iraq and Syria; the forced internal displacement or mass exodus of millions of Syrians and Iraqis; a global refugee crisis; a wave of terrorist attacks around the globe—and these are just some of the consequences that receive news coverage. ISIS's actions also have had highly destabilizing effects in Western societies. The terror attacks in Paris, Brussels, Nice, Orlando, and San Bernardino, for instance, resulted in calls to restrict immigration laws and the free movement of peoples, and also revived ethnonationalist movements in much of Europe and even in the United States.

Given the enormity of these implications for the region and the West, it is striking that no systematic accounting of the costs associated with chronic state failure has been issued to date. This is all the more remarkable given the long-established causal link—as identified by numerous studies by political scientists—between state failure and terrorism.[25] That the consequences of state failure transcend borders and can cross vast oceans is a much-studied phenomenon by social scientists; and yet it is increasingly overlooked by policymakers and state agencies burdened with overly specialized personnel, short-term mandates, and limited resources. Another key issue is the misunderstanding (or the conceit) that somehow only the United States or the great powers can or should rectify state failures. Hence the conclusion that no progress can be made to either build up state capacities or eradicate transnational terrorism without an explicit political, military, and economic commitment by a great power. To be sure, great power leadership is tremendously important in corralling other states and international organizations to share in the financial and military burdens necessary for successful state-building, but as the postinvasion period in Iraq made abundantly clear, even a superpower as economically and militarily well endowed as the United States cannot by itself (or even in cooperation with the U.K.) address issues arising from power-sharing, institution-building, ethnic and religious strife, corruption, and economic degradation. State capacity-building is tough, multigenerational work, which is why it must be entrusted to long-term institutional processes that extend beyond the momentary concerns of the great powers and policymakers.

Bearing in mind these realities and limitations, a synthetic framework that bridges the gap between the international and regional responses would consist of three major components. First, there must be an international commission tasked with investigating the permissive conditions under which ISIS first emerged and has since thrived. The commission's report should also provide empirical metrics for assessing the annual costs associated with the collapse of key state institutions and provisions in Syria and Iraq since ISIS's inception (including the losses of life, human capital, public health, economic output, and foreign investment; international restrictions placed on the country; and the like). Second, the findings and recommendations made by the commission would form the basis of a "regional trusteeship" that could act as a cooperative among the major powers in the region—Iran, Saudi Arabia, Turkey, and Egypt—for streamlining political, economic, military, and humanitarian policies. The objective here would be to establish trust between Shia- and Sunni-majority states around the twin imperatives of deradicalization and state capacity-building. Last, there should be a UN

Security Council resolution authorizing the establishment of a multinational antiterror force for the Middle East tasked with carrying out the mission of the U.S.-led Global Coalition. The rationale for such an initiative is to include major stakeholders—such as Russia, Iran, and China—that are excluded from the coalition's military, political, financial, and anti–ISIS propaganda efforts.

These proposals, to be sure, require a great deal more reflection and elaboration. At any rate, they do not constitute the main purpose of this chapter, which is to provide an overview of the existing international and regional responses to ISIS and to cast a critical eye on the differences and contradictions between them. It is my hope that the preceding has shed light on some of the more glaring gaps between diagnostic analyses of ISIS's rise and the policy prescriptions implemented or proposed. In particular, I have endeavored to demonstrate how the counter-ISIS campaign, both internationally and regionally, is undermined by a muddled understanding of ISIS as both a symptom and a cause of state failure in the region. Just as the post-9/11 fascination with degrading and destroying al Qaeda unwittingly resulted in the neglect of underlying causes and permissive conditions, so too, alas, have the current approaches to countering ISIS been too narrowly focused on merely removing the existing threat. It is high time that the corrosive consequences of dispossession and extremism that arise in failing or collapsed states are met with appropriate remedies.

Notes

1 ISIS's unforeseen offensives deep into Iraqi and Syrian territories also constituted an intelligence failure on the part of Western intelligence agencies. For more on this, see Erik Dahl's chapter in this volume.
2 The White House, "Statement by the President on ISIS," Washington, September 10, 2014 (www.whitehouse.gov/the-press-office/2014/09/10/statement-president-ISIS-1).
3 U.S. Department of Defense, "Operation Inherent Resolve," Special Reports, December 2, 2016 (www.defense.gov/News/Special-Reports/0814_Inherent-Resolve).
4 Ibid.

5 Global Coalition, "Plenary Meeting of the Global Coalition–Progress Up-date," Washington, November 28, 2016 (http://theglobalcoalition.org/us -led-plenary-meeting-to-discuss-progress/).

6 Department of State, "Factsheet: The Global Coalition to Counter Daesh," Washington, July 21, 2016 (www.state.gov/s/seci/261626.htm).

7 A June 2014 report estimated that ISIS's financial fortunes exceeded $2 billion, which would make it the richest jihadist organization in the world. Martin Chulov, "How an Arrest in Baghdad Revealed ISIS's $2 Billion Jihad-ist Network," *The Guardian*, June 15, 2014 (www.theguardian.com/world /2014/jun/15/iraq-isis-arrest-jihadists-wealth-power).

8 Terrence McCoy, "ISIS Just Stole $425 million, Iraqi Governor Says, and Became the 'World's Richest Terrorist Group,'" *Washington Post*, June 12, 2014.

9 For early reporting on Saudi and Qatari financing of ISIS, see Josh Rogin, "America's Allies Are Funding ISIS," *Daily Beast*, June 14, 2014 (www .thedailybeast.com/articles/2014/06/14/america-s-allies-are-funding-isis .html); Patrick Cockburn, "Iraq Crisis: How Saudi Arabia Helped ISIS Take Over the North of the Country," *The Independent*, July 12, 2014 (www .independent.co.uk/voices/comment/iraq-crisis-how-saudi-arabia -helped-isis-take-over-the-north-of-the-country-9602312.html); Steve Clemons, "'Thank God for the Saudis': ISIS, Iraq, and the Lessons of Blowback," *The Atlantic*, June 23, 2014; Lori Plotkin Boghardt, "Qatar Is a U.S. Ally. They Also Knowingly Abet Terrorism. What's Going On?," *New Republic*, October 6, 2014 (https://newrepublic.com/article/119705/ why-does-qatar-support-known-terrorists).

10 Global Coalition, "Countering Daesh Financing and Economic Resources—Progress Update," Washington, July 29, 2016 (http://theglobalcoalition.org /countering-daesh-financing-economic-resources-progress-update/).

11 "Sectarianization" is too complex and broad a category to be examined in isolation from regional dynamics. For a comprehensive and recent consid-eration of this dynamic in the Middle East, see Nader Hashemi and Danny Postel, eds., *Sectarianization: Mapping the New Politics of the Middle East* (Lon-don: Hurst, 2016).

12 Jacob Silverman, "'Paris Is on Fire," *Politico Magazine*, November 14, 2015 (www.politico.com/magazine/story/2015/11/paris-is-on-fire-213359).

13 Patrick Cockburn, "Whose Side Is Turkey On?," *London Review of Books* 36 (November 6, 2014): 8. Also see Cockburn's excellent book on the for-mation of ISIS, *The Rise of Islamic State: ISIS and the New Sunni Revolution* (London: Verso, 2015).

14 See books by Joby Warrick, *Black Flags: The Rise of ISIS* (New York: An-chor Books, 2015) and Fawaz Gerges, *ISIS: A History* (Princeton University Press, 2016).

15 Curtis Ryan, "Regional Responses to the Rise of ISIS," *Middle East Report* 45, no. 276 (Fall 2015) (www.merip.org/mer/mer276/regional-responses -rise-isis).

16 David Kilcullen, the former chief strategist in the Office of the Coordinator for Counterterrorism in the State Department, put it more directly: "There Undeniably Would Be No ISIS if We Had Not Invaded Iraq," *The Independent*, March 4, 2016 (www.independent.co.uk/news/world/middle -east/iraq-war-invasion-caused-isis-islamic-state-daesh-saysus-military -adviser-david-kilcullen-a6912236.html).

17 For a geopolitical account of Iran's role as the guardian of Shia interests in the region, see Vali Nasr, *The Shi'a Revival: How Conflicts within Islam Will Shape the Future* (New York: W.W. Norton, 2006).

18 For a recent and excellent historical study of the Guards, see Afshon Ostovar, *Vanguard of the Imam: Religion, Politics, and Iran's Revolutionary Guards* (Oxford University Press, 2016).

19 W. Andrew Terrill, "Iran's Strategy for Saving Asad," *Middle East Journal* 69 (Spring 2015): 222–36.

20 Ray Takeyh and Reuel Marc Gerecht have argued that, in fact, Iran has used the ISIS threat as a pretext for further consolidating its power base in Iraq and Syria. "Iran's ISIS Trap," *Foreign Affairs*, November 15, 2015 (www .foreignaffairs.com/articles/syria/2015-11-15/irans-isis-trap). Although there is some truth to this assertion, the historical record also clearly demonstrates that the Islamic Republic's support of Shia militias in Iraq and of military and economic aid to the Syrian regime predate the advent of ISIS.

21 For an in-depth analysis of the Saudi efforts at counterrevolution tactics, see Project on Middle East Political Science, "The Saudi Counter-Revolution," POMEPS Briefing 5, August 9, 2011 (www.pomeps.org/wp -content/uploads/2011/08/POMEPS_BriefBooklet5_SaudiArabia_web .pdf). On Qatar's role, see Kristian Coates Ulrichsen, *Qatar and the Arab Spring* (Oxford University Press, 2014). It must also be noted that a major dimension of these dynamics is the political economy of oil, which, as the historian Toby Craig Jones has argued, is a major imperative, especially in Saudi strategic thinking, affecting Iran's relations with Western powers. As he rather bluntly puts it: "Saudi counterrevolution is not just about an oppressive regime being oppressive. Nor does it simply aim to rescue the authoritarian order and the close-knit family of tyrants that has long dominated the political status quo in the region. There is another imperative at work. It is the desperate urge to protect the kingdom's regional hegemony and, most important, the advantage it garners from an oil-dependent, global political economy." Toby Craig Jones, "Saudi Arabia versus the Arab Spring," *Raritan* 32 (Fall 2011): 44–45.

22 For a definitive account of Saudi Arabia's sectarian domestic and foreign policy, and its relations to Saudi Shia, see Toby Matthiessen, *The Other Saudis: Shiism, Dissent and Sectarianism* (Cambridge University Press, 2014). In response to Sheikh Nimr's execution, the Saudi embassy in Tehran was attacked and set on fire.

23 A case in point was Turkey's handling of a major suicide bombing in late July 2015 in the border town of Suruç, which marked the beginning of Turkey's participation in the coalition against ISIS. As Ian Bremmer noted at the time, "In response to the Suruç bombing, Turkish police launched security raids across the country, rounding up more than 1,300 suspects in a matter of days. But the number of PKK militants detained outnumber ISIS affiliates more than 6 to 1. Between July 23 and July 26, 75 Turkish jets flew 155 sorties against 400 or so PKK targets. Number of ISIS targets hit? Three." Ian Bremmer, "These 5 Stats Explain Turkey's War on ISIS— and the Kurds," *Time*, July 31, 2015.

24 Conflict Armament Research, "Tracing the Supply of Components Used in Islamic State IEDs," London, February 2016 (www.conflictarm.com /publications/).

25 James A. Piazza, "Incubators of Terror: Do Failed and Failing States Promote Transnational Terrorism?," *International Studies Quarterly* 52, no. 3 (2008): 469-88; Robert I. Rotberg, ed., *State Failure and State Weakness in a Time of Terror* (Brookings Institution Press, 2003).

8

Regional Constraints on the U.S. Confrontation of ISIS

Feisal al-Istrabadi

Perhaps no utterance by a president of the United States has been so quickly and so thoroughly proven wrong as when President Barack Obama asserted that the Islamic State in Iraq and Syria (ISIS) was a "jayvee team," a locution that national security official Antony Blinken also used. It was telling that the man who described ISIS as a strategic threat to U.S. interests was fired as secretary of defense, while, by contrast, Blinken was elevated to the number two position at the Department of State. Within a matter of months, ISIS rampaged through Iraq, occupying its second largest city, Mosul, in four hours. The Iraqi Army initially collapsed under the onslaught, though the Americans would claim that the Iraqi prime minister ignored intelligence warnings delivered just days earlier.

The United States and regional powers began engaging in military operations in June 2014 to dislodge ISIS, first from Iraq, but also from Syria. The military campaigns to defeat ISIS and liberate lands it had occupied have been officially declared over in both Iraq and Syria, though ISIS cells continue to operate in both countries. Still, insufficient attention has been paid to what a post-ISIS dispensation in Iraq and Syria might be. This is partly due to an incoherent alliance structure, in which the disparate states engaged to varying degrees in the fight do not share a strategic objective. While some of the international and regional powers were genuinely engaged in a fight to rid the region of this terrorist menace, others had competing agendas that often superseded the fight against ISIS. These competing interests often resulted in hampering the U.S. effort.

U.S. policy over the years, certainly throughout the Obama administration, has also hampered the fight against ISIS by failing to consider adequately what a post-ISIS political settlement would consist of. Indeed, for more than a decade U.S. policy has consisted of supporting personalities in Iraq, rather than pursuing good governance and the institutions of government. It also largely disengaged from Iraqi politics from 2012 to 2014, except to the extent that it put its weight against a constitutional effort to engender a parliamentary vote of no-confidence in the then-incumbent prime minister. The United States did so not because there was any constitutional infirmity in the parliamentary move, but because it supported the person who was then in office and could not conceive of a replacement. The blood of many Iraqis and American soldiers was spilled as a result of that decision, which drove many in the Iraqi Sunni community to acquiesce—at least at a critical juncture—to ISIS as an alternative to the government in Baghdad. No more thought has since been given to a political settlement in post-ISIS Iraq. The same situation exists in Syria, where the United States has never had a cogent political strategy.

After this introduction, the first section outlines the strategic interests of Iran, the Arab states, Turkey, and Russia. The competing motivations of these players are considered, in contrast to U.S. interests with respect to ISIS. Throughout this chapter it is assumed that the United States had a vital national security interest in defeating ISIS, both militarily and as an ideology. The latter, of course, is a much more difficult proposition and cannot be accomplished through military force. The chapter concludes by assessing the implications for future U.S. policy. In the absence of inclusive political settlements in Iraq and Syria, new iterations of ISIS are likely to appear in the future, each of which will require U.S. involvement.

An Incoherent Alliance Structure and
Constraints on U.S. Policy

The Obama administration left a legacy of a complicated, and at times irreconcilable, network of alliances and rivalries across the Middle East, one that defies easy characterization. The United States is allied with the Baghdad government, which is itself allied with Iran in the fight against ISIS. In Syria, in contrast, the Obama administration took an exceptionally hard rhetorical line against Iran's long-term ally, Bashar al-Assad, whom both the Iraqi and Iranian governments have supported with men and materiel. Turkey, a NATO ally, played an ambivalent role in both Syria and Iraq with respect to ISIS, at least during the Obama administration, though it has since adapted itself to Russia's efforts in Syria. Turkey's president, Recep Tayyip Erdoğan, initially demanded Assad's departure, but now accommodates Russia's support of him, more concerned with Kurdish aspirations in Syria than with the fight against ISIS. Iran's expanding influence in the region motivates America's Arab allies in the Gulf and beyond. For its part, the Trump administration encouraged an open rift in the delicate alliance structure of the Gulf states. A contretemps between Saudi Arabia, the United Arab Emirates, and Bahrain, on the one hand, and Qatar, on the other, has erupted into a major diplomatic row, with Kuwait and Oman maintaining neutrality between the competing states. No clear U.S. strategy exists in the region unifying the various players, even with respect to ISIS and any of its future incarnations.

Beyond the regional players, the United States was forced to confront the reality of the Russian pro-Assad intervention in September 2015. Having failed to act in Syria over the span of five years, the United States may well have been frozen in contemplation of what a Russian reaction to U.S. intervention might entail. Instead, the United States was surprised that it may have encouraged Russian action by its own inaction. In the event, Russia initially intervened only to stabilize Assad, whose regime appeared to be on the verge of collapse. Once Assad was sufficiently secure, Russia ceased its intervention. Only later did it reengage, escalating its support for the Assad regime to ensure not merely his survival but his control over significant parts of Syria. The second phase of Vladimir Putin's intervention has put an end to talk of a post-Assad Syria—for now.

Candidate Donald Trump pledged to support whoever was fighting ISIS. That, of course, would include Iran, since there is no doubt that Iran has been fighting ISIS in Iraq. Syria is more problematic because, as several studies have shown, neither the Assad regime nor the Russians principally targeted ISIS. Instead, they have as a rule attacked the non-ISIS opposition to Assad in a transparent effort to ensure to the extent possible that the choice remained between ISIS and an unrepentant Assad. That strategy has largely worked and more or less set the stage that confronts U.S. policymakers in 2018 and will do so going forward. The complication from an American point of view, however, is that it ensures Iran's longest-term ally in the region survives the civil war and continues to be a player, to the chagrin of most of America's Arab allies in the region. Undoubtedly, Saudi Arabia and its regional allies will see Assad's survival—in whatever form—as a win for Iran and concomitantly a loss for them. These divergent concerns operate as a constraint on U.S. policy, making coherent choices very difficult. The interests and roles of each of these countries are considered in detail in the rest of the chapter.

Iran

ISIS's rise in Syria and Iraq challenged Iran's regional hegemonic ambitions directly. Although ISIS was never a threat to unseat the new dispensation in Baghdad, where the Shia are a large majority, the minority Alawite government in Damascus could easily have been brought down by action, whether coordinated or not, of non–ISIS and ISIS factions. Moreover, even if Baghdad's government was unlikely to have fallen to ISIS, the total and complete chaos that would result from ISIS going unchallenged in Iraq would be dangerous to Iran's own security, especially as ISIS gained a foothold in Diyala Governorate on the Iranian border with Iraq. Aside from a direct danger to Iran, much of the so-called strategic depth that Iran has amassed since the overthrow of the Shah lay at risk.

Iran's role in the region has undergone a remarkable metamorphosis since the Islamic revolution of 1979. At that time, Iran was isolated from regional affairs, becoming rather a pariah after being the first Middle Eastern state proper to legislate its version of political Islam. As a revolutionary regime it sought to export its revolutionary zeal to the region.[1] It is worth recalling that Khomeini's discourse in the early days of the revolution was couched in terms of a more popular appeal to Islam generally, not Shiism as such. The response of the Gulf monarchies, as well as other Arab states, was to "brace for war" in the hope that Iraq could be an effective bulwark to restrain Iran.[2] Thus, from the very beginning of the Iranian Revolution, many of the Arab governments looked upon Iran as expansionist and sought to curb its ambitions.

Of the major Arab states in the region, only Syria's Baathist government, bitter rival of its Iraqi counterpart by the time of the commencement of hostilities, tilted toward Iran.[3] This set the stage for what has been a Syrian-Iranian alliance of nearly forty years' standing. The benefits, of course, were mutual. Hafez al-Assad, Bashar's father, saw in Iran a counterpoise to two neighboring rivals, Israel on the one hand (this was in the days leading up to the Camp David Accords) and Iraq on the other. For his part, Khomeini found in Assad an ally who could act as a conduit for the Shia in Lebanon, including especially Hezbollah.[4] Yet lest a sectarian narrative be assumed, it should be recalled that Iran's influence would extend into the Gaza Strip over Hamas, a Sunni religio-political organization akin to the Muslim Brotherhood.[5]

Thus, over the decades after the revolution, Iran slowly acquired greater regional influence. By 2003 the United States had removed Iran's bitter enemy, Saddam Hussein, from power, and a Shia political class, much of whose leadership had spent decades in exile in Iran or Syria, was ensconced in Baghdad. From 1979 to the time of ISIS's spectacular apogee in 2014, Iran went from an isolated, besieged revolutionary state to one that had regional influence that extended from the Persian Gulf through Baghdad, Damascus, southern Lebanon, and Gaza, the latter all on the Mediterranean Sea. Thus, to borrow a phrase from the geopolitics of another part of the world, Syria has remained Iran's "near abroad," an important lynchpin in Iran's rise and continued influence, and death and succession within the Assad family did nothing to alter this relationship.

Iran's strategic interest in Syria in light of ISIS has been clear: it is to ensure not merely the survival of the Alawite dispensation in Damascus, but also the personal survival of Bashar al-Assad. In this respect, at least considering the first incarnation of Russia's intervention, there was a rhetorical divide between Russia and Iran. Initially, Foreign Minister Sergei Lavrov indicated that Russia did not have the personal survival of Assad as a strategic goal. Whether that was mere rhetoric even at that stage, there had been no indication that Iran would brook a change of personality that the Lavrov statement might have suggested. By the time of the second incarnation of Russia's involvement, it seems both countries were firmly on the same side: if Obama said Assad had to go, Russia and Iran agreed that Assad must stay. At this writing, they are attempting to return control over most, if not all, of Syria to Assad. For both Russia and Iran the ideal would be a return to a unitary state with Assad firmly at the helm.

Iran's calculation in fighting ISIS in Iraq is quite different. The last thing Iran wants is a stable, strong state. Here, U.S. and Iranian calculations diverge significantly and irreconcilably. It is in the U.S. interest to achieve a coherent, stable Iraq and its various subparts, including the Kurdistan region of Iraq. Revanchist tendencies jeopardize American interests by threatening to engulf the region in even greater wars in the future, both among the new statelets and between new and precursor states.

For Iran, however, in contrast to its ideal resolution in Syria, a coherent, stable Iraq approaches an existential threat. Much of the current political and military leadership in Iran was burnished during the Iran-Iraq War. Supreme Leader Ali Khamenei, for instance, was president of Iran throughout most of the war. The commander of the Quds Brigade of the Iranian Revolutionary Guard Corps, Major-General Qasem Soleimani, was a twenty-three-year-old officer when the war began. (How ironic it was that he assumed the responsibility of coordinating the defense of Baghdad against a feared ISIS attack in 2014. He did the same for Erbil, even as the United States bombed ISIS positions when the group sought to take the regional capital.) For the Iranian leadership a reemergence of strong state institutions in Baghdad is a nightmare. American policymakers in the George W. Bush and Obama administrations seemingly never understood this reality, assuming instead that if they accommodated Iran's "legitimate" interests in Iraq they would work to strengthen Baghdad's institutions. This was always an American fantasy. Whether the Trump administration eschews it remains to be seen.

But the total collapse of the Iraqi state is not in Iran's interest either. ISIS's obtaining a permanent foothold in Iraq threatens Iran in several ways. It does so directly in that ISIS would naturally regard Iran's Shiite theocracy as apostate and could well take its campaign of terror across a rather porous border. The route for exporting such terror might not be so far-fetched. ISIS initially established a beachhead in Diyala Governorate, on the Iranian border with its Khuzestan Province. Khuzestan, of course, is a predominantly Arab province, where there is a Sunni minority. ISIS might well think it could find supporters in that population and would no doubt look for those who were disenchanted with Tehran. In the event, Iran could not take that chance, and Diyala was one of the first and most active engagements of IRGC ground forces in Iraq, an area where the United States simultaneously targeted ISIS from the air, in effect supporting Iranian ground action. While the total chaos of June 2014 is anathema to Iran, as Denise Natali stated once in a panel on which this author also served, the ideal for Iran is Nuri al-Maliki's Iraq in 2013: internecine fighting preventing the rise of rational and stable state institutions, occasional al Qaeda attacks to keep Baghdad off balance, but not total chaos.

While Iran's policy has been to defend against the possibility that ISIS might genuinely threaten the predominantly Shii dispensation in Baghdad, it has no necessary allegiance to one or another particular political figure in Iraq as it does in Syria. Any of a range of political actors would satisfy its strategic interests in Iraq, principally because the major political figures from the Shii religious parties are not a threat to basic Iranian interests in Iraq. To the contrary, they are willing to accommodate those interests. Nothing exemplifies Iran's flexibility more than its prior support for Nuri al-Maliki until he became a liability when he proved wholly inadequate in the face of ISIS's rise in 2014. With U.S. coordination, Iran dumped Maliki and supported the rise of Haider al-Abadi, who became prime minister of Iraq in 2014. As Maliki tries to undermine his successor in order to return to power, it remains to be seen what Iran's response will be: to support him, Abadi, or some other candidate.

There is perhaps an exception—or at least a codicil—to the proposition that Iran does not support any particular individual in Iraq. The IRGC clearly has its favorites in Iraq, most particularly in the Popular Mobilization Units (PMUs). These individuals include Hadi Ameri, Abu Mahdi al-Muhandis, and Qais al-Khazali. It is likely that these militia leaders, who operate within the established Iraqi chain of command officially but not in reality, represent an insurance policy that the Iranian regime maintains against less-than-compliant political figures. It is also possible that Iranian officialdom is itself divided on Iraq, with different Iranian factions supporting different individuals within the Iraqi polity. It is quite likely that such a cacophony of voices exists in Iranian policy toward Iraq, though the overarching strategic interest against Iraq becoming a stable, coherent state remains.

The Arab States

Much of what motivates current thinking in the Arab states is a desire to check perceived Iranian dominance over what King Abdullah II of Jordan once infelicitously described as a "Shia crescent."[6] The fear—a great deal of it unfounded—is of a nascent neo-Persian empire that stretches through Iraq, Bahrain, Yemen, Syria, and southern Lebanon. Thus, when members of the Shia majority in Bahrain demonstrated in Pearl Roundabout in Manama, Saudi Arabia sent troops—at the invitation of the king of Bahrain—to crush the protests. The Gulf states saw the hand of Iran in these demonstrations, rather than a disenfranchised population seeking its legitimate rights. Similarly, when a civil war between Yemeni factions resulted in the Houthis taking the capital, Iran's sinister hand was seen in the region, and Saudi Arabia and its allies unleashed a war in Yemen that continues to pulverize that hapless country, though to what end is unclear.

In this context, most of the Arab states have been far less concerned with ISIS's rise than with Iran's. The most definitive action taken by Saudi Arabia in light of the rise of ISIS in the summer of 2014 was not to send its ample air force to pound ISIS targets, but to build a wall on its border with Iraq.[7] Lost, perhaps, on the Saudi leadership was that, while the border wall might prevent a land invasion by ISIS, it would do nothing to appease ISIS sympathizers who lived within the kingdom or reduce their ability to plan and carry out terrorist attacks there. Saudi Arabia and the Gulf states simply do not perceive the existence of ISIS as the existential threat that it is for Iraq. The congruence of much of Wahhabism and Salafism, ideologies present throughout the Gulf states and elsewhere in the region, with that of ISIS and the ease with which the former could lead to the latter, has caused no urgency in these states to defeat ISIS. If the defeat of ISIS is a matter of priority to the Gulf states, they have kept the fact safely secret.

The Arab states generally do not appear to share America's concerns about the threat that ISIS poses. As the United States ramped up its fight against ISIS in Iraq, and as the Trump administration spoke of cooperating with Russia in the Syrian theater, the Arab states made no indication that they regard ISIS as a threat to their interests or to regional stability. Indeed, in chapter 7 of this volume Hussein Banai argues that the Gulf states regard ISIS as a positive, a check on Iran's ambitions. The Trump administration has spoken of a need to accelerate the effort against ISIS in Iraq, and candidate Trump spoke of the possibility of creating safe havens in Syria. Both strategies would have entailed expending far greater resources in personnel as well as materiel, yet none of the Arab states indicated a willingness to assist in the effort.

Instead, Saudi Arabia, the Gulf states, Jordan, and their allies have focused their wrath on Yemen—with American logistical support—and the perceived Iranian role there. What the strategic objective of these countries is seems opaque. If it is to restore the presidency of Abdrubbuh Hadi, the literature on restoring governments defeated in civil wars should not buoy the coalition's hopes. It is more likely that they will "prolong the conflict, producing more death and devastation" and "[overstress] the intervening state—especially when that state has limited capabilities and internal problems of its own."[8] This, of course, while draining their own resources. Notwithstanding these dangers to the interveners, they nonetheless made intervening in Yemen a strategic priority over defeating ISIS.

Saudi Arabia's challenge to Iran has become so central to its regional policy that it has co-opted several competing imperatives of long standing. Acting with the United Arab Emirates and Bahrain, Saudi Arabia has shattered the veneer of unity, for decades its hallmark, of the Gulf Co-operation Council (GCC), by confronting Qatar over its economic ties to Iran and its supposed support for Islamist extremists in the region. Qatar does indeed have to guard its economic relationship with Iran, with whom it shares its principal asset—other than the U.S. air base it hosts—the world's largest nonassociated natural gas field. Qatar also does support Islamist militant groups in places like Syria, amongst others, but here its sin seems to be in choosing the wrong flavor of militants: the other Gulf states also support various other Islamist groups in the region. Kuwait and Oman, the other two members of the GCC, have tried but failed to broker a compromise between the factions, again contributing to the evident fracturing of the GCC. The end result has been to push Qatar closer to Turkey and possibly to Iran, too. The other imperative shattered by the current Saudi leadership—though its implications are far beyond the scope of this chapter—is the all-but-open cooperation between the kingdom and Israel in their mutual confrontation with Iran, an effect that has been brewing since the Obama administration concluded the Joint Comprehensive Plan of Action with Iran.

Of course, it cannot be gainsaid that these Arab states' ignoring the ISIS threat is also in keeping with popular sentiment in their respective countries. Jordan's example in actively and publicly participating in the initial days of the fight against ISIS is instructive. When ISIS burned Lt. Muath al-Kasasbeh alive, the immediate reaction in Jordan and the Arab states was fury, calling for quick and overwhelming retaliation.[9] But once tempers cooled (and Jordan initially did undertake massive retaliations that included the execution of ISIS members caught in Jordan), there was reporting to the effect that ordinary citizens had begun wondering out loud why Jordan was participating in the "West's" war on ISIS.[10] The Jordanian government for its part quietly dropped out of the coalition against ISIS and instead joined the Saudi-led effort in Yemen.

Aside from domestic public opinion—no small consideration—it is curious that these states so abandoned the fight against ISIS. The radical group surely represents as great a threat to Jordan as it does to Iraq. Recalling that Abu Musab al-Zarqawi, the leader of al Qaeda in Iraq, a predecessor organization of ISIS, was Jordanian, it is easily predictable that, in Jordan and other Arab states, ISIS's nihilistic ideology will find supporters. Although these states are not weak like Iraq or Syria, still, as ISIS is defeated and predictably changes its tactics to those of a classical terrorist organization, these regional Arab states will be no less susceptible than Iraq to violent convulsions. It was shortsighted for these states not to engage ISIS directly and in a sustained fashion, except that, perhaps, they expected Uncle Sam to do the heavy lifting—to their ultimate benefit—while they engage in Yemen.

Above all, the coalition of states led by Saudi Arabia fears a new Sykes-Picot Agreement emerging a century after the original. Sykes-Picot, contrary to modern myths made a century later, did not devise the current borders of the Middle East, nor did it purport to do so. Instead, in 1916 it divided the Middle East into spheres of influence between the presumptively victorious powers, though Russia dealt itself out of the deal through the intermediation of the revolution. The Arab states today fear a de facto concession to Iran that it may reliably maintain its spheres of influence throughout the northern Gulf to the Mediterranean. Indeed, President Obama's statement to the effect that Saudi Arabia must learn "to share" the Middle East with Iran, could be interpreted in no other way in Riyadh and its allied capitals.[11]

From Obama's perspective, the statement may have merely reflected reality. The United States was unwilling to invest troops or resources to counter Iran in Lebanon, Syria, or Iraq. It was, however, willing to do so in Yemen, presumably because it is in the Saudi sphere of influence. The Saudis have not been sanguine about Obama's remark, and some in the Saudi leadership view it as another example of Obama's fecklessness or weakness, especially where Iran is concerned. Trump's anti-Iranian expressions are thus music to their ears. Whether the new administration will be any more willing to expend resources in the effort to dislocate Iran from its sphere remains to be seen, although whether the U.S.

taxpayer is eager for another confrontation in the Middle East is doubtful.

Iraq's interests are treated very briefly in this section. It suffices now to say that Iraqis had few goals in common, even if they generally shared one important one: to defeat ISIS. In this respect Iraq was a much easier place in which to combat ISIS than Syria, because all the players in the country were shooting in the same direction, though there were relatively minor skirmishes after the referendum in Baghdad's reassertion of its constitutional authority over disputed territories. The situation is distinctly different in Syria, where it has been by no means clear that all the various factions are united in confronting ISIS. As noted, the Syrian government itself, along with its Russian allies, at least delayed confronting ISIS as it destroyed non-ISIS opponents. Iraq was different. All Iraqi forces—regardless of sect or ethnicity—were united in an offensive that has eliminated ISIS in Iraq, at least as a force capable of gaining and holding territory. The problems in Iraq relate to the inability of its politicians, and repeated American policy failures over the years, to develop a political modus vivendi that allows a calming of fears and the reconstitution of a reasonably coherent state.

Turkey

It is not an exaggeration to say that, for Turkey, ISIS has been an afterthought. Like the Arab states, it has been motivated by considerations other than the inherent dangers that ISIS poses to the region and the international community. It is concerned by the possibility of Kurdish autonomy in Syria and what had been talk of Kurdish independence in Iraq. Turkey, in general, wholly failed to assist in the U.S. effort against ISIS, notwithstanding it being a NATO ally. It did cooperate with Russia in Syria, after some earlier erratic behavior on its part.

Early in the Syrian civil war, when it looked as if the Assad regime was headed for a certain fall, Turkey announced its own version of the Obama statement that Assad had to go. This must have come as a surprise in Damascus, as the Assads and the Erdoğans had been known to be friends and taken couples' vacations together. It was an unanticipated about-face, but it came at a time when Erdoğan seemed to be pining openly for a reconstituted neo–Ottoman Empire under his tutelage. Perhaps he sought to expand his regional influence, especially with Saudi Arabia and Iran, by getting out ahead of what at the time seemed inevitable.

Assad's fortunes turned, of course. This was partly due to U.S. inaction and its failure to support a moderate opposition at a time when it might have become an effective force. It was also partly due to the fragmentary nature of the opposition to Assad. Still, Turkey, like the rest of the world, was surprised when Vladimir Putin committed Russian military forces to prop up Assad, the single most decisive factor in Assad's survival. But in the days of this first phase of the Russian intervention, Turkey remained implacably opposed to the Syrian tyrant. Significantly, it downed a Russian Air Force jet that had strayed (perhaps intentionally) over its airspace, the first time a NATO country had done so since the Korean War. Turkey remained defiant and obtained the public support of its NATO allies. (There can be no doubt that Putin had been testing NATO defenses in Turkey and elsewhere, though one might still think it a foolhardy escalation to shoot to kill, even if Erdoğan has yet to suffer any comeuppance from Putin for doing so.)

Ankara changed its blustery tone in Syria when it became clear that the Russian strategy had metamorphosed into a second phase. By then Russia's intervention was not intended merely to prevent Assad from falling, but to help him regain lost ground and hang on to power, even if in a de facto "rump" Syria. As the Russian strategy appeared to be working, Turkey recalculated its interests, too. If Assad was to survive, Turkey could not take a chance that he might make a peace with the Syrian Kurds that would be distasteful to Ankara and its decades-old fight with the PKK, allied with the Kurdish militias in Syria. If Turkey wanted to affect the status of the Syrian Kurds in a post–civil war dispensation that still included Assad, it needed to be a player on the winning side— or at least not be associated with the losing side. Thus another Turkish about-face ensued with respect to Russia (though not to Assad).

Turkey continues not to support Assad. It continues to support opposition groups on the ground. Its principal mission in Syria, however, is to ensure that Kurdish YPG forces allied with the PKK, which it considers a terrorist organization, do not gain a foothold akin to that of Iraq's Kurds. To that end, and no doubt giving in to the Realpolitik consideration that Russia has the muscle to ensure Assad's survival, Turkey appears to have worked out an arrangement with Russia to ensure that Kurdish aspirations in Syria are managed more to its satisfaction. The quid pro quo for Putin is that he has gained an ally in the effort to defeat ISIS as he fights to expand Assad's control over territory he had previously lost.[12] It is fair to say that Turkey had been fighting ISIS as such only episodically.

Any such agreement between Turkey and Russia puts Turkey on a direct collision course with U.S. policy. Inherent in the Turco-Russian understanding is that the Russians will not arm YPG fighters. Turkey is adamant that YPG fighters not be armed or even used to fight ISIS.[13] For its part, the United States has committed to both arming and utilizing the YPG in the confrontation with ISIS in Syria.[14] This will be a very difficult circle to square in US-Turkish relations, as the Trump administration has announced that fighting ISIS is its priority in the Middle East. This fight simply has not been, and foreseeably will not be, the top priority for Turkey. Keeping Kurdish separatism in Syria in check will continue to be Turkey's first priority. At this writing, Turkey is actively attacking U.S-supported Kurdish forces in Afrin and other areas, despite the (so far only rhetorical) objections of the Trump administration.

In Iraq, Turkey's calculation is slightly different, though not altogether dissimilar. Before the 2003 downfall of the Saddamist regime in Iraq, Turkish foreign policy officials would become apoplectic at the mention of federalism in Iraq. Three successive Iraqi prime ministers from the Shiite Dawa Party, however, have demonstrated to Turkey what it regards as Baghdad's undue closeness to, and reliance on, Tehran. In this environment Turkey has, at least at times, played Erbil, the Iraqi Kurdistan regional capital, off against Baghdad. The game is clear: Turkey is leaving the option open to itself to create a buffer between it and a greater Iran, as Iranian dominance over the politics and security of Baghdad and points south has grown.

As recently as 2012, Ankara was clearly toying with the idea of Iraqi Kurdish independence. It has since backed away, partly under pressure from the United States, but also as the realities of what an independent Kurdish state in northern Iraq might mean for Syrian Kurds, and ultimately for Turkey's own Kurdish population. Still, relations between Erbil and Ankara are outstanding, including both political and economic relations, though Iraqi Kurdistan's abortive independence referendum severely tested those relations. Indeed, Turkey has a dominant hand in the economy of Iraqi Kurdistan, with Turkish agricultural and manufactured goods flooding the market. Some in Iraqi Kurdistan see this as their insurance policy that Turkey will have to maintain good relations with the regional government. Given the relative size of the two economies, however, it is certain that Turkey regards itself as having the upper hand, as any interruption of the trade between Turkey and Iraqi Kurdistan would have an immediate calamitous effect in the latter. Of course, Iraqi Kurdistan has two centers of power, one in Erbil, the other in Sulaimania. While Turkey enjoys good relations with Sulaimania too, it is evident that Iran has the lion's share of influence there.

Turkey has a third significant strategic objective in Iraq, one relating directly to its internal politics and security. Long before the fall of the previous regime in 2003, there were PKK bases in northern Iraq. Since that time, Turkey has undertaken periodic security operations in northern Iraq to maintain what is essentially a cordon sanitaire on the Iraqi side of the frontier. Both Baghdad and Erbil look away when Turkey undertakes these operations. This puts the Iraqi Kurdistan regional government in something of a delicate, even embarrassing, position. On the one hand, it allows Turkey to bombard PKK positions within Iraqi Kurdistan. On the other hand, it is allied with the PKK and its allies the PYG in Syria. It is not only the United States that has an intricate and sometimes contradictory web of alliances in the Middle East.

Russia

Russia's role in Syria is discussed at length in the earlier sections of this chapter, and those points will not be repeated here. It is worthwhile noting, however, that Russia's entry into the Syrian civil war constitutes its first major and direct foray into Middle Eastern politics since Anwar Sadat expelled the Soviet Union from Egypt in 1972. Clearly the Russian

Federation seeks to balance the United States and the other Western powers in the region. The Chinese have also joined this enterprise, though they have so far only used their weight against the United States and its allies in the corridors of the UN Security Council.[15]

It should be noted that the relationship between Russia and Syria has always been a mutually utilitarian one, at least according to one scholar, not one based on ideological empathy. Roy Allison has observed that the Soviets were well aware—having penetrated the Syrian Foreign Ministry and the Syrian embassy in Moscow, and even by bugging Hafez al-Assad's apartment on his visits there—that the elder Assad was a comparatively unenthusiastic ally.[16] Still, Syria gained arms and technical expertise while presumably the Soviet Union gained perceived benefit, including international prestige, by maintaining a foothold in the region. Allison is of the view that Russia and Syria now genuinely share a Weltanschauung regarding the sacrosanct nature of international borders and traditional concepts of sovereignty when it comes to regime change à la Iraq or Libya.[17] Paradoxically, he says that Syria was among the first states to support the Russian incursion into Georgia. He might also have noted that Syria's respect for the sovereignty of Lebanon is roughly equivalent to Russia's respect for Ukraine's. Still, Allison's larger point is intuitively correct that, at least in the Middle East, neither state wants Western powers to intervene, and certainly not to redraw the political map.

That is not to say, however, that Russia necessarily intervened to save Assad personally. Instead, Allison, writing before the first phase of the Russian military intervention in Syria, notes that Putin wishes to demonstrate personal steadfastness with his allies.[18] That is no doubt correct; in addition, he may have wanted to frustrate the United States and its allies in the region. Although initially Lavrov made a point of not arguing that it was necessary to keep Assad in power, that calculation might well have changed, at least for the nonce. In any case, more may be at play in Syria than Russia's steadfastness and joy at frustrating U.S. policy.

Angela Stent maintains that Russia's military intervention in Syria (she was writing during what this chapter refers to as the "first phase" of Russia's intervention) demonstrates that Russia "once again intends to be accepted as a global actor and play a part in every major international decision."[19] Rather disturbingly, she argues that Putin's steps in Syria represent a sort of inferiority complex, a response to Russia's "perceived exclusion from the post–Cold War European security order."[20] Here she references specifically NATO's expansion to include states once allied with—or part of—the Soviet Union. In her view, Putin's moves in Syria signal a desire for Russia to establish a sphere of "privileged interests," her explanation for his incursions into Georgia and Ukraine, too.[21]

In any event, there is one significant and noteworthy achievement that Russia has realized, and policymakers in Washington would do well to take note of it. According to Jeffrey Goldberg's interview with Obama,[22] administration officials were constantly concerned that an intervention in Syria would spiral out of control, using Vietnam as a cautionary tale. They regularly debated the pros and cons of committing in excess of 100,000 U.S. troops, à la Iraq, or standing by and doing nothing. Vladimir Putin proved—despite the use of indiscriminate bombing of civilians that caused horrific casualties—that it is possible for a power to intervene in the Middle East for a limited strategic purpose, and to do so without committing massive numbers of ground forces or sustaining high levels of casualties. That has been true in both phases of the Russian intervention, both the initial intervention to prevent the fall of Assad and the second phase to ensure he regained control of territory. Of course, Russia achieved these strategic aims in cooperation with Syrian ground forces (though that was almost certainly unnecessary in the first phase, where aerial bombardment was devastatingly sufficient). The point is that it is a strategy—now foreclosed after five years of civil war—the United States could also have deployed: arm and train Syrian opposition forces and support them from the air, at least sufficiently to convince Assad that he needed to negotiate. The failure of the Obama administration to do so constitutes an opportunity lost.

Conclusion: Implications for U.S. Foreign Policy in the Future

There was much talk over the years about "degrading and destroying" ISIS in the Obama administration. The Trump administration changed the rhetoric to "demolishing and destroying" the terrorist group. Such locutions suggest that what is required to destroy the group is mere martial vigor. Proponents of this language must think that an effort akin to that made in the Second World War, reduced in proportion given the threat, will suffice to destroy this group. They are mistaken.

To be sure, it was appropriate to destroy ISIS physically, to liberate the territories it once occupied, and to allow people whose homes are in those areas an opportunity to rebuild their lives. This is not merely advocacy of a philanthropic exercise on the part of the United States. It is a part of the vital national strategic interests of the country. There can be no doubt that, if it could, ISIS would launch attacks against the United States in a manner similar to the September 11 attacks. Its maintaining territory in Iraq and Syria meant that a particularly virulent and violent terrorist group had freedom of movement and the ability to establish terrorist training camps on a large scale to threaten the United States and its allies the world over. Indeed, the masses of refugees fleeing ISIS in Iraq, Syria, and elsewhere constitute a problem that has rocked the post–Cold War dispensation in Europe, with concomitant effects on U.S. foreign policy. Moreover, ISIS's existence on territory it took from host states constituted a kind of success that could have bred other "successes" in its efforts to radicalize others.

Still, it is well to recall that ISIS is quintessentially an ideology, however heinous and repulsive it may be. No ideology can be destroyed with guns and bombs alone. That much should be clear from the resurgence of neo-Nazi groups throughout Europe and, indeed, the United States. Its physical destruction, therefore, will not rid the world of this menace.

Rather, political settlements in both Iraq and Syria will be required to ensure that other iterations of ISIS do not arise again. As ISIS continues to lose ground, thus shrinking its so-called caliphate, it will predictably metamorphose into a classical terrorist organization that will simply engage in what are effectively hit-and-run tactics, albeit with suicide bombers. Indeed, it has already carried out such attacks in Iraq, even in the wake of losing the territory it once controlled.

The danger of failing to engender post-ISIS polities in which politics takes the place of violence is that it risks new iterations of ISIS becoming attractive again in the future as a short-term tactic for dealing with political disenfranchisement. This is what occurred in Iraq in 2014. A sufficient number of the Sunni there decided to look the other way as ISIS began to infiltrate Anbar and Ninevah Governorates, because they found Maliki's authoritarian policies and practices intolerable. If the politics of the country are not settled well, that process will predictably recur, and the United States will find itself back in the region fighting the next generation of terrorist organizations.

All factions in Iraq were clearly fighting against ISIS. That has been true since 2014. What is not clear, however, is what exactly the Iraqis have been fighting *for*. Certainly, ordinary rank-and-file soldiers in the Iraqi armed and security forces were fighting for a reunited Iraq. Just as certainly, Kurdistani Peshmerga forces were *not* fighting for a unified Iraq. But what of the Shia PMUs? Were they fighting to reunite Iraq under Baghdad's federal government or only to protect Baghdad and the predominantly Shia south from further incursions by terrorist groups? These are fundamentally political questions, but they are absolutely essential, because if the politics are not settled well, any military victory will be entirely ephemeral.

The United States has thus far failed to articulate a strategic vision for a post-ISIS Iraq. The U.S. Iraq team, originally appointed by Obama and kept in place by Trump, has been focused like a laser on retaking the next square meter from ISIS. It continues to believe in supporting individuals, rather than using the weight and expertise of the United States to help engender institutions of good governance. Current policy is and has been that, if Iraq's current prime minister successfully retakes territory occupied by ISIS, then his political fortunes will be strengthened and he will be able to make agreements for the post-ISIS dispensation.

This reasoning ignores that the current Iraqi prime minister is being undermined from within his own governing coalition, even as Iraqi and U.S. forces succeeded in eradicating ISIS from territories it occupied. Maliki, the former prime minister, clearly is moving to oust him, though even he is the object of jockeying for leadership. This is to say nothing of various PMU leaders who clearly have ambitions to higher office. In any event, no political leader has the strength to dictate terms, and if he could, he would merely ensure that another insurgency eventually emerges.

It is essential that U.S. policy identify a political settlement that is achievable in Iraq and that it pursue that settlement as diligently and methodically as it has pursued the military objectives. A new team with fresh thinking and new ideas will be necessary.

The United States periodically convinces itself that its influence in Iraq is diminished. There is a familiar pattern to this cyclical thinking. After the United States acts as if it has no influence, a crisis occurs. The Iraqis then turn to the United States to help solve it, and the United States realizes that, in fact, it continues to wield considerable influence within the Iraqi political class. The events of 2014 are the latest example of this phenomenon, when in May then-current and former U.S. officials argued that U.S. influence in Iraq was nearly nonexistent. The United States must realize that, in fact, it is hardwired into the Iraqi political class, as former U.S. ambassador Ryan Crocker once said. This does not mean that the United States can dictate terms to the Iraqis. It cannot. It is, however, an important and influential player, unless it chooses not to be, as it did in the period from 2011 to 2014, which led to disastrous consequences.

A number of items must top the agenda of U.S. policy in Iraq. First, Iraq's various constituent groups must be genuinely enfranchised—not only ethnic and sectarian minorities, but political minorities as well. Genuine power-sharing is essential. The Iraqi population has grown impatient with the sectarian spoils system that has been in place since 2003. Competent officials are a prerequisite—not merely technocratic ministers, but competent technocrats throughout ministry structures. There is no point in appointing a competent minister if the rest of the ministry staff are incompetent political hacks.

Corruption must also top the U.S. agenda in Iraq. It is not lost on the ordinary Iraqi citizen that its government is one of the most corrupt in the world. In this connection, the United States should posit its further engagement and assistance to the Iraqis not only on relatively corruption-free institutions of governance, but on the provision of services. The failure of successive Iraqi governments since 2004 (and the Coalition Provisional Authority before that) to provide even basic services has undermined the legitimacy of the Iraqi state for years. Calls for autonomous regions in the south—the creation of which will only further strengthen Iran—are not based on ideological or nationalists impulses (as they are in Iraqi Kurdistan), but on utter frustration with the corruption in Baghdad and the lack of basic services.

If genuine reconciliation efforts are not undertaken in Iraq, the blood of Iraqi and American service men and women spilled since June 2014 will have been in vain. There has been much talk about reconciliation from American officials since 2003. No action of any meaningful nature has actually obtained, however, and Iraqi politicians who ignore U.S. advice about reconciliation have never paid a price for doing so. Indeed, the current leadership of the U.S. team on Iraq policy convinced the Obama administration to treat the arrests and trials of senior Sunni elected officials as an internal matter in 2012. That neglect resulted directly in the rise of ISIS in 2014. If the lessons from the mistakes of the past are not learned, the mistakes will be repeated.

The Iraqi armed and security forces may play a critical role in any reconciliation effort. After the U.S. administrator in Iraq disbanded these services in 2003, he put forward a plan for reconstituting them. The plan called for certain parties represented in the Iraqi Governing Council to put forward the names of the first set of recruits, both officers and enlisted men. The parties asked to provide these recruits were the religious parties, both Sunni and Shii, and the two Kurdish parties. Predictably, this resulted in the nascent Iraqi Army and Security Forces, from their inception, being based on sectarian and ethnic considerations. It also meant that the first loyalty of these officers and enlisted personnel was almost certainly to the parties that had nominated them, not to the state of Iraq.

The post-ISIS period will be an opportunity to cleanse this original sin. It is true that under Prime Minister Abadi, Iraqi Army units are far less likely to carry Shii sectarian banners than they were under his predecessor, and that is a very positive development. Still, U.S. policy should insist on the continued professionalization of armed and security services and the full integration of units from across ethno-confessional lines. Ideas floated in Washington about having only the ethno-confessional group of a particular region secure that region are a recipe for the continued Balkanization of the country. If ISIS proved one thing in 2014 it is that such an insular approach to the security of the country is bound to fail. Only a truly integrated Iraqi force can maintain peace and public order in the country. Having fully integrated units—as existed in Iraq before 2003—will promote further national cohesion and help bind the wounds of the past, contributing in no small part to national reconciliation.

On a related issue, it has already been noted that the Iraqi Army collapsed with incredible speed in the face of a force it vastly outnumbered. This collapse should not have been altogether surprising. American officials knew long before the withdrawal of U.S. forces in 2011 that Prime Minister Maliki was coup-proofing the army by cashiering experienced, professional officers and replacing them with cronies whose loyalty lay with him personally. He further weakened the regular army by undertraining and underequipping it. Moreover, units in Mosul had so abused the local population that, as ISIS began to advance into the city, the Maliki-loyalist officers fled, fearful of what might happen to them should they fall into the hands of the locals. Naturally, when ordinary soldiers saw their officers running, they could not be expected to fight. Had this unfortunate chain of events occurred with any other army in the world, it is almost certain that the results would have been similar.

The U.S. response to Maliki's dismantling of the regular Iraqi Army was to do precisely nothing. Indeed, it continued to support him, especially during the no-confidence effort in 2012. This was the case even though his coup-proofing efforts had been under way for years by then and even though U.S. officials were well aware of those efforts. U.S. policy must mediate in favor of creating cohesive, integrated armed and security forces that are strong enough to maintain public order, fend off threats from violent groups, and defend national borders, while simultaneously ensuring that those forces are manned by professionals and not cronies who might support the rise of the next dictatorship.

Syria is a far more complicated matter. The Trump administration speaks of cooperating with Russia in fighting ISIS. That is understandable, though it is also problematic. Assad will never be an effective interlocutor in putting the country back together. His personal survival means a fragmented Syria into the foreseeable future. A fragmented Syria without effective governmental controls will be a cauldron for violence and, again, the possible rise of other terrorist groups that will have the ability to threaten U.S. and allied interests.

A U.S. policy that acknowledges that Russia has reasserted itself into the Middle East after an effective absence of more than four decades is rational. But it ought to extract a quid pro quo. The person of Assad has become so heinous to the broad range of Syria's population that he simply cannot be a part of the solution to Syria's problems. The United States should work with the Russian Federation to secure his retirement to a dacha in Russia. An acceptable interlocutor must be found who can engage the regime's non-ISIS-affiliated opposition if there is any hope for reuniting the country.

One thing must be recalled, however. There is very little doubt that Syria's minority Alawi population has noted what happened in Iraq when the Sunni minority fell from power: it lost everything. That lesson was not lost on the Alawi elites who govern, or on ordinary citizens. As in Iraq, genuine power-sharing and reconciliation will be necessary to avoid repeating the past.

Notes

1 Pierre Razoux, *The Iran-Iraq War*, translated by Nicholas Elliott (Belknap Press of Harvard University Press, 2015), pp. 3–4 (quoting the Ayatullah Ruhullah Khomeini as saying, "We want to found an Islamic State gathering the Arab, the Persian, the Turk, and other nationalities under the banner of Islam"). Razoux is mistaken in asserting, however, that Saddam Hussein, the Iraqi dictator, appeared in February 1980—seven months before the launch of the war—"wearing his traditional olive green uniform" (idem, p. 1). Hussein, who was not a military officer, was accustomed to appearing in custom-tailored French suits and ties before this time. He began to wear his "traditional olive green uniform" as a rule only after the commencement of hostilities in September 1980.

2 Ibid., pp. 4, 55.

3 Ibid., pp. 54–55, 107–09.

4 Mohsen Milani, "Why Tehran Won't Abandon Assad(ism)," *Washington Quarterly* 36, no. 4 (2013): 79–93, 80.

5 Relations between Iran have ebbed and flowed since 2011, with at least one expert attributing the break between the two to sectarian differences after the Syrian civil war began. Hanin Ghaddar, "The Marriage and Divorce of Hamas and Hezbollah," Wilson Center, August 26, 2013 (www.wilsoncenter .org/article/the-marriage-and-divorce-hamas-and-hezbollah). There appears to have been an attempted rapprochement between Iran and Hamas in early 2017, though there are still no obvious signs of success at this writing. Adnan Abu Amer, "Hamas Insists Ties with Iran Strong, Despite Regional Polarization," translated by Mohammed Khalili, *Al-Monitor,* February 9, 2017 (www.al-monitor.com/pulse/originals/2017/02/hamas-iran-relations -support-military.html).

6 See Matt Purple, "Why Saudi Arabia Is Hammering Yemen," *National Interest,* April 12, 2016 (http://nationalinterest.org/feature/why-saudi-arabia -hammering-yemen-15748).

7 Richard Spencer, "Revealed: Saudi Arabia's 'Great Wall' to Keep Out Isil," *The Guardian,* January 14, 2015 (www.telegraph.co.uk/news/worldnews /middleeast/saudiarabia/11344116/Revealed-Saudi-Arabias-Great-Wall-to -keep-out-Isil.html).

8 Kenneth M. Pollock, "The Dangers of the Arab Intervention in Yemen," Brookings, March 26, 2015 (www.brookings.edu/blog/markaz/2015/03 /26/the-dangers-of-the-arab-intervention-in-yemen/).

9 "Jordan Pilot: Anger Dominates Mideast Media Response, BBC News, February 4, 2015 (www.bbc.com/news/world-middle-east-31129326).

10 See, for example, Tom Finn, "Calls for Revenge in Jordan as Nation Mourns Slain Pilot," *Middle East Eye,* February 15, 2015 (www.middleeasteye.net /news/calls-revenge-jordan-village-slayed-jordanian-pilot-1570457587).

11 Jeffrey Goldberg, "The Obama Doctrine," *The Atlantic,* April 2016.

12 "Common Ground on Syria Unites Russia and Turkey against the West," *The Guardian,* December 21, 2016 (www.theguardian.com/world/2016 /dec/21/common-ground-on-syria-unites-russia-and-turkey-against -the-west).

13 Samia Nakhoul and Nick Tattersall, "Turkey, U.S. on Collision Course over Kurdish Role in Battle for Syria's Raqqa," Reuters, March 2, 2017 (www.reuters.com/article/us-mideast-crisis-syria-turkey-usa-analy-id USKBN16925O).

14 Paul McLeary, "U.S.-Backed Fighters in Syria Worry More about Turkey than ISIS," *Foreign Policy,* February 24, 2017 (http://foreignpolicy.com /2017/02/24/u-s-backed-fighters-in-syria-worry-more-about-turkey -than-isis/).

15 For a discussion of the Sino-Russian role in frustrating the United States, the United Kingdom, and France in Syria, see Feisal Amin Rasoul al-Istrabadi, "The Limits of Legality: Assessing Recent International Interventions in Civil Conflicts in the Middle East," *Maryland. Journal of International Law* 119 (2014): 134–42.

16 Roy Allison, "Russia and Syria: Explaining Alignment with a Regime," *Crisis International Affairs* 89, no. 4 (2013): 801.

17 Ibid., p. 804.

18 Ibid.

19 Angela Stent, "Putin's Power Play in Syria: How to Respond to Russia's Intervention," *Foreign Affairs,* January–February 2016, p. 106.

20 Ibid., p. 108.

21 Ibid.

22 Goldberg, "The Obama Doctrine."

PART V

U.S. Interests

9

Territorial Havens and the Risk of Complex Terrorist Attacks in the United States

Risa Brooks

When the 9/11 Commission issued its final report in July 2004, it offered several recommendations for how to prevent future terrorist attacks against the United States.[1] Foremost among them was eliminating terrorist safe havens of the kind Al Qaeda enjoyed in Afghanistan before the 2001 attacks.[2] Since that time, preventing terrorist sanctuaries from emerging in the Middle East has been a central goal of U.S. foreign policy and a principal rationale for the country's overseas wars.[3] The George W. Bush administration's war in Afghanistan and 2003 invasion of Iraq were both fueled in part by concerns about terrorist sanctuaries.[4] President Obama similarly prioritized the threat posed by terrorist havens in his foreign policy and military actions in the Middle East.[5] Officials in the Trump administration have similarly cited the threat posed by havens, as have military leaders.[6]

After its dramatic military gains in June 2014, ISIS's control of territory in Syria and Iraq also raised the specter of a transnational group plotting terrorist attacks in the United States from an overseas sanctuary.[7] Indeed, preventing ISIS from retaining a terrorist sanctuary soon emerged as a major rationale for military action against the group under both the Obama and Trump administrations.[8] Since 2014 those efforts to retake ISIS-controlled land have diminished the territorial control of ISIS in Iraq and Syria considerably. Still, ISIS leaders show no sign of relenting in their pursuit of territory in support of their self-declared caliphate. In addition, many of their affiliates today retain significant areas of territorial control in Asia, North Africa, the Middle East, and beyond.

How does a militant group's—and ISIS's in particular—control of overseas territory affect its ability to engage in attacks against the United States? I argue that the threat is far more limited than is commonly appreciated: control of territory enhances a group's capabilities, but that territory is not sufficient to allow it to carry out attacks from overseas in the United States, especially what I term "complex" terrorist plots. Not all sanctuaries are created equal. In particular, they vary in how close to or remote from the area of operations they are. That is, they vary according to whether the sanctuary encompasses the area of attacks, or provides ready access to it, or is separated from the target by major logistical and security obstacles. Although the territorial basis of a sanctuary—the physical control of territory—can provide several advantages and contributes to a group's organizational capacity and capabilities, without local access and security in the area of operations, it is limited in what it can do. Hence, as long as an ISIS haven is remote from the United States, the threat it poses is circumscribed.[9] For this reason Americans should be cautious not to overestimate the threat that an ISIS sanctuary in the Middle East and North Africa poses to their security.

This chapter proceeds as follows. I begin by defining and discussing the importance of "complex" terror attacks. I discuss the advantages territoriality provides groups such as ISIS in planning terrorist attacks. I then analyze the disadvantages and obstacles the remoteness of that sanctuary poses to the group. In this regard, I highlight the *inability* to provide security for its operatives as they seek access to and then prepare plots within the United States, and the vital role the lack of "community sanctuary" plays in insulating the country from complex attacks. I argue that, unlike in some parts of Europe, ISIS has been prevented from realizing important synergies between its remote territorial sanctuary and a local community safe haven. Consequently, the group faces several significant challenges in engaging in complex attacks in the United States. In the final section I review the implications of the analysis and offer several practical guidelines for countering a resurgent ISIS sanctuary threat.

The Importance of Complex Terrorist Attacks

In recent years many terrorism analysts and officials in the United States have been heavily focused on preventing attacks perpetrated by "lone wolves."[10] These attacks, as usually conceived, are basic in nature: they are perpetrated independently by solo actors, or intimates (brothers, married couples), against unsecured targets, using easily accessible weapons (vehicles, knives, and firearms). ISIS has regularly called on its sympathizers to engage in such acts, and a small number have been perpetrated in recent years.[11]

Complex attacks are significantly more challenging to carry out than basic attacks. These are attacks that exhibit one or more properties: a network of operatives; targets that are hardened by security defenses; phased or simultaneous attacks or a campaign of temporally clustered attacks; and lethal and technically sophisticated weapons. These attacks require technical ability as well as skills in terrorist tradecraft to execute successfully. These include aptitude in surveillance, secured communications, tactical coordination, and often, fabrication of explosives. Because of the number and nature of precursor steps required to plan and prepare them, these plots also entail a high risk that they will be detected and exposed to authorities. They place considerable demands on a group's capacity to retain operational security and the ability to deny information about their plans to authorities.[12]

In comparison with the lone-wolf challenge, considerably less attention has been paid to the prospect that ISIS could engage in complex attacks of this kind in the United States. This may reflect the country's counterterrorism successes and al Qaeda core's failure to execute any successful spectacular attacks on the United States since 9/11.[13] It may also reflect ISIS's own stated priority of establishing a caliphate in the Middle East, which heretofore has required it to focus its energies on acquiring and protecting territory in the region.[14]

Avoiding complex attacks, however, remains vitally important for the United States. Should ISIS redirect more of its energies toward transnational attacks, the threat could in principle intensify. Indeed, there may be incentives for ISIS to do this during the Trump administration, given several of its officials' hawkish views of the threat posed by "radical Islamic terrorism."[15] If the aim is to incite the United States into launching a ground war in the Middle East, as ISIS's ideology and propaganda suggest,[16] then there may be in the future greater incentives for the group to focus on provoking such a response with a terrorist spectacular.

The political effects of a successfully executed complex attack are apt to be far-reaching. Complex attacks have important propaganda value and may increase recruitment, sympathizers, and fundraising opportunities for militant groups. Complex attacks also signal a group's capability and power to do harm to an adversary and its allied population. They may be strategically effective to the extent that they generate more intense levels of terror in the target audience. Research shows that the psychological consequences of a terrorist attack are affected by the "quality and extent" of exposure to the event.[17] Complex attacks may incite enduring and intense levels of fear in the target population. Indeed, terrorists rely on this in order to induce an overreaction from the state and capitalize on opportunities to mobilize new supporters in its wake.[18]

An ISIS-perpetrated complex attack is likely to further mobilize Americans who already profess elevated fears of terrorism.[19] The 2015 ISIS attack in Paris, for example, increased worries among Americans about terrorist attacks at home.[20] Should an ISIS-coordinated complex attack occur in the United States, officials will experience intense pressure to invest more heavily in the overseas military fight against the organization. A reasoned assessment of ISIS's capacity to engage in such an attack is essential.

ISIS's Sanctuary in Iraq and Syria

ISIS's seizure of the Iraqi town of Mosul in June 2014 and its ensuing take-over of large pieces of territory in Syria and Iraq took many analysts by surprise.[21] Since a coalition of Western and regional actors were mobilized to retake this territory,[22] ISIS has lost control of much of it in both Syria and Iraq.[23] Still, it is worth remembering that ISIS in its previous incarnation as al Qaeda in Iraq (AQI) was once nearly defeated. Just as ISIS reemerged from its marginalized status to capture the world's attention with its military successes in 2014, it is important not to discount the potential revitalization of the organization. The leadership and organization remain intact, if reduced in size. Barring some transformation in the political conditions that facilitated its revitalization, the entity is unlikely to go away and could regroup in some new form. Similarly, there are places in the Middle East and North Africa in which it has established strongholds and seeks to expand influence, most notably in Libya, but also in Afghanistan and in the Sahel. Hence concerns about overseas terrorist havens are likely to remain a major fixation of the United States, as they have been since 2001.

In this context it is useful to think carefully about the implications of territorial control for the group's ability to mount complex terrorist attacks. Although control of territory provides several advantages to ISIS, such territory is still of limited benefit because it is "remote" from targets in the United States.[24]

The Importance of Controlling Territory

The importance of territorial sanctuaries, or cross-border havens, for insurgents employing guerrilla warfare or tactics of conventional warfare has been well established.[25] Perhaps less obvious is why holding territory is beneficial to groups employing terrorist tactics against an adversary. Strategically, terrorism does not directly challenge a state's military or involve tactical engagements with it; terrorist organizations do not require land to base an armed force. Rather, strategies of terrorism rely on a coercive or punishment logic. A "provocation" strategy of terrorism uses attacks to incite fear and disorientation in a population, provoke an overreaction from the government, and capitalize on its ensuing delegitimization to mobilize new supporters for the militants' cause. An "armed pressure" strategy aims to generate costs that a target population must bear in order to coerce policy change from their state.[26] Whether the aim is to elicit an overreaction or to generate costs, however, being able to perpetrate complex attacks is often strategically advantageous for groups employing terrorist methods.

Holding territory, in turn, can help facilitate the execution of complex attacks by making it possible for a group to strengthen its capabilities.[27] Camps within the zone of control can facilitate extensive training and preparation of operatives, as well as the cultivation of specialized expertise, such as engineers skilled in the fabrication of explosive devices.[28] The engineer who fabricated the explosives for the Paris (2015) and Brussels (2016) attacks was apparently cultivated by ISIS in this manner.[29] Control of territory may also allow militants to exploit natural resources or operate illicit markets to raise funds, and in some cases to build commercial or industrial enterprises. Many of these activities have been observed in regard to ISIS.[30]

Within a territorial sanctuary, leaders can also vet recruits, evaluating their capacity to withstand the pressures of a complex plot by putting them in situations of intense stress.[31] Camps provide for indoctrination and build cohesion within a group preparing a plot. As Thomas Hegghammer observes, for example, the militants engaged in a terrorist campaign in Saudi Arabia in 2003 had previously benefited enormously from their experiences in Afghan camps, which provided for their "acculturation, indoctrination, training and relations building."[32] As other analysts put it, "Training camps provide more than seclusion and security. They also allow for the creation of a controlled environment where the recruits can be immersed fully into the new group, continually evaluated and tested, and gradually initiated into the organization."[33] Bin Laden was able to evaluate recruits within the Afghan sanctuary, for example, and selected operatives for 9/11 in this way.[34]

In addition, control of territory allows for the development of specialized expertise and leadership, which can provide essential support and guidance in planning and preparing a complex attack. ISIS has been able to vet operatives who have traveled to Syria, including the European ringleader of the Paris and Brussels attacks. ISIS's leadership has been able to establish infrastructure and routines in support of external operations. In the Brussels and Paris attacks, for example, ISIS managers provided contacts and guidance to the local organizer in Europe.[35]

The Limitations of "Remote" Sanctuaries

Although ISIS's capacity to control territory in the Middle East and larger region enhances its ability to engage in terrorist attacks, it would still faces serious obstacles to executing complex attacks in the United States. These obstacles stem from the fact that such havens are separated from the area of operations by security and logistical barriers that render the sanctuary "remote" from the United States. Physical obstacles such as the Atlantic Ocean, as well as security measures related to port security and significant investments in intelligence and domestic counterterrorism initiatives by the United States complicate access to the country and the ability to engage in covert terrorist-related activities within it. Also crucial is the absence of local communities in the United States that would tolerate or support militant activities and provide the group security and resources. These obstacles both complicate movement into the United States and increase the challenges and security risks of carrying out the many antecedent activities essential to a complex plot.

Specifically, the remoteness of a territorial sanctuary creates three sets of obstacles to engaging in complex attacks. A first obstacle is locating operatives within the United States who can prepare and execute the attacks. In principle, there are two ways that the group could do this. Each, however, poses challenges and creates obstacles to successfully executing an attack. First, ISIS might try to infiltrate the country with foreign operatives (that is, trained and vetted foreign nationals sent to execute a plot). Doing this, however, requires evading security barriers at ports and borders as well as immigration controls. Second, the group can rely on self-recruits. Self-recruits include individuals in the United States who are recruited online by leaders located in the remote sanctuary but otherwise operate autonomously. The track record of aspiring militants in the United States who act without training and guidance, however, suggests that recruits of this kind would be hard-pressed to successfully organize a complex attack. Such self-initiated plotters have trouble fabricating even simple bombs, such as those made from pressure cookers, and often have made egregious errors in operational security.[36] There is little evidence that self-recruits in the United States can on their own successfully organize a network of operatives to attack a hardened target or multiple targets with sophisticated weapons.

Alternatively, residents with travel documents from the area to be targeted might on their own initiative travel to the remote sanctuary for training with the intention of returning home to plot an attack (or be recruited to do so by the militant group's leaders).[37] Individuals who self-select to join the militant group, however, are apt as a general pool to be inferior in skill and character to vetted recruits. The psychological impulses that drive them to seek out the group may render them violent and difficult to manage.[38] Those who travel to the sanctuary zone to receive training and guidance may also be tracked by law enforcement.

Moreover, even if they avoid detection and scrutiny, it is unclear whether the training they receive within the remote territorial sanctuary will be sufficient. Consider, for example, that in both of the most serious plots by al Qaeda involving sophisticated explosive devices post-9/11, the individuals had been trained extensively by overseas militant organizations. Faisal Shahzad, who sought to bomb Times Square in 2009, was trained by the Pakistani group Tehrik e Taliban.[39] Najibullah Zazi, who plotted in 2009 to bomb the New York subway, had received instruction from al Qaeda. Yet, once back in the United States, neither Shahzad nor Zazi successfully managed to manufacture their respective explosive devices. Shahzad's fertilizer-based car bomb failed to explode, and Zazi was caught when he e-mailed an overseas contact seeking clarification about how to construct his TATP bombs.[40] These cases illustrate another difficulty facing militant groups that rely on infiltrators and self-recruits within the United States: because their operatives will lack the help of managers, experts, or mentors in the local environment, they will have to rely on electronic communications, which may expose them to operational security detection.

A second problem relates to getting information about local targets essential to a plot. These include details about security measures and access to targets, escape routes, timing, and positioning of weapons. Once again, electronic resources might prove useful in this regard. Militants may be able to view online floor plans, live traffic feeds, or GPS and satellite data. But even when available, these sources of information are likely to be insufficient to provide a complete survey of local conditions. Even basic plots, such as a foiled effort to bomb New York City's Herald Square, require on-the-ground surveillance.[41]

A complex plot involves even more detailed information. Consider the surveillance undertaken by American David Headley as he prepared to execute the 2008 Mumbai attacks. These attacks might not seem to have required extensive surveillance, given that they were aimed at soft targets, such as a train station and hotels. Headley, however, undertook five extended trips to Mumbai in order to scout targets, beginning in March 2008.[42] He hired fishermen to take him on private tours of the Mumbai harbor and took surveillance video to determine landing points for the attackers.[43] He also stayed in the Taj Majal Palace Hotel (one of his main targets) at least twice. Like Headley, the 9/11 attackers also engaged in scouting and surveillance of targets, including numerous rides on commercial aircraft to assess security conditions and a surveillance flight up the Hudson River corridor.[44]

A third problem afflicts both self-recruits and infiltrators: both will have to retain operational security as they communicate, coordinate, undertake surveillance, fabricate weapons, and the like, in preparation for an attack. Foreign infiltrators who lack situational knowledge and familiarity with the local environment may raise suspicion.[45] And local residents recruited for an attack will lack experience and expertise in terrorist tradecraft related to counterintelligence.

There is, despite these obstacles, one possible route for militants operating from a remote sanctuary to overcome the lack of access and local security: vet and train infiltrators so well in terrorist tradecraft that they are able to carry out all these tasks without being detected and without any guidance and support from local handlers and mentors. In other words, in principle the training of recruits could be so comprehensive, and the operatives so talented and dispositionally suited to the task, that they could circumvent all the obstacles facing a group trying to plot an attack from a remote territorial sanctuary.

But given current security precautions in the United States, the obstacles ISIS (or any other group for that matter) faces to thoroughly training recruits in this way remain extremely high. The 9/11 attacks are instructive in this regard. The attacks are commonly viewed as the most creative and skillfully executed attacks committed by a terrorist organization. The plot itself was years in the making. The nineteen men selected to carry out the plot were vetted. Before coming to the United States, they were extensively trained by Khaled Sheikh Mohammed (KSM), the plot's principal mastermind.

Despite all these advantages, the al Qaeda operatives committed numerous errors in operational security in the months leading up to the attacks. Two of the hijackers, Nawaf al-Hazmi and Khalid Mihdhar, were especially careless. When they sought to take flight lessons in San Diego, their behavior was so bizarre that the instructors became suspicious. The men, for example, asked to skip training on small planes and instead focus on large Boeing aircraft; and they showed little interest in learning how to take off or land.[46] Mihdhar subsequently left without KSM's approval to see family in Yemen when he became homesick.[47] Hazmi bragged to his roommate that he would soon be famous.[48] He also apparently told fellow employees at a gas station something about a potential plot. According to the 9/11 Commission report, some of these station attendants were expecting in August 2001 to be questioned in regard to Hamzi's comments, and at least one individual is suspected of knowing some details about the plot.[49] Zacarias Moussaoui, another al Qaeda operative in the United States, also raised suspicions at a flight school in Eagan, Minnesota, prompting the instructor to report him to authorities and leading to his arrest on immigration charges.[50] Mohammed Atta, the plot's tactical ringleader, violated his own admonitions to the other hijackers not to contact their relatives before the attack and called his father.[51] In short, even under nearly ideal circumstances, the militants made numerous errors in operational security—errors that if made today would have been much more likely to expose the plot. For these reasons, any plan by ISIS to rely on training to overcome the obstacles presented by remoteness would be fraught with difficulty and perhaps impossible to execute.

The Absence of Community Sanctuaries in the United States

The United States has one other major advantage that limits the ability of ISIS's leaders to engage in complex attacks within the country's borders: it lacks "community sanctuaries." Such sanctuaries could provide added security and help a group of infiltrators or self-recruits avoid exposure while they prepared complex plots in the United States. These sanctuaries are unlike territorial sanctuaries, which are based on physical control of land and where the need to remain clandestine is mitigated. Community sanctuaries occur in areas where geographically concentrated populations (such as a neighborhood or town) tolerate or support militant activity for any number of complex reasons. A group operating within such an environment must remain clandestine to avoid detection by law enforcement or counterterrorism efforts by the state. But the added security provided by community members and by embedding in social networks insulates the militants against exposure. Analysts of terrorist organizations have long highlighted the importance of social support of this kind in aiding clandestine terrorist groups.[52]

Less appreciated is the impact on militant groups of the opposite of community support: community opposition. Communities can be integral players in counterterrorism when they *reject* militancy and assist state authorities in exposing it. Dense social networks become dangerous to militants because they make it easy to detect outsiders and aberrant behavior. Securing communities against the willingness of members to tolerate or support extremism is thus a vital means of safeguarding against terrorist attacks. When those measures are combined with effective security and intelligence efforts, the security environment becomes even more hostile to aspiring militants.

The United States has significant advantages on both fronts. The government has invested heavily in counterterrorism since 9/11, and although the efficacy and necessity of some aspects of those investments may be debated, the infrastructure for detecting terrorist-related activity in the United States has been transformed.[53] In addition, there is little evidence that ISIS militants benefit from security within community sanctuaries in the United States. Although there are incidences of individual Muslims engaging in terrorist violence, and some individuals may profess support for extremist causes, there is also evidence that the vast majority of American Muslims reject militancy and view ISIS with the same suspicion as other Americans.[54] ISIS lacks geographic pockets of supporters: there are no Molenbeeks, Bogsides, French banlieues, or Finsbury Park mosques in the United States that could provide the kind of cover and concealment that ISIS might seek. There is considerable evidence that immigrant communities of Muslims are vibrant and integrated, especially in comparison with their European counterparts.[55] Moreover, there is evidence that the rejection of militancy has had a beneficial effect on counterterrorism. Muslim community members have provided tips that have exposed a significant percentage of extremists in the United States since 9/11.[56] In fact, so wary was KSM of the dangers these communities pose to aspiring militants that he warned the 9/11 hijackers to steer clear of them once they relocated to the United States.[57]

The absence of community sanctuaries in the United States is a vital source of resilience against the perpetration of complex attacks by ISIS. It prevents the group from benefiting from the synergies that emerge when militants combine a "remote territorial" with a "local community" sanctuary. To see this, consider patterns in the complex al Qaeda and ISIS attacks that have occurred in Europe since 9/11. In each case, individuals involved in the plots had been trained or received instruction in foreign sanctuaries. Militants also then benefited from the security they found within neighborhoods in Europe where many details of the plot were worked out and preparations undertaken. In 2005 the 7/7 bombers in London found added security in areas of Leeds, and especially in social networks centered on a local bookstore and community institutions. The attackers responsible for the 2004 explosions on Madrid trains prepared their plot in safehouses where some of their activities were observed by outsiders. More recently, the 2015 Paris and 2016 Brussels attacks were facilitated by the security available to them in the Brussels neighborhood of Molenbeek.[58] In fact, several of the perpetrators and weapons involved in attacks in Europe in recent years have been traced in one way or another to Molenbeek, including the 2015 attack in Paris on the office of the satirical newspaper *Charlie Hebdo.*[59]

Revisiting the 9/11 attacks also provides reassurance that the contemporary threat of complex attacks posed by ISIS is limited. The tendency among observers is to focus on the advantages the group's Afghan sanctuary provided the group in preparing the plot. But equally important to remember is how different the United States was domestically. This is critical to understanding al Qaeda's success. Political mobilization against the threat posed by al Qaeda was limited, and significant investment in counterterrorism had not been forthcoming. Equally important, there were weaknesses in intelligence and law enforcement. As is well known, problems within the CIA and FBI meant that breaches in operational security by the militants in the United States, and other opportunities for detecting the plot, were not pursued.[60] In addition, the militants operated in an environment where there was a lack of awareness about the possibility that malevolent actors might seek to prepare complex terrorist attacks. In other words, 9/11 is the product of *both* its external sanctuary and the pre-9/11 security environment in the United States.

Today, however, the United States is a different place. Not only have there been the aforementioned improvements in counterterrorism, but American society (perhaps for better and for worse) has been transformed by the attack. Today Americans are primed to identify aberrant behavior, and there are numerous examples of individuals providing tips to authorities.[61] Consequently, it would be much more difficult for ISIS to infiltrate operatives or for self-recruits without extensive training to undertake the steps necessary to prepare a complex attack without risk of exposure or failure. The mistakes and errors made by the hijackers are vital to bear in mind (mistakes that occurred despite their comprehensive training). In today's environment, it is difficult to imagine that at least one of those errors, if not the preparatory actions they undertook, would not result in the plot's exposure.

Implications for U.S. Counterterrorism Strategy

The analysis, in turn, has several implications for how we assess the terrorist threat to the United States posed by an ISIS territorial sanctuary in Iraq should they succeed in reestablishing one in the future, or the retention of a territorial haven elsewhere in the region.

First it suggests that the threat is more qualified than it is sometimes characterized. Control of territory provides a militant group such as ISIS opportunities to augment its capabilities. It can retain significant bureaucratic infrastructure and a leadership hierarchy that provides guidance, management, and training in support of a complex plot in the United States. In principle it could identify recruits, such as Americans or foreign infiltrators, who could travel from the region to the United States to prepare and plot such attacks. The threat seen from this vantage point certainly seems ominous.

Crucially, however, ISIS lacks the access and security in the United States that would allow it to capitalize on those advantages. Recruiting trained or experienced operatives is one obstacle. Of the few dozen Americans who have successfully traveled to the Middle East to fight with ISIS, a significant number have been killed or been arrested.[62] Whether those individuals who survive will retain the ambition to engage in attacks in the United States, or could return and prepare a plot without having their actions monitored, is questionable.[63] The latter constraint, in particular, requires ISIS to rely on individuals whose travels have not been monitored, which might be hard for it to verify; in any case, it also yields a finite pool of qualified recruits. Relying on foreigners poses its own different and serious obstacles, as discussed earlier.

In turn, should a network coalesce and seek to prepare a complex plot, the group faces a serious risk of exposure as it prepares to execute the attack. Carrying out pre-attack steps such as surveillance against hardened targets, coordination, communication, fabrication, and practice with sophisticated weapons generates opportunities for detection. ISIS lacks local community sanctuaries in the United States, which might provide added security and insulate against intelligence and law enforcement counterterrorism efforts. In fact, Muslim communities have in many documented cases proven to be hostile environments to extremists; and through some combination of community tips or intelligence and monitoring, all but a small number of attacks since 9/11 have been foiled or failed. And these failed attacks were all basic attacks requiring minimal coordination, premeditation and tradecraft, or technical expertise. The impermissive security environment in the United States is a major obstacle to carrying out complex attacks.

The analysis has two final implications for what should be the strategy and approach to countering the transnational terrorist challenge posed by ISIS. The first relates to the need to support Muslim communities' demonstrated willingness to expose suspected extremists in their midst. Some of the counterterrorism methods that law enforcement employs, such as the use of informants, monitoring of religious institutions, and the use of sting operations, are controversial in this regard.[64] Although some contend they are necessary expedients, they may also undermine the long-term resiliency of these communities and therefore their capacity to expose extremism. A community's ability to expose militancy depends on the maintenance of social trust and vibrant social networks within it. Initiatives aimed at outreach and support for communities may be less likely to corrode this social trust, and therefore ongoing investments in measures of this kind are essential.

Second, the analysis bears on U.S. strategy toward ISIS in the Middle East. The analysis suggests that *eliminating* ISIS's territorial foothold through aggressive action by the U.S. military is not necessary to sharply limit the terrorist threat to the country. A strategy premised on rolling back territorial gains through airpower and support to local armed forces has to date showed promise in eroding the amount and nature of territorial control.[65] Long-term occupation or a future commitment of ground forces in a combat role is not only unnecessary, but could be counterproductive if it generates more resilient community support in the region for the militants.

If ISIS's top leadership is kept on the run and contained within a small territorial footprint, the United States can employ counterterrorism methods that have been proven effective against al Qaeda's core leadership, including the use of drones and special operations forces. As Daniel Byman has argued, drones and special operations troops can distract and degrade militant organizations.[66] These methods render the territorial sanctuary porous, degrading the security the militants employ. Without freedom of movement, investments in infrastructure and organizational stability are less viable. The quality and utility of the territorial sanctuary is eroded and with it the benefits it has to the group. This is an important strategic effect.

These methods are not without downsides. The propaganda benefit of inevitable mistakes and civilian deaths from drone attacks are serious problems. These mistakes can invigorate "community sanctuaries" in the region and beyond. There is no obvious formula for measuring the costs against the benefits of eroding the group's territorial sanctuary. Still, the drones and special operations counterterrorism approach may be the best available, assuming it is married with a clear strategy for supporting community resilience against militancy in the United States. An ISIS with a weakened and attenuated territorial sanctuary will be handicapped in its capacity to plan a complex plot against Americans at home. Without a local foothold and sympathizers in community sanctuaries in the United States, its ability to prepare and execute such an attack are further hampered. For these reasons, the ISIS "sanctuary threat" to the United States remains limited.

Notes

1 *The 9/11 Commission Report: Final Report of the National Commission on Terrorist Attacks upon the United States* (New York: W. W. Norton, 2004).

2 CRS Report to Congress, "Removing Terrorist Sanctuaries: The 9/11 Commission Recommendations and U.S. Policy," Francis T. Miko, August 10, 2004 (www.fas.org/irp/crs/RL32518.pdf). In this chapter, the terms "safe haven" and "sanctuary" are used interchangeably.

3 The concern with sanctuaries dates to the Reagan era, but intensified post-9/11. See Ryan Lizza, "ISIS, Terrorist Sanctuaries and the Lessons of 9/11," *New Yorker*, November 19, 2015.

4 See, for example, the rationale in Bush's letter notifying Congress of military action in Iraq on March 21, 2003 (http://georgewbush-whitehouse.archives.gov/news/releases/2003/03/print/20030321-5.html).

5 A good example is Obama's July 2016 rationale for maintaining 8,400 troops in Afghanistan. See "Statement by the President on Afghanistan," July 6, 2016 (www.whitehouse.gov/the-press-office/2016/07/06/statement -president-afghanistan).

6 See "Remarks by President Trump on the Strategy in Afghanistan and South Asia," August 21, 2017 (www.whitehouse.gov/the-press-office/2017 /08/21/remarks-president-trump-strategy-afghanistan-and-south-asia); also see comments by General John W. Nicholson, "Statement for the Record," February 9, 2017(www.armed-services.senate.gov/imo/media/doc /Nicholson_02-09-17.pdf).

7 To be sure, there are a variety of reasons beyond the direct terrorist threat to the United States that justify concern about ISIS. See Peter Krause's chapter in this volume. Also see Daniel Byman, "The Islamic State Threat to the Middle East," Brookings, August 1, 2016 (www.brookings.edu/blog/markaz /2016/08/01/the-islamic-state-threat-to-the-middle-east/).

8 See Ash Carter's references to safe havens in "Opening remarks at Counter-ISIS Defense Minister Meeting," July 20, 2016 (www.defense.gov/News /Article/Article/850655/carter-welcomes-frances-increased-counter-isil -support/). Michele Flournoy and Richard Fontaine, "An Intensified Approach to Combatting the Islamic State," Policy Brief (Washington: Center for a New American Security, August 2015).

9 Other scholars also emphasize ISIS's physical distance from the United States as an important factor in limiting its capabilities. Daniel Byman, "Europe versus America: Comparing the Terrorism Threat," Brookings, April 5, 2016 (www.brookings.edu/blog/order-from-chaos/2016 /04/05/europe-vs-america-comparing-the-terrorism-threat/). The aim of this chapter is to explain in detail why and how that distance (as well as other security obstacles) limits the group's capacity to engage in attacks.

10 Doina Chiacu, "FBI Chief Warns of Islamic State Recruits, Lone Wolf Attacks," Reuters, March 12, 2015.

11 Josh Levs and Holly Yan, "Western Allies Reject ISIS Leader's Threats against Their Civilians," CNN, September 22, 2014 (www.cnn.com/2014 /09/22/world/meast/isis-threatens-west/). See the data available on the New America Foundation's website, "Terrorism in America after 9/11" (www.newamerica.org/in-depth/terrorism-in-america/). Also see the annual reports by Charles Kurzman, including "Muslim-American Involvement with Violent Extremism, 2015" (https://kurzman.unc.edu/ files/2016/02/Kurzman_Muslim-American_Involvement_in_Violent_ Extremism_2015.pdf).

12 Blake W. Mobley, *Terrorism and Counterintelligence: How Terrorist Groups Evade Detection* (Columbia University Press, 2012).

13 See the comments by former acting director of the CIA Michael Morell in Rocco Parascandola, "No Terror Group Capable of a 9/11 Type Attack: Ex-CIA Chief," *New York Daily News*, February 17, 2015.

14 Audrey Kurth Cronin, "ISIS Is Not a Terrorist Group," *Foreign Affairs*, March/April 2015.

15 Guy Taylor, "Donald Trump's Team Puts 'Radical Islam' Front and Center in Terror Fight," *Washington Times*, November 23, 2016.

16 William McCants, "ISIS Fantasies of an Apocalyptic Showdown in Northern Syria," Brookings, October 3, 2014 (www.brookings.edu/blog/markaz/2014/10/03/isis-fantasies-of-an-apocalyptic-showdown-in-northern-syria/).

17 See A. Stith Butler, A. M. Panzer, and L. R. Goldfrank, eds., *Preparing for the Psychological Consequences of Terrorism: A Public Health Strategy*, Institute of Medicine Committee on Responding to the Psychological Consequences of Terrorism (Washington: National Academies Press, 2003), pp. 56–57.

18 Andrew H. Kydd and Barbara H. Walter, "The Strategies of Terrorism," *International Security* 31 (Summer 2006): 49–80; Peter R. Neumann and M. L. R. Smith, *The Strategy of Terrorism: How It Works and Why It fails* (London: Routledge, 2008), chap. 3.

19 "Americans Name Terrorism as No. 1 Problem," (www.gallup.com/poll/187655/americans-name-terrorism-no-problem.aspx); "Gallup: U.S. Public Opinion on Terrorism" (www.gallup.com/opinion/polling-matters/186665/gallup-review-public-opinion-terrorism.aspx).

20 Scott Clement and Juliet Eilpern, "Americans More Fearful of a Terror Attack in the United States, Poll," *Washington Post*, November 20, 2015.

21 See the chapters by Erik Dahl and Jim Wirtz in this volume.

22 Christopher M. Blanchard and Carla E. Humud, "The Islamic State and U.S. Policy," Congressional Research Service, February 2, 2017 (https://fas.org/sgp/crs/mideast/R43612.pdf).

23 See the maps in "Islamic State and the Crisis in Iraq and Syria in Maps," BBC News, January 10, 2018 (www.bbc.com/news/world-middle-east-27838034).

24 Broadly defined, a terrorist sanctuary is a place or a setting that provides a group's members "security" to engage in the militant activities essential to preparing and executing violent attacks. For a similar definition, see "Ungoverned Areas and Threats from Safe Havens," Final Report of the Ungoverned Areas Project, prepared for the Office of the Undersecretary of Defense for Policy by the Office of the Deputy Assistant Secretary of Defense for Policy Planning, 2007.

25 Daniel Byman, "Deadly Connections: States that Sponsor Terrorism" (Cambridge University Press, 2005); Idean Salehyan, "Rebels without Bor-

ders" (Cornell University Press, 2009). Some analysts distinguish insurgents from terrorists on the grounds that only the former hold territory. Luis de la Calle and Ignacio Sanchez-Cuenca, "What We Talk about When We Talk about Terrorism," *Politics and Society* 39 (2011): 451–72.

26 Kydd and Walter, "Strategies of Terrorism"; Neumann and Smith, *The Strategy of Terrorism.*

27 Many of the benefits that the terrorism expert Byman and his colleagues discuss in relation to insurgents are also relevant for terrorists. See Daniel Byman and others, *Trends in Outside Support for Insurgent Movements* (Washington: Rand, 2001), p. 84.

28 On terrorist camps, see James J. F. Forest, "Training Camps and Other Centers of Learning," in *Teaching Terror*, edited by James J. F. Forest (Oxford: Roman and Littlefield, 2006). See also Michael Kenney, "Beyond the Internet: *Metis, Techne,* and the Limits of Online Artifacts for Islamist Terrorists," *Terrorism and Political Violence* 22 (April 2010); Petter Nesser, "How Did Europe's Global Jihadis Obtain Training for Their Militant Causes?," *Terrorism and Political Violence* 20, no. 2 (2008): 234–56.

29 Alissa J. Rubin, "Radicalization of a Promising Student Turned Bomb Maker in Brussels," *New York Times*, April 8, 2016.

30 Jamie Hanson-Lewis and Jacob Shapiro, "Understanding the Daesh Economy," *Perspectives on Terrorism* 9, no. 4 (2015) (www.terrorismanalysts.com /pt/index.php/pot/article/view/450).

31 Devin R. Springer, James L. Regens, and David N. Edger, *Islamic Radicalism and Global Jihad* (Georgetown University Press, 2008), p. 154; Nesser, "How Did Europe's Global Jihadis Obtain Training?"

32 Thomas Hegghammer, "The Failure of Jihad in Saudi Arabia," Occasional Paper (Combating Terrorism Center at West Point, February 25, 2010).

33 Springer and others, *Islamic Radicalism*, p. 153.

34 *The 9/11 Commission Report*, pp. 232–35.

35 Rukmimi Callimachi, "State Dept. Identifies ISIS Operative Suspected in Paris and Brussels Plots," *New York Times*, November 22, 2016.

36 Michael Kenney, "'Dumb' Yet Deadly: Local Knowledge and Poor Tradecraft among Islamist Militants in Britain and Spain," *Studies in Conflict and Terrorism* 33 (October 2010): 914–15; Daniel Byman and C. Christine Fair, "The Case for Calling Them Nitwits," *The Atlantic,* July/August 2010, pp. 106–08; *Terrorism since 9/11: The American Cases*, edited by John Mueller (Mershon Center, Ohio State University, March 2016).

37 Thomas Hegghammer and Petter Nesser, "Assessing the Islamic State's Commitment to Attacking the West," *Perspectives on Terrorism* 9, no. 4 (2015) (www.terrorismanalysts.com/pt/index.php/pot/article/view/440/html); Nesser, "How Did Europe's Global Jihadis Obtain Training?"

38 David Rohde, "Foreign Fighters of Harsher Bent than Taliban," *New York Times*, October 30, 2007; Daniel Byman, "The Homecomings: What Happens When Arab Foreign Fighters in Iraq and Syria Return," *Studies in Conflict and Terrorism* 38 (2015): 581–602); Hegghammer and Nesser, "Assessing the Islamic State's Commitment to Attacking the West."

39 *United States* v. *Shahzad,* Government Memorandum in Connection with the Sentencing of Faisal Shahzad, No. 10, Cr. 541 (S.D.N.Y., September 9, 2010). The government has established tracking for aluminum nitrate fertilizer (used in both the Oklahoma City and the first World Trade Center bombings in 1993). As a result, militants must rely on more complicated and difficult-to-fabricate weapons using inferior-grade fertilizer or unstable explosives such as triacetone triperoxide (TATP).

40 See Peter Bergen, "The Threat of al Qaeda," Testimony for the Intelligence, Information Sharing and Terrorism Risk Assessment Subcommittee of the House Homeland Security Committee, November 19, 2009.

41 Craig Horowitz, "Anatomy of a Foiled Plot," *New York Magazine,* May 21, 2005.

42 Bruce Hoffman, "American Jihad?," *National Interest*, May/June 2010.

43 "Chicagoan charged with conspiracy in 2008 Mumbai attacks in addition to foreign terror plot in Denmark," Department of Justice, Office of Public Affairs, December 7, 2009.

44 *The 9/11 Commission Report*, pp. 242–45.

45 Hanson-Lewis and Shapiro, "Understanding the Daesh Economy"; Byman, "The Homecomings," p. 590.

46 *The 9/11 Commission Report*, pp. 221–22.

47 Ibid., p. 222.

48 Kenney, "Dumb, but Deadly," p. 916; 9/11 Commission Report, p. 222.

49 *The 9/11 Commission Report*, pp. 249–50.

50 Ibid., 246–47.

51 Ibid., 249.

52 See Christopher Paul, "How Do Terrorists Generate and Maintain Support ?," in *Social Science for Counterterrorism: Putting the Pieces Together*, edited by Paul K. Davis and Kim Cragin (Washington, Rand, 2009).

53 Risa Brooks, "Muslim 'Homegrown' Terrorism in the United States: How Serious Is the Threat?," *International Security* 36, no. 2 (2011): 7–47.

54 See "Muslims and Islam: Key Findings in the U.S. and around the World," Pew Research Center, July 22, 2016 (www.pewresearch.org/fact-tank /2016/07/22/muslims-and-islam-key-findings-in-the-u-s-and-around -the-world/).

55 On the assimilation and success of American Muslims, especially the immigrant population, see Byman, "Europe versus America"; Dave Phillips,

"Muslims in the Military: The Few, the Proud, the Welcome," *New York Times*, August 2, 2016.

56 See the data available on the New America Foundation's website, "Terrorism in America after 9/11" (www.newamerica.org/in-depth/terrorism-in-america/).

57 *The 9/11 Commission Report*, pp. 215–16.

58 Roger Cohen, "The Islamic State of Molenbeek," *New York Times*, April 11, 2016.

59 Andrew Higgins, Kimiko De Freytas-Tamura, and Katrin Beinhold, "In Suspect's Brussels Neighborhood, a History of Petty Crimes and Missed Chances," *New York Times*, November 16, 2016.

60 Amy Zegart, *Spying Blind: The CIA, the FBI and the Origins of 9/11* (Princeton University Press, 2009); Austin Long, Joshua Rovner, and Amy Zegart, "Correspondence: How Intelligent Is Intelligence Reform?," *International Security* 30 (Spring 2006): 196–208.

61 Peter Bergen, "Jihadist Terrorism since 9/11: A Threat Assessment," New America Foundation, September 8, 2016 (www.newamerica.org/international-security/policy-papers/jihadist-terrorism-15-years-after-911/).

62 Bergen, "Jihadist Terrorism since 9/11."

63 Byman, "The Homecomings"; Hegghammer and Nesser, "Assessing the Islamic State's Commitment to Attacking the West."

64 Eric Lichtblau, "FBI Steps Up Use of Stings against ISIS," *New York Times*, June 7, 2016.

65 See Barry Posen, "Contain ISIS" *Atlantic* November 20, 2015; Brian Michael Jenkins, "Disrupting Terrorist Safe Havens," *The Hill* 18 August 2014; Jenna Jordan and Lawrence Rubin, "An ISIS Containment Doctrine," *The National Interest*, July 21, 2016.

66 Daniel Byman, "Why Drones Work: The Case for Washington's Weapon of Choice," Brookings, July/August 2013. See also, for example, Joby Warrick, "ISIS's Second-in-Command Hid in Syria for Months," *Washington Post*, November 28, 2016.

10

A State, an Insurgency, and a Revolution

Understanding and Defeating the Three Faces of ISIS

Peter Krause

The United States has been politically, economically, and militarily involved in the Middle East for over half a century. Despite the war-weariness of the American public and growing support for a grand strategy of restraint, direct U.S. engagement in the region will continue into the foreseeable future.[1] Notwithstanding the difficulties of identifying (let alone pursuing and achieving) the "least bad option" in the Syrian civil war, the Israeli-Palestinian conflict, and the unwelcome tension between supporting democratization and stability, the United States has a number of core interests in the Middle East. These include preventing the rise of a regional hegemon, nuclear proliferation, and significant terrorist attacks on the homeland, as well as ensuring access to oil and the security of regional allies.

These interests provide a backdrop for the most prominent regional threat to emerge in recent years: the Islamic State of Iraq and Syria, or ISIS. The good news is that ISIS poses little threat to the most crucial U.S. regional interests, such as preventing the rise of a regional hegemon and the proliferation of nuclear weapons. The bad news is that ISIS still presents a significant threat to a number of other U.S. interests, such as the stability of regional allies and the prevention of terrorist attacks. Furthermore, the group's unique structure makes it more difficult for the United States and its allies to defeat, as ISIS is not simply a terrorist group. Rather, it is at once a state that has controlled and governed territory the size of Indiana, a transnational insurgency that seeks to spread chaos and overthrow regimes across the region, and a revolutionary movement that works to reshape societies and spread an extreme ideology and apocalyptic vision.

A failure to understand and combat any one of these parts of ISIS will ensure a long, frustrating future of tactical victories and strategic defeats, as ISIS uses any remaining part of its organization to prepare the ground to regenerate the others. Therefore, although the recapture of territory from ISIS in Iraq and Syria from 2015 to 2018 is an important and necessary step toward the group's defeat, it is only the first of many.[2] Nonetheless, the news is not all bad. Just as ISIS's hydra heads reinforce each other, they also present additional vulnerabilities for the group. By tying the attractiveness of a revolution to the fate of a fragile "state," and by dooming that state to economic and popular failure due to an extreme, apocalyptic ideology, ISIS helps to sow the seeds of its own demise.

First, I detail U.S. interests in the region and discuss the extent to which ISIS threatens each of them. Next, I present and analyze the three faces of ISIS and how they help explain the group's past and future behavior. Finally, I conclude with prescriptions for how the United States and its allies can defeat ISIS and protect their core interests in the Middle East.

U.S. Interests in the Middle East

The United States has five primary interests in the Middle East (see figure 10-1). First, the United States seeks to avoid the rise of a regional hegemon—a single strong state that dominates the region along with its military and economic resources.[3] A regional hegemon could not be

FIGURE 10-1   U.S. Interests and ISIS Threats in the Middle East

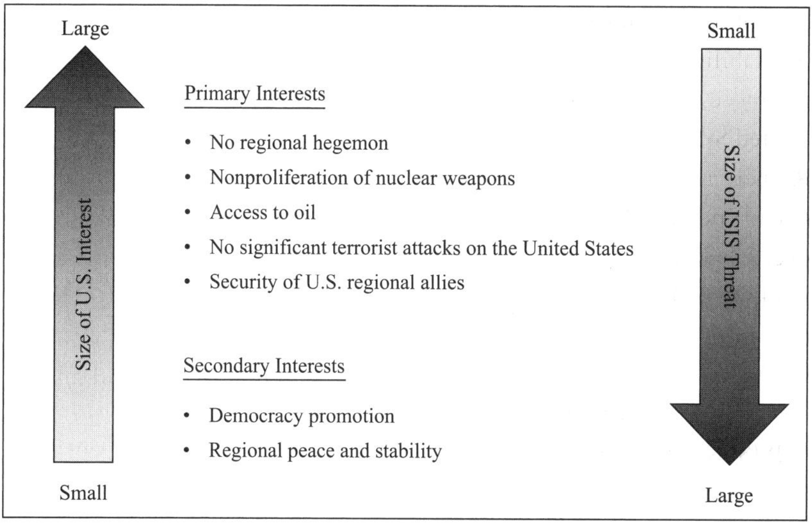

balanced by its neighbors in the Middle East alone, meaning that it would also present a significant security challenge for the United States and its allies in Europe, Africa, and Asia given the Middle East's central geographic location. Furthermore, a hegemon in the Middle East would control a significant portion of the world's oil reserves, giving it the power to potentially destabilize the market or hold the United States and other nations hostage to high prices or low output. U.S. intervention against Iraq's 1990–91 occupation of Kuwait and threat to Saudi Arabia was driven in part by these concerns.

Second, the United States aims to prevent the proliferation of nuclear weapons in the Middle East. Despite some scholarly claims and historical evidence that the presence of nuclear weapons can help stabilize relations between enemies, the process of creating a nuclear arsenal before the achievement of a secure second-strike capability is inherently destabilizing and dangerous. Furthermore, the stability-instability paradox suggests that even if multiple Middle Eastern states were to acquire secure nuclear arsenals without arms races and intentional or unintentional use, the number and intensity of conventional wars and insurgencies in the region could increase.

Third, the United States has a strong interest in ensuring access to the large oil supplies in the region, which are needed to power the U.S. and global economies. Although oil-rich states have an interest in exporting these resources, some may also have an incentive to cut off the supply chain for political or economic leverage. Therefore U.S. military presence may be required to deter such blockades or swiftly remove them.

Fourth, the United States aims to prevent significant terrorist attacks in general, and on its homeland in particular. Although nonnuclear terrorism is not an existential threat, history has shown that the impact of surprising and deadly attacks on civilians can have outsized economic, political, and social effects. Minimizing such attacks is thus a primary U.S. interest identified by leading politicians and the American public alike.

The fifth primary U.S. interest is ensuring the security of its key allies in the Middle East, including Egypt, Israel, Jordan, Saudi Arabia, Turkey, and the new Iraqi government. The domestic politics of every one of these countries has concerned Washington in recent years, from the jailing of academics and journalists to the spread of settlements and the promotion of sectarianism. Nonetheless, the United States has a long history of political, military, and economic support for these countries and their people, and they, not the United States, are the ones who will largely determine whether the region will become stable, prosperous, and free.

To a lesser extent, the United States also has an interest in peace and stability across the region, as well as in the promotion of democracy.[4] These are certainly admirable objectives with a number of benefits, but their absence does not pose a significant threat to the United States. Furthermore, democratization is often in tension with stability in the short term, and the United States has often not been consistent in its support for the former, especially in the Middle East. Therefore, these are still U.S. interests, but they are less important and less pursued than the five primary interests previously identified.

ISIS Threats to U.S. Regional Interests

ISIS threatens some U.S. interests, but the most significant U.S. interests face the least significant threat from ISIS, and vice versa. For starters, ISIS poses little to no threat to regional hegemony or nuclear proliferation in the Middle East. Despite its grand territorial designs for its "caliphate," the group has no chance of becoming as powerful as leading states like Saudi Arabia, Iran, and Turkey, let alone surpassing them to become the hegemon that dominates the region. Furthermore, because ISIS has been fighting a multifront war against almost every state in the region simultaneously, the group is not hastening the rise of another hegemon through the disproportionate weakening of any of the regional challengers.

Similarly, as much as ISIS would like to obtain and employ a nuclear weapon, its chances of acquiring one are quite low, and its chances of building one are even lower.[5] The threat ISIS poses does not significantly affect the desire of regional states to initiate or accelerate their own nuclear programs, which is driven more by regional and international rivalries with other states. Most states in the region desire nuclear weapons for regime security, but ISIS is unlikely to be deterred from attacking nuclear-armed states—indeed, it has already done so on numerous occasions. Therefore nuclear weapons would hold little deterrent effect on the group, and so ISIS does not increase the likelihood of nuclear proliferation by other state actors.

ISIS poses a small threat to the free flow of oil and a small-to-medium threat to the security of U.S. regional allies. ISIS forces have controlled scattered oil fields in eastern Syria and western Iraq; however, they lost many of those in late 2017 and are unlikely to capture larger, more lucrative oil fields in neighboring areas, and they have sold oil from the fields they captured in any case (including to their enemies). They are very unlikely to carry out an operation that could significantly slow the flow of Middle East oil, such as a blockade of the Strait of Hormuz, which is a questionable prospect even for far more capable and better-positioned states like Iran.[6] At best, their major attacks could shake up oil markets, but they do not have the power to control them or shut them down.

The threat to U.S. allies posed by ISIS differs. For Israel, ISIS poses no existential threat, but it may spark violent escalation spirals in Gaza and the Sinai as it attempts to expand its foothold there by outbidding Hamas for leadership in the jihadi community. For Egypt, Jordan, Saudi Arabia, and Turkey, ISIS poses a threat to the stability of their regimes, not simply through violence, but also through the delegitimization of their forms and effectiveness of governance. ISIS has lost significant territory, but it has a number of members in these countries, which pose significant security threats and can polarize local politics.

Outside the Middle East, ISIS poses a significant security and military threat to Europe, and one that is likely to increase now that ISIS has lost territory and is shifting its focus to what it sees as a region rife with ethnic tension and disaffected Muslim populations.[7] Despite increased security measures put in place after attacks in Belgium, France, and elsewhere, the presence of a significant number of trained ISIS operatives can ensure a series of deadly attacks and ethnic polarization. Beyond the violence, ISIS has already had a significant impact on the politics of European countries; its violence and the refugees it purposely helped create have pushed European politics to the right, and nationalist parties continue to win unprecedented support at the polls by espousing counterterrorism and nativist platforms.[8]

ISIS poses a significant threat to the U.S. interests of regional peace and stability and the prevention of terrorist attacks. Between 2014 and 2016 the group committed nearly 3,000 terrorist attacks (nearly three per day), causing tens of thousands of deaths.[9] From January 1, 2014, through October 31, 2015, in Iraq alone, ISIS killed 18,802 and wounded 55,047 people.[10] ISIS has played a pivotal role in escalating the civil wars in Iraq and Syria, committing ethnic cleansing and genocide against minority populations and stirring up sectarianism that will long outlast the conflicts themselves. Furthermore, ISIS has shown the willingness and ability to carry out and inspire terror attacks both inside and outside the Middle East, including in Europe and North America. The continued loss of territory will likely increase these risks, especially in the short term, as ISIS aims to demonstrate its continued vitality to supporters and detractors alike and the group shifts its focus to new areas.

The best way to remove the threat ISIS poses to U.S. interests is to destroy the organization itself. Its multifaceted nature makes that more easily said than done, however, especially given a lack of understanding of its component parts both by policymakers and by the American public. In the next section, I detail the three faces of ISIS and the best approaches to defeating each one.

ISIS's Three Parts: Insurgent Group, State, and Revolutionary Movement

To defeat ISIS, it is necessary to understand each of its three faces: insurgent group, state, and revolutionary movement.

ISIS as an Insurgent Group

Much of the confusion surrounding ISIS and how to defeat it stems from a misunderstanding of what exactly ISIS is. First, ISIS leads a transnational insurgency that is actively fighting to overthrow regimes—not only in Iraq and Syria, but also in Libya, Nigeria, Algeria, Saudi Arabia, Pakistan, and Yemen, among others.[11] The thousands of ISIS fighters in Iraq and Syria have included a mix of former Iraqi military officers and battle-hardened insurgents from a decade of fighting, as well as foreign fighters from abroad, many of whom came with little or no military know-how or experience.[12] The prominence of former Iraqi military and intelligence officers may seem surprising given the ideological disconnect between the apocalyptic Salafi jihadists of ISIS and the secular Arab nationalism of the Baath Party. However, their common enemy (Shiite political parties and militias), common base of support (the Sunni heartland), and shared power position on the outside looking in after the fall of Saddam Hussein made for an initial marriage of convenience that, for many, became much more. For example, Abu Muslim al-Turkmani was an Iraqi military officer who served under Saddam Hussein and then became ISIS's second-in-command and governor for all of its territories in Iraq until he was killed in a U.S. drone strike in 2015. In fact, former Saddam military officers have run three of ISIS's most important ministries: security,

military, and finance.[13] Ayad Hamid-Jumaili was a former Saddam-era
intelligence officer from Fallujah. Until his death in March 2017, he
oversaw all of ISIS's security and intelligence operations, which mirror
those of the Baathists with their reliance on an extensive network of informants and harsh reprisals for any act of disloyalty.

The combination of these former Iraqi military officers and battle-
hardened insurgents has led to impressive, innovative performances by
ISIS on the battlefield. Its crowning success was the capture of Iraq's
second largest city, Mosul, in 2014 with as few as 800 fighters against
30,000 Iraqi soldiers, many of whom fled in the face of ISIS fighters
and their reputation for extreme brutality.[14] ISIS's desire and ability to
take and hold territory allowed the group to gain control of more than
9 million people from Mosul in the east to the edge of Aleppo in the
west, from the Turkish border in the north to Iraq's Anbar Governorate in the south—an area the size of Great Britain at its peak in 2014.[15]
The group's reach expanded even further through its network of affiliates, which have often grown at the expense of its rival, al Qaeda. Itself
a former affiliate of al Qaeda (al Qaeda in Iraq), ISIS has flipped major
groups like Boko Haram into its network and set up affiliates of its
own amidst ongoing conflicts in Egypt, Yemen, Somalia, Libya, and
elsewhere.[16]

The capture of Mosul and retreat of the Iraqi Army helped provide
ISIS with the tools it needed for the group's most deadly and effective
tactic: mass suicide bombings. ISIS acquired 2,300 armored Humvees
from fleeing Iraqi forces, more than two-thirds of the 3,000–3,500 Humvees the United States had supplied to the Iraqi Army.[17] These vehicles
enable highly effective suicide attacks. Their chassis can support a tremendous amount of weight, allowing for heavier explosive payloads and
more powerful bombs. Their armored exterior makes them difficult to
disable as they speed toward their target, and their familiar appearance
makes it difficult for Iraqi forces to recognize them as enemy vehicles until
it is too late. ISIS has used these weapons in conjunction with their large
ranks of willing suicide bombers to devastating effect. The group took
Ramadi in May 2015 by detonating *thirty* suicide car bombs in the center of the city, "10 of which each were comparable in power to the Okla-

homa City truck bomb of 1995 [which killed 168 people]."[18] In other cases, they have overrun Iraqi and Syrian army checkpoints by blasting through their defenses with multiple suicide car bombs.

Even as ISIS has faced a massive onslaught from a multinational coalition that has retaken over 70 percent of the territory captured by the group, surprise attacks revealed the enduring morale of its fighters and sophistication of its operations under duress. In October 2016, ISIS attackers pushed into the heart of the Iraqi metropolis of Kirkuk despite the ongoing siege against its stronghold in Mosul. Witnesses describe the attack as "ambitious and carefully planned," as about 100 ISIS fighters gathered in nearby Hawija, an ISIS enclave, and entered the city by truck.[19] The ISIS fighters not only took over key parts of the city, but they also anticipated and set up ambushes for Kurdish reinforcements that responded to the attack. One hundred and sixteen people were killed and 265 wounded in the fighting, including numerous police officers, Kurdish Peshmerga, and civilians. The commander of the Kurdish counterterrorism force, Polad Talabani, said, "What they did to us inside Kirkuk was by far the worst we have ever seen."[20] As ISIS's territorial holdings continue to shrink in 2018, the group will attempt to plan similar strikes to destabilize vulnerable areas and prepare to fill the vacuum created by weak states and polarized societies.

ISIS as a State

The capture and control of territory by ISIS allowed it to expand into its second sphere: statehood. Although no other state formally recognized the "Islamic State" declared in 2014, ISIS developed a state in practice, with a hierarchy of governing institutions and ministries, courts, schools, and other social services. One ISIS fighter claimed, "You look only at the executions. But every war has its executions, its traitors, its spies. We set up soup kitchens, we rebuilt schools, hospitals, we restored water and electricity, we paid for food and fuel. While the UN wasn't even able to deliver humanitarian aid, we were vaccinating children against polio."[21] The majority of the funds ISIS had to pay for such projects came not from oil or foreign donations, but from a variety of taxes the group imposed on the 3 to 4 million people within the territories it controlled, from commercial taxes on businesses to the *jizya* tax on non-Muslim individuals.[22]

According to some who lived under its rule, ISIS was more efficient and effective at governing than its Baghdad or Damascus predecessors. By instituting sharia and brutal punishments, the group claims to have largely eliminated corruption and kidnappings, while maintaining or improving the distribution of resources and social services. Needless to say, its brutality is itself the cause of many civilian deaths, but it also can deter wrongdoing and convince people to adhere to its rule.[23] ISIS nonetheless continued certain practices of the pre-conflict Syrian and Iraqi regimes, especially concerning food distribution. The group continued to subsidize the cost of flour and opened bakeries when necessary to ensure there would be bread for the population under its control.

Of course, the group claims that it is not just any state, but rather the Islamic Caliphate reborn under the guidance of its leader, Abu Bakr al-Baghdadi. The vast majority of the world's Muslim scholars and civilians reject the legitimacy of this "caliphate" and ISIS's claims, including key religious leaders from Egypt's Al-Azhar to Saudi Arabia's Grand Mufti. Nonetheless, the credentials of the declared caliph—al-Baghdadi is a descendant of Prophet Muhammad and has a PhD in Quranic Sciences—coupled with ISIS's claims about fully instituting sharia law and a "pure" Islamic society have proven attractive to its members and some individuals both inside and outside of its territory.[24] One need only watch a few segments of ISIS's plentiful propaganda videos to realize that it was at pains to portray the "normal," happy life inside its "caliphate" in order to keep its subjects content and try to attract more.

Indeed, the establishment of a "state" is ISIS's most unique and signature accomplishment. Al Qaeda and like-minded jihadis always supported the concept of a caliphate and believed one should be established, but only far in the future once the ground was prepared after the expulsion of the "far enemy" (that is, the United States and the West) and the conversion of more Muslims to their particular strain of jihadism. ISIS turned that conventional game plan upside down. The group argued that the governance of territory and the establishment of the caliphate were both a religious duty and a strategic boon, as these would attract recruits and provide a true base for expansion and the removal of foreign influence. Furthermore, ISIS exhibited far fewer qualms about using extreme force to establish and maintain its "state" than al Qaeda, whose leadership constantly tried to restrain ISIS in its earlier guises before the rupture in 2014.[25] Although the significant loss of territory all but dissolved the Islamic State "caliphate" by 2018, the fact that it emerged and functioned for multiple years will serve as a milestone, a reminder, and a potential example for the future.

ISIS as a Revolutionary Movement

Finally, ISIS represents a revolutionary movement that seeks to reshape societies in the Middle East and beyond, as well as redefine what it means to be a Muslim.[26] An insurgent group is a military entity, a state is a political entity, and a revolutionary movement is both of these, as well as a social, cultural, and ideological entity. Revolutions do not simply seek to replace presidents and generals; they aim to overturn the existing social order and replace it with a new vision for how life should be for individuals, their community, and their polity. The nature of ISIS's revolution can be seen in the other two spheres, as its "state" directly aims to upset the borders and bargains of the Westphalian nation-state system rather than integrate within it.[27] Its insurgencies do not merely seek to replace an unfavorable leader with a favorable one, but to change the demographic makeup of the territory and the mores within it through ethnic cleansing and "religious policing." The loss of territory may help cripple ISIS's state, but not necessarily its revolution, as former ISIS propaganda leader and organizer of foreign operations Abu Muhammad al-Adnani explained: "Whoever thinks that we fight to protect some land or some authority, or that victory is measured thereby, has strayed far from the truth."[28] "O America," Adnani said. "Would we be defeated and you be victorious if you were to take Mosul or Sirte or Raqqah? . . . Certainly not! We would be defeated and you victorious only if you were able to remove the Koran from Muslims' hearts."[29]

Indeed, ISIS's position as a revolutionary movement goes far beyond its insurgent and statist cloaks. First, the group's ideology sets it apart, as it not only aims to convert Muslims to its extreme interpretations but also emphasizes apocalyptic Islamic themes that al Qaeda and other jihadi groups have downplayed. For example, ISIS preaches that the Mahdi will come soon and that ISIS has to prepare to fight alongside him. A series of setbacks in 2006 and 2007 tempered ISIS's use of apocalypse as a strategic blueprint, but the group still uses related language and ideas to motivate followers and change conceptions of the present and future.[30] This has significant implications for group behavior, as a world that is about to end in massive battles between the forces of Islam and "Rome" is one in which extreme violence and degradation are not only acceptable, but expected.

Second, ISIS has spent a great deal of time and effort trying to inculcate youth with these ideas and train the next generation of jihadis. ISIS has used its control of mosques and schools within its "state" to recruit and control children, who are desensitized through exposure to beheadings and mass killings and initially used as informants and spies.[31] Those selected to be "cubs of the caliphate" undergo training for months, take part in the killing of prisoners, and graduate to become suicide bombers and frontline fighters.[32] Even those not selected for such missions have ISIS's worldview and ideology drilled into them. Like children everywhere, not all will remember or agree with what they are taught, but some will, and even a small increase in the number of ISIS sympathizers can change the future trajectory for the group and the region.

Third, to attract those it cannot drill in person, ISIS has made more extensive use of social and conventional media to spread its message globally than any previous jihadi group. A 2015 report noted that ISIS "releases, on average, 38 new items per day—20-minute videos, full-length documentaries, photo essays, audio clips, and pamphlets, in languages ranging from Russian to Bengali."[33] This propaganda helped the group attract more foreign fighters (approximately 30,000) than any other in history, including more than the combined total of al Qaeda and other insurgent groups during the war in Afghanistan against the Soviet Union.[34] ISIS's open approach to media and violence is also revolutionary. It crowd-sources the creation and distribution of its propaganda, and it makes attacks by lone wolves in distant lands a key part of its strategy. ISIS claims credit for these unaffiliated but inspired individual attackers, honoring them as soldiers of ISIS in a way that other jihadi groups have not and using them to polarize their societies and lay the groundwork for ISIS's ideas to take root.[35]

How to Defeat ISIS in Three-Level Chess

The challenge for analysts and states alike is not simply that ISIS has three faces, but rather that ISIS is simultaneously an insurgent group, a state government, and a revolutionary movement (see figure 10-2). Understanding and defeating any one of these entities is challenging; effectively addressing all three at once is nearly impossible given the tensions

FIGURE 10-2   The Three Faces of ISIS

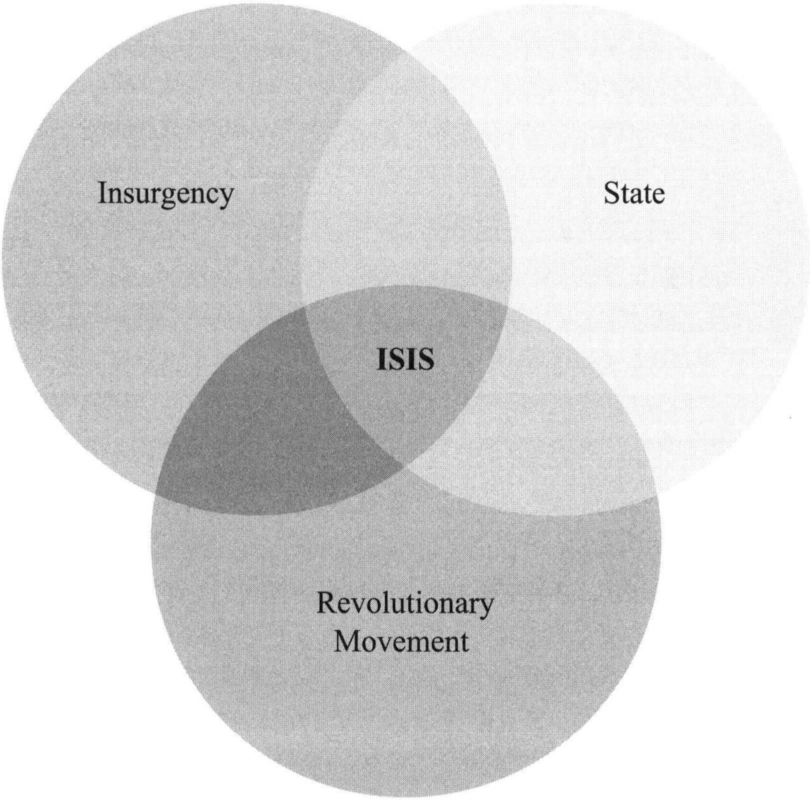

in priorities and policies between them. For its part, the United States is far better positioned to defeat some aspects of ISIS than others. The marginalization of ISIS will therefore require a multilateral, multistage effort across a number of fronts: a war of bombs, a war of governance, and a war of ideas. I offer a series of policy recommendations for how these three separate struggles can be pursued in complementary fashion, rather than in isolation or contradiction.

Defeat Sectarianism and Polarization

Polarization is *the* engine to ISIS's growth and success in all three areas. ISIS launches attacks across ethnic lines to generate animosity and provoke reactions by the local government and targeted groups, which further inflame sectarian tensions. This strategy polarizes communities and makes individuals less likely to challenge ISIS's authority and warped ideology and more likely to join the organization itself. The violence also helps create a new set of political grievances against the existing government, opening a vacuum for ISIS to fill with its own governance. The initial rise of al Qaeda in Iraq (AQI) and its comeback as ISIS were not random events: the organization's surge was due in large part to the ramping up of the civil war in Iraq from 2004 to 2006 and the civil war in Syria from 2011 to 2014, as well as the group's ability to plug into both as engines for growth. ISIS has followed this blueprint of vampyric radicalization and "demographic engineering" from its days as AQI to today in Iraq, Europe, and beyond.[36] Indeed, ISIS details this strategy explicitly, noting that it aims to eliminate the "gray zone" between true Muslims and non-Muslims by violent provocation and polarization.[37]

END REGIONAL CIVIL WARS: To lessen the polarization and sectarianism that ISIS feeds off of, the United States and its allies in the Middle East must first work tirelessly to end regional civil wars. Nothing radicalizes populations and marginalizes moderates more than these conflicts because it is most dangerous for individuals to be neutral in civil wars, as all sides target such people as a threat.[38] The United States and its allies might believe they have an interest in keeping these wars at a slow burn in order to bleed and bankrupt rivals like Iran and Russia. However, what strength is sapped from problematic but deterrable state rivals is trans-

ferred to dangerous and less deterrable jihadis, not to mention the radicalization of the states themselves who become embroiled in long-term
sectarian civil conflicts. Given that over 85 percent of all terrorist attacks
globally occur in five countries experiencing ongoing civil wars (Iraq,
Syria, Afghanistan, Nigeria, and Pakistan), ending these wars would be
the single most effective counterterrorism tactic.[39] Since many of these
civil wars have become proxy wars as part of a new Middle East cold war,
U.S. diplomacy with allies and rivals alike at the state level can have major
downstream effects on the power and threat posed by nonstate actors like
ISIS.[40]

   FIGHT THE WAR OF IDEAS INDIRECTLY: Second, the United States
must fight the war of ideas against ISIS, but it must do so indirectly.[41]
ISIS fights its own war of ideas across multiple levels. Its victories on the
battlefield allow it to capture territory; it then uses these victories to trum-
pet its ideology online and in the classroom within its newly acquired
state; this spreading of the message attracts more supporters to its revolutionary movement and insurgency, and the cycle continues. As a secular
government the United States does not win by—and should avoid—
engaging in theological debates with ISIS, just as it does not expound on
Christianity, Judaism, or other religions. The U.S. brand is so poor in
the Middle East that attempts to actively lead a debate against ISIS would
only hurt those in the region who are able to engage and discredit the
organization. Instead, the United States can help the vast majority of Muslims who reject ISIS more effectively win the debate by shaping the environment in which it takes place.

   In addition to ending civil wars to sap radicals and empower moderate voices, the United States can also topple and prevent the reemergence
of the physical "caliphate." Although not normally thought of as a step
in the war of ideas, all of the major transnational revolutionary movements in the region centered on states who drove them—and faltered
when those states collapsed. Communism in the region—which supported and was championed by numerous political parties and rebel
groups—faced major setbacks with the fall of the Soviet Union, while
Arab nationalism rose and fell with the fortunes of the United Arab Republic (Egypt). On the other hand, the modern Shia Islamist movement

that ISIS finds itself fighting directly was driven by the Iranian Revolution, and the current state's decades-long push to spread its ideas and influences throughout the region sustains it. Should Iran's Islamic regime fall, the impact on its revolutionary ideas across the region would be tremendous. In this sense, ISIS's tying of its fortunes to a physical state creates significant vulnerabilities for the group, and its toppling delegitimizes it in the minds of many. The United States may do many things poorly in the region, but if there is one thing it has proven to be good at it is overthrowing regimes. A slow squeeze of the caliphate in which ISIS gradually lost funds, could not provide social services, and ruled over an increasingly insecure and unruly population may have been strategically beneficial by further discrediting the group and leaving memories of disorder rather than of effective governance that was swiftly pulled away by outsiders.

On the Internet, it is far less important (and wise) for the U.S. government to directly respond to ISIS propaganda than to work with private corporations to weaken their message and allow other critics to defeat them. Twitter's commitment to banning ISIS accounts that advocate violence and violate their terms of service help weaken the group's message. Google's Jigsaw program places counter-ISIS websites at the top of searches alongside pro-ISIS ones, which help ensures that any aspiring supporters will be exposed to criticisms and failures alongside any praise and successes.

FIGHT POLARIZATION IN THE UNITED STATES: Given the significant polarization in American society today, defeating sectarianism in the Middle East is easier said than done. However, U.S. attempts to address polarization in American society can represent an example of humble self-criticism and solidarity, as well as a bulwark against ISIS attempts to gain a foothold on U.S. shores. President George W. Bush was criticized for not asking Americans to make any sacrifices in the struggle against terrorism. U.S. leadership should change course and ask Americans to improve social bonds in their communities across ethnic and religious lines. Not only are such actions in line with American values, but they also help to prevent social alienation, which is one of the most common causes of individuals lashing out and responding to ISIS's attempts to recruit lone wolves.

Roll Back ISIS Territorial Control with a Revised "Afghan Model"

ISIS has proven that it is often at its best on the battlefield. ISIS not only conquered territory the size of Indiana, but it simultaneously fought nearly every state and group in the region for years and is still standing. Nonetheless, the group can lose, and has lost, territory when facing versions of the "Afghan model" of warfare, where indigenous ground forces partner with U.S. advisers and air strikes to degrade and defeat it. The key to this approach is not simply the capability of these combined forces, but also how their makeup thwarts ISIS's designs on the battlefield and the "day after" it retreats.

ISIS cared so much about the supposed coming apocalyptic battle in Dabiq, Syria, that it named its English-language magazine after the town. Then, when the invading forces came, ISIS was swiftly removed with little fanfare on the group's part. Why? It was in part because the attacking forces were Syrian Arabs backed by Muslim Turks, rather than non-Arab, non-Muslim Westerners as anticipated and hoped for. ISIS may be somewhat flexible in its religious prophecies, but it is difficult for ISIS to sell a narrative of Islam versus the West when Arab Islamic forces are the ones directly fighting and defeating them.[42]

As the situation in Afghanistan reveals, the "Afghan model" has a number of shortcomings. Initial battlefield gains have not translated into a stable, cohesive state despite a decade and a half of effort.[43] Many of these failures stem from an inability to appreciate the significant regional interests behind the Taliban (such as Pakistan), however. Although collective action challenges remain, ISIS lacks a similar regional backer and is an avowed enemy of all states in the region.[44] ISIS can therefore be pushed back more easily. However, the greater problem of the "Afghan model" with both the Taliban and ISIS is the failure to provide credible, effective governance after battlefield success.

Help Allies Win the War of Competitive Governance

Defeating ISIS as a state requires far more than removing them from control of territory. To ensure that the "Islamic State" does not come back—and is not welcomed back by civilians on the ground—regional powers need to engage in and win at competitive governance.[45] Local governments need to demonstrate to their citizens that they can provide public goods like security and transportation, and private goods like jobs, health care, and schools. On top of this, they need to make citizens feel that they have a stake in the state and its future, especially if they are a minority ethnic or religious community. If and when governments fail to do one or more of these things, those affected individuals will become more susceptible to an extremist group like ISIS that promises safe streets, free schools, and an end to corruption, which some are willing to tolerate in exchange for increased restrictions on freedom. As former U.S. ambassador to Syria Robert Ford explained, "If the new rulers don't have local support, the Islamic State will always be able to recruit people, especially if the water isn't turned on, the schools aren't open and the electricity is off."[46]

As much as media coverage focuses on ISIS's extreme violence, the group rose to power in Syria from 2011 to 2014 by focusing on building and governing a state in the Sunni borderlands, while Bashar al-Assad focused on destroying those groups that focused on overthrowing him. Operations that aim at degrading the "Islamic State" and its resources should therefore be understood in the context of delegitimizing its governance in the eyes of its population as much as loosening its physical control of territory. The "economic war" waged on ISIS in 2015 and 2016 forced the group to significantly increase taxation of its constituents and cut its military salaries in half, which led to increased unrest and defections.[47] Even though many residents liked the services that ISIS provided, they did not like the increasing amount of money they had to pay for them. In this sense, the slow squeeze before the recapture of Mosul and Raqqah may prove to be a positive. It forced ISIS to provide poorer governance with fewer resources and so degraded perceptions of its rule in the eyes of civilians over time, rather than disappearing in one fell swoop while memories of reliable, incorruptible ISIS governance remained fresh.

The fact that ISIS is a transnational organization unfortunately means that this competition over governance must be won not just in one place, but in countries across the region. Otherwise the group will certainly try to capitalize on any weak link where there are discontented Sunnis. The discussion of a "ghost caliphate" relies precisely on this concept of

ISIS biding time before seeping back into cracks left by failing local governance, as the group did once before in Iraq and Syria.

Although the struggle over governance is central to defeating ISIS on multiple fronts, it is one in which the United States cannot play the lead role. Nonetheless, the United States can and should set the stage by providing political, economic, and—when needed—military heft to help enact power-sharing deals both within and between Middle Eastern states. The key challenges to quality and inclusive governance in the region are the struggles between groups and states over the distribution of resources and power. The United States can provide incentives and international pressure to help regional states reach and enact deals that give all ethnic and religious communities a seat at the table and a stake in the country. They can also work with key allies like Saudi Arabia, Turkey, and Egypt and key rivals like Russia and Iran to establish realistic agreements on power-sharing and spheres of influence in the region. Conflicts and disagreements will remain, but the sobering costs of endless proxy wars that go nowhere and help strengthen a common threat like ISIS should help these negotiations move toward a more stable regional order.

Match Means to Ends

All of the greatest failures of U.S. intervention in the Middle East can be traced back to a mismatch between available means and desired ends. Despite coming to office having criticized President Bush for his failed intervention in Iraq after the overthrow of Saddam Hussein, President Obama noted that his biggest foreign policy mistake was failing to adequately plan for the "day after" Gaddafi was overthrown in Libya.[48] Nonetheless, the Obama administration called for the end of the Assad regime in Syria, yet only devoted enough resources to prevent the rebels from losing, rather than actually winning. After initially criticizing the Obama administration for its Syria policy, the Trump administration similarly stated in April 2017 that Assad should go, but did not subsequently devote resources adequate to the task.[49] Scholars and policymakers debate the merits of intervention and restraint, but there should be no debate over the folly of pursuing the *goals* of the former with the *resources* of the latter. The United States has received a dose of humility, having

experienced how little even the world's superpower can do in a distant
region of proud, capable individuals and states with their own interests,
about which the United States exhibits little understanding. ISIS can be
defeated, but only with strong regional partners and only if the fight is not
folded into broader projects of foreign-imposed regime change and poorly
formulated plans for democratization. The key to defeating ISIS is to recognize and understand its three faces and capitalize on the vulnerabilities
such a multifaceted group presents.

Notes

1 Paul Lewis, "Most Americans Think U.S. Should 'Mind Its Own Busi-
ness' Abroad, Survey Finds," *The Guardian*, December 3, 2013 (www
.theguardian.com/world/2013/dec/03/american-public-mind-its-own
-business-survey); Barry R. Posen, *Restraint: A New Foundation for U.S.
Grand Strategy*, Cornell Studies in Security Affairs (Cornell University Press,
2014).

2 Eric Schmitt, "Thousands of ISIS Fighters Flee in Syria, Many to Fight
Another Day," *New York Times*, February 4, 2018.

3 Ian S. Lustick, "The Absence of Middle Eastern Great Powers: Political
'Backwardness' in Historical Perspective," *International Organization* 51, no. 4
(1997): 653–83.

4 Unfortunately, democratization is often a destabilizing process. Edward D.
Mansfield and Jack Snyder, "Democratization and the Danger of War,"
International Security 20 (July 1, 1995): 5–38.

5 Keir Lieber and Daryl Press, "Why States Won't Give Nuclear Weapons to
Terrorists," *International Security* 38, no. 1 (2013).

6 Caitlin Talmadge, "Closing Time: Assessing the Iranian Threat to the Strait
of Hormuz," *International Security* 33, no. 1 (2008): 82–117.

7 "Global Terrorism Index 2016," Institute for Economics and Peace, No-
vember 2016 (http://economicsandpeace.org/wp-content/uploads/2016/11
/Global-Terrorism-Index-2016.2.pdf); Julian E. Barnes, and Benoit Faucon,
"Islamic State Threat in Europe Shifts," *Wall Street Journal,* July 28, 2016.

8 Gregor Aisch, Bryant Rousseau, and Adam Pearce, "How Far Is Europe
Swinging to the Right?," *New York Times*, May 22, 2016.

9 National Consortium for the Study of Terrorism and Responses to Terrorism (START), Global Terrorism Database [data file], 2016 (www.start
.umd.edu/gtd); Esri Story Maps, and PeaceTechLabs, "2016 Terrorist Attacks," n.d. (http://storymaps.esri.com/stories/2016/terrorist-attacks/).

10 "Report on the Protection of Civilians in the Armed Conflict in Iraq: 1 May–31 October 2015," United Nations High Commission for Human Rights, United Nations Assistance Mission for Iraq, n.d. (www.uniraq.org/images/humanrights/UNAMI-OHCHR_%20POC%20Report_FINAL_01%20May-31%20October%202015_FINAL_11Jan2016.pdf).

11 William Arkin, Robert Windrem, and Cynthia McFadden, "New Counterterrorism 'Heat Map' Shows ISIS Branches Spreading Worldwide," NBC News, August 3, 2016 (www.nbcnews.com/storyline/isis-terror/new-counterterrorism-heat-map-shows-isis-branches-spreading-worldwide-n621866).

12 William M. Arkin and Robert Windrem, "ISIS Numbers Drop by Half, but Fighters Now Attacking around the World," NBC News, July 13, 2016 (www.nbcnews.com/storyline/isis-uncovered/isis-numbers-drop-fighters-now-attacking-around-world-n604206).

13 Isabel Coles and Ned Parker, "The Baathists: How Saddam's Men Help Islamic State Rule," Reuters, December 11, 2015 (www.reuters.com/investigates/special-report/mideast-crisis-iraq-islamicstate/#article-the-baathists).

14 "Islamic State: What Has Happened since the Fall of Mosul?," BBC, June 10, 2015 (www.bbc.com/news/world-middle-east-32784661).

15 Henry Johnson, "Mapped: The Islamic State Is Losing Its Territory—and Fast," Foreign Policy, March 16, 2016 (http://foreignpolicy.com/2016/03/16/mapped-the-islamic-state-is-losing-its-territory-and-fast/).

16 Bethan McKernan, "All the Groups Worldwide that Have Pledged Their Allegiance to ISIS," The Independent (www.indy100.com/article/all-the-groups-worldwide-that-have-pledged-their-allegiance-to-isis—WyppUO47Kg).

17 "TSG IntelBrief: The Devastating Islamic State Suicide Strategy," May 29, 2015 (http://soufangroup.com/tsg-intelbrief-the-devastating-islamic-state-suicide-strategy/).

18 Justin Fishel, "Fall of Ramadi: 30 Car Bombs, 10 as Big as Oklahoma City Blast, U.S. Official Says," ABC News, May 20, 2015 (http://abcnews.go.com/ABCNews/fall-ramadi-30-car-bombs-10-big-oklahoma/story?id=31188102).

19 Michael R. Gordon, "Seeking Clues to ISIS Strategy in Corpses and Cellphones Left in Kirkuk," New York Times, October 29, 2016.

20 Ibid.

21 Michael Georgy, "Mosul under Islamic State: Hardship, Terror and Swift 'Justice,'" Reuters, November 2, 2016 (www.reuters.com/article/us-mideast-crisis-mosul-islamicstate-idUSKBN12X2AS).

22 Joseph Thorndike, "How ISIS Is Using Taxes to Build a Terrorist State," Forbes, August 18, 2014. See also Patrick Johnston and others, "Foundations of the Islamic State: Management, Money, and Terror in Iraq, 2005–2010,"

Rand Research Report, 2016 (https://www.rand.org/pubs/research_re
ports/RR1192.html).

23 Mara Revkin and William McCants, "Experts Weigh In: Is ISIS Good at
Governing?," Brookings, 2015 (www.brookings.edu/blog/markaz/2015/11
/20/experts-weigh-in-is-isis-good-at-governing/).

24 William McCants, "The Believer: How Abu Bakr Al-Baghdadi Became
Leader of the Islamic State," Brookings Institution (http://csweb.brookings
.edu/content/research/essays/2015/thebeliever.html).

25 "Letter from al-Zawahiri to al-Zarqawi," July 9, 2005 (www.globalsecurity
.org/security/library/report/2005/zawahiri-zarqawi-letter_9jul2005.htm).

26 For more on this, see Scott Atran, "Why ISIS Has the Potential to Be a
World-Altering Revolution," *Aeon* (https://aeon.co/essays/why-isis-has-the
-potential-to-be-a-world-altering-revolution).

27 Barak Mendelsohn, "The Jihadi Threat to International Order," *Washington Post*, May 15, 2015.

28 Robin Wright, "After the Islamic State," *New Yorker*, December 12, 2016.

29 Ibid.

30 William McCants, *The ISIS Apocalypse: The History, Strategy, and Doomsday
Vision of the Islamic State* (New York: Macmillan, 2015).

31 John Horgan and Mia Bloom, "This Is How the Islamic State Manufac-
tures Child Militants," VICE News, July 8, 2015 (https://news.vice.
com/article/this-is-how-the-islamic-state-manufactures-child-militants).

32 Mia Bloom, "Cubs of the Caliphate," *Foreign Affairs*, July 21, 2015.

33 Brendan Koerner, "Why ISIS Is Winning the Social Media War—And
How to Fight Back," *WIRED*, April 2016 (www.wired.com/2016/03/isis
-winning-social-media-war-heres-beat/).

34 Ashley Kirk, "Iraq and Syria: How Many Foreign Fighters Are Fighting
for ISIL?," *The Telegraph*, March 24, 2016 (www.telegraph.co.uk/news
/2016/03/29/iraq-and-syria-how-many-foreign-fighters-are-fighting
-for-isil/).

35 Jessica Stern and J. M. Berger, *ISIS: The State of Terror* (New York: Ecco,
2015).

36 Sarah Kenyon Lischer, "Security and Displacement in Iraq: Responding to
the Forced Migration Crisis," *International Security* 33 (Fall 2008): 95–119.
On the impact of demographic engineering on territorial control, see Peter
Krause and Ehud Eiran, "How Human Boundaries Become State Borders:
Radical Flanks and Territorial Control in the Modern Era," *Comparative
Politics* 50, no. 4 (July 2018).

37 *Dabiq*, no. 7; David A. Lake, "Rational Extremism: Understanding Terrorism in the Twenty-First Century," *Dialogue IO* 1, no. 01 (January 2002):
15–29.

38 Roger Petersen, *Resistance and Rebellion: Lessons from Eastern Europe* (Cambridge University Press, 2001); Stathis Kalyvas, *The Logic of Violence in Civil War* (Cambridge University Press, 2006); Yuri Zhukov, "Population Resettlement in War: Theory and Evidence from Soviet Archives," *Journal of Conflict Resolution* 59, no. 7 (2015): 1155–85.

39 "Global Terrorism Database" (www.start.umd.edu/gtd/).

40 F. Gregory Gause III, "Beyond Sectarianism: The New Middle East Cold War," Brookings Doha Center Analysis Paper 11 (July 2014) (www .brookings.edu/~/media/Research/Files/Papers/2014/07/22-beyond -sectarianism-cold-war-gause/English-PDF.pdf?la=en).

41 Peter Krause and Stephen Van Evera, "Public Diplomacy: Ideas for the War of Ideas," *Middle East Policy* 16, no. 3 (2009) (http://go.galegroup.com/ps/i .do?id=GALE%7CA210368258&v=2.1&u=mlin_m_bostcoll&it=r&p =AONE&sw=w&asid=b20627907965fb19ed21309c3b709df1).

42 This is one of the main reasons that bin Laden and al Qaeda wanted to first remove the "far enemy" before fighting the "near enemy," and if recent trends continue he may be proved right (at least in his disagreement with ISIS and its predecessors). Rashmee Roshan-Lall, "The Unfulfilled Dabiq Prophecy an Omen for ISIS," *Arab Weekly*, October 23, 2016 (www .thearabweekly.com//Opinion/6827/The-unfulfilled-Dabiq-prophecy-an -omen-for-ISIS).

43 Peter Krause, "The Last Good Chance: A Reassessment of U.S. Operations at Tora Bora," *Security Studies* 17, no. 4 (2008): 644–84.

44 See chapter 8 by Feisal al-Istrabadi and chapter 7 by Hussein Banai in this volume.

45 William McCants and Mara Revkin, "Experts Weigh In: Is ISIS Good at Governing?," Brookings, November 20, 2015.

46 "The Islamic State Has Been a Catastrophe for Sunnis," *Washington Post*, November 23, 2016.

47 Eric Robinson and others, "When the Islamic State Comes to Town: The Economic Impact of Islamic State Governance in Iraq and Syria," Rand Research Report, 2017 (www.rand.org/pubs/research_reports/RR1970 .html).

48 Scott Shane and Jo Becker, "A New Libya, with 'Very Little Time Left,'" *New York Times*, February 27, 2016; Jeffrey Goldberg, "The Obama Doctrine," *The Atlantic*, April 2016.

49 David Graham, "What Is Trump's Syria Policy?," *The Atlantic*, April 11, 2017.

Contributors

Hussein Banai is assistant professor of international studies at the School of Global and International Studies at Indiana University. He is also a research affiliate at the Center for International Studies at MIT, where he is a co-convener of the Critical Oral History Workshop on U.S.-Iran relations.

Risa Brooks is Allis Chalmers associate professor of political science at Marquette University. She is a nonresident fellow in security studies at TRENDS, an Abu Dhabi–based think tank, and currently an adjunct scholar at the Modern War Institute at West Point.

Erik J. Dahl is an associate professor of national security affairs at the Naval Postgraduate School in Monterey, California, and the author of *Intelligence and Surprise Attack: Failure and Success from Pearl Harbor to 9/11 and Beyond* (Georgetown University Press, 2013).

Sumit Ganguly is professor of political science and holds the Rabindranath Tagore Chair in Indian Cultures and Civilizations at Indiana University. His most recent book (with William R. Thompson) is *Ascending India and Its State Capacity* (Yale University Press, 2017). He is a member of the Council on Foreign Relations and a fellow of the American Academy of Arts and Sciences.

Feisal al-Istrabadi is founding director of the Center for the Study of the Middle East and professor of the practice of international law and diplomacy at the Maurer School of Law and the School of Global and International Studies at Indiana University. He is a fellow of the American Academy of Arts and Sciences and a member of the Council on Foreign Relations.

Peter Krause is associate professor of political science at Boston College and research affiliate with the MIT Security Studies Program. He is the author of *Rebel Power: Why National Movements Compete, Fight, and Win* (Cornell University Press, 2017) and coeditor of *Coercion: The Power to Hurt in International Politics* (Oxford University Press, 2018).

Kevin W. Martin is a member of the School of Historical Studies at the Institute for Advanced Study in Princeton, New Jersey, and a senior fellow at the Center for the Study of the Middle East at Indiana University. His first book was *Syria's Democratic Years: Citizens, Experts, and Media in the 1950s* (Indiana University Press, 2015).

Nukhet Sandal is associate professor of political science at Ohio University and director of Global Studies at the Center for International Studies. Her latest book is *Religious Leaders and Conflict Transformation* (Cambridge University Press, 2017).

Amin Tarzi is director of Middle East Studies at the Marine Corps University and adjunct professor of practice (international relations) at University of Southern California's Dornsife, Washington, D.C. Program, and senior fellow, Program on the Middle East, at the Foreign Policy Research Institute.

James J. Wirtz is dean of the School of International Graduate Studies, Naval Postgraduate School, Monterey, California. He is coeditor of *Intelligence: The Secret World of Spies* (Oxford, 2018). He was honored as a Distinguished Scholar in 2016 by the Intelligence Studies Section of the International Studies Association.

Index